Copyright Acknowledgments

Table 3.1, pages 54-55, originally appeared as Table 2-1, pages 40-41, "Foreign Policy Formation Viewed Cognitively," pp. 18-54 in Robert Axelrod (ed.) Structure of Decision: The Cognitive Maps of Political Elites, by Ole Holsti. Copyright 1976 by Ole Holsti. Reprinted with permission.

Figure 3.1, page 67, originally appeared as Figure 1, page 28, "Indicators of Stress in Policymakers During Foreign Policy Crises," Political Psychology, Volume 1, No.1, Spring, 1979 by Margaret G. Hermann. Copyright 1979 by International Society of Political Psychology. Reprinted with permission.

Figure 3.2, page 84, originally appeared as Figure 1, page 900, "Attitudes, Values and Related Concepts: A System of Classification," Social Science Quarterly, Volume 55, No.4, March, 1975, by Jay Meddin. Copyright 1975 by the University of Texas Press. Reprinted with permission.

Figure 3.3, page 93, originally appeared as Figure 4.3, page 102, A Psychological Examination of Political Leaders, by Margaret Hermann and Thomas W. Milburn (eds.). Copyright 1977 by the Free Press (a division of the Macmillan Publishing Co., Inc.). Reprinted with permission.

Figure 3.4, page 100, originally appeared as Table 4-1, page 83, Structure of Decision: The Cognitive Maps of Political Elites, by Robert Axelrod (ed.). Copyright 1976 by Princeton University Press. Reprinted with permission.

Figure 4.1, page 118, originally appeared as Figure 6.1, page 107, The Nature of Human Values, by Milton Rokeach. Copyright 1973 by the Free Press (a division of the Macmillan Publishing Co., Inc.). Reprinted with permission.

Table 5.9, pages 168-169, originally appeared as Table 5.22, pages 160-161, The Nature of Human

Values, by Milton Rokeach. Copyright 1973 by the Free Press (a division of the Macmillan Publishing Co., Inc.). Reprinted with permission.

Figure 6.1, page 190, originally appeared as Table 12-1, page 192, Understanding Foreign Policy Decisions: The Chinese Case, by Davis Bobrow, Steve Chan, and John Kringen. Copyright 1979 by the Free Press (a division of the Macmillan Publishing Co., Inc.). Reprinted with permission.

behavior. More generally, a variety of concepts and theories from evolutionary biology can be applied to the study of political and other forms of human behavior. Advocates of ethological, sociobiological, and similar biological perspectives maintain that, at the least, mainstream social science in the twentieth century has seriously underestimated the impact of genetic endownment and failed to recognize the interplay of nature (genetic inheritance) and nurture (environmental factors, learning, culture) in accounting for human behavioral patterns and the dynamics and processes of social and political systems.

Political theorists interested in the biology and politics nexus have reintroduced biology (e.g., sociobiology and ethology) into discussions of human nature. In a comparative analysis of marmots (rodents such as the woodchuck) and humans, for example, Masters (1978e: 64) maintains that natural selection could simultaneously favor both (intragroup) aggressiveness and altruistic tendencies (i.e., defense of the group).

Masters (1975, 1976, 1978c, 1978d, 1978e) and others who advocate and employ ethological and sociobiological approaches to political behavior have focused on concepts ranging from crowding, altruism, and territoriality to dominance, aggression, and charisma. As Somit et al. (1978: 22) point out, ethology and sociobiology assume that an organism's behavior is the product of interaction among:

- The environment;
- The organism's prior learning; and
- The genetically-transmitted tendencies characteristic of the species to which the organism belongs.

In a concrete illustrative study, Masters (1978a) uses the concept of "attention structure" to study presidential campaigns in the U.S. Originally developed by Michael Chance, the concept of attention structure is designed to demonstrate that the identification of dominance with aggressive behavior in ethology is inadequate. According to Chance, primate social group coherence can be characterized in terms of two "modes" of "attention:" the agonic (persistently cohesive and rigid) or the hedonic (fluctuating social cohesion). In human social systems, certain situations (e.g., the mass media) are predominantly hedonic and others (e.g., centralized bureaucracy) are agonistic (Masters, 1978a). Unlike many social theories, Masters (1978a: 7) emphasizes, the concept of "attention structure" entails the recognition that humans can be both hedonic and agonistic, depending on the context.

Masters (1978) applies the attention structure concept to the 1972 U.S. presidential campaign. The degree to which candidates serve as the focus of attention is clearly fundamental to the analysis of a particular campaign or political processes more generally. The successful candidate is likely to be the one who constitutes "the primary focus of attention <u>for the relevant public or constituency</u> [Masters, 1978a: 14; emphasis in the original]." During the Democratic prenomination period, this was clearly Senator George McGovern (over Senator Edmund Muskie and the other challengers); during the campaign, however, the focus was on Richard Nixon, the incumbent.

Masters (1978a) provides several examples of the utility of an attention structure approach. In the process of gaining the nomination, he (1978a: 42) notes, McGovern concentrated on controlling the Democratic Convention and thereby lost control of the national attention structure. McGovern's inability to accept the nomination until 2:48 A.M. (because of the tolerance for the proliferation of frivolous vice-presidential candidates earlier in the evening) symbolized his alleged "weakness" to the general public. This and ensuing events (the Eagleton affair, the rejections by a host of potential running mates) resulted in an immediate and ultimately fatal loss of control over the public attention structure.

In terms of photographic coverage in major newsmagazines, McGovern peaked in June and July of 1972, with Nixon assuming and maintaining predominance after August. Overall, Masters (1978a) concludes, the media—by its role in eliminating Muskie, its relentless exposure of weaknesses and embarassing incidents in the McGovern campaign, and in other ways—contributed significantly to Nixon's landslide victory in 1972. This conclusion (which is hardly consistent with the prevailing perceptions of the media's role and biases by everyone involved at the time, including Nixon and his inner circle) illuminates the relative impact of the media as a shaper of attention structure (which concerns symbolic images of leadership and dominance) vis-a-vis the actual preferences and

The use of paralinguistic and nonverbal techniques surmounts the problem of accessibility and simultaneously provides a nonreactive measurement technique. The two features, <u>of assessment "at a distance"</u> and <u>nonreactive measurement</u> enhance the attractiveness of such techniques as substitutes for (and supplements to) such standard direct methods for acquiring manifest content data as interviews and surveys.

An illustrative study is Frank's (1977) psycho-political examination of George McGovern and Hubert Humphrey in their first televised debate in the 1972 California Presidential primary.[17] Frank videotaped the debate and coded responses for both candidates for three types of nonverbal behavior (nods, blinks, and gross body movements) and two types of paralinguistic behavior (speech disturbances and "nonimmediacy" frequencies). Interestingly, McGovern apparently experienced anxiety when he attacked Humphrey; Humphrey's anxiety, in contrast, seemed to be aroused by defenses of his own record. Frank employed the data to probe the relationship between issue type and stress responses. While only the two indicators of nods and blinks differentiated between high and low stress topics for Humphrey, all of the indicators did so for McGovern.

Nonverbal and psychophysiological data are particularly appropriate for two types of research concerns in the study of foreign policy-makers. One is the high stress situation; the other is the decision process mode of analysis.

Psychophysiological indicators are ideal for detecting emotional states generally and especially for identifying peaks of arousal (whether the latter is physically- or psychologically-based). When an individual experiences a high level of threat, anxiety, and psychic stress, this is mirrored by certain internal bodily changes. For example, some of the eccrine sweat glands respond to stress and other external (psychological) stimuli (Hassett, 1978). Stress and tension also lead to increases in the cardiovascular, the digestive, and other systems. While the relationship is not uniform or simple, psychologically experienced stress is reflected in the organisms's physical system. The invariant emotion-arousal linkage forms the basis for Wiegele's research on voice stress, which is summarized below.

Chapter 1 distinguished between source analysis (measured by various overt traces) and process analysis. The latter is usually not revealed in explicit verbal output, which represents the end-product of an elaborate set of information processing and decision-making processes. Although the empirical lacunae and theoretical uncertainties are still troublesome, the work of Donchin and other cognitive psychophysiologists provides a foundation for an eventual psychophysiological theory of at least some components of the complex internal processes referred to as "thinking," "cognition and perception," or "decision-making." Donchin's work on one particular brain electrical activity component--the P300--constitutes the second case study below.

Voice Stress Analysis

The work of Wiegele (1978b) on the psychophysiology of elite stress in international crises represents research of very high potential relevance to the political psychologist concerned with foreign policy elites.[18] Wiegele focuses on the debilitating conditions of high psychological stress in the context of five international crises: (1) Truman's July, 1950 address on the North Korean invasion of South Korea; (2) the July, 1961 report by Kennedy concerning the Berlin crisis; (3) Kennedy's October, 1962 speech during the Cuban missile crisis; (4) Johnson's August, 1964 address on the Gulf of Tonkin affair; and (5) Johnson's January, 1968 speech about the crisis following North Korea's capture of the U.S. intelligence ship Pueblo.

The bulk of the verbal research on foreign policy elites has been indirect; given the inescapable intrusiveness of most psychophysiological techniques, most such research must be direct. The attractiveness of Wiegele's voice stress analysis (VSA) methodology is that it is simultaneously direct and remote; VSA therefore does not require the cooperation of the subject but, like other psychophysiological methods, nevertheless provides a direct means of securing data about elite decision-makers.

Wiegele's VSA research is closely associated with the concept of "signal leakage." Signal leakage can be defined as "the unintended verbal or nonverbal emission of a measurable clue to a psychological state by an individual human being [Wiegele, 1979e: 73]." In contrast to much of the work on the manifest (verbal) content of elite signals, which analyzes the explicit and intended "tip of the iceberg" of elite output, nonverbal and psycho-

Political Psychology and Biopolitics

Other Titles in This Series

Presidents, Secretaries of State, and Crises in U.S. Foreign Relations: A Model and Predictive Analysis, Lawrence S. Falkowski

U.S. Policy in International Institutions: Defining Reasonable Options in an Unreasonable World, edited by Seymour Maxwell Finger and Joseph R. Harbert

Congress and Arms Control, edited by Alan Platt and Lawrence D. Weiler

Crisis Resolution: Presidential Decision Making in the Mayaguez and Korean Confrontations, Richard G. Head, Frisco W. Short, and Robert C. McFarlane

U.S.-Japan Relations and the Security of East Asia: The Next Decade, edited by Franklin B. Weinstein

Communist Indochina and U.S. Foreign Policy: Postwar Realities, Joseph J. Zasloff and MacAlister Brown

National Interests and Presidential Leadership: The Setting of Priorities, Donald E. Nuechterlein

Arms Transfers to the Third World: The Military Buildup in Less Industrial Countries, edited by Uri Ra'anan, Robert Pfaltzgraff, Jr., and Geoffrey Kemp

Political Leadership in NATO: A Study in Multinational Diplomacy, Robert S. Jordan

Psychological Models in International Politics, edited by Lawrence S. Falkowski

Lend-Lease, Loans, and the Coming of the Cold War: A Study of the Implementation of Foreign Policy, Leon C. Martel

Nuclear Energy and Nuclear Proliferation: Japanese and American Views, edited by Ryukichi Imai and Henry S. Rowen

Presidential Decisionmaking in Foreign Policy: The Effective Use of Information and Advice, Alexander L. George

The Security of Korea: U.S. and Japanese Perspectives in the 1980s, edited by Franklin B. Weinstein and Fuji Kamiya

Westview Special Studies in International Relations

*Political Psychology and Biopolitics:
Assessing and Predicting Elite Behavior
in Foreign Policy Crises*

Gerald W. Hopple

The interface between psychology and politics has been an area of sustained inquiry for several decades. More recently, the nexus between psychopolitical factors and international politics--linkages among biopolitics, political psychology, elite analysis, foreign affairs, and world politics--has been explored.

This volume reviews and assesses the major studies and frameworks in the field, looking at belief systems research, operational code analysis, cognitive mapping, and other psychological indicators, and highlighting the relevance of this kind of inquiry to the phenomena of crisis and war. Throughout there is a concern with predicting elite behavior, and in the final chapter new cross-sectional data for foreign policy elites in thirty-nine countries are presented and evaluated as predictors of actual behavior in the international arena.

Gerald W. Hopple is senior research analyst, International Public Policy Research Corporation.

Political Psychology and Biopolitics: Assessing and Predicting Elite Behavior in Foreign Policy Crises

Gerald W. Hopple

Westview Press / Boulder, Colorado

Westview Special Studies in
International Relations

All rights reserved. No part of this publication may be reproduced or transmitted in any form or by any means, electronic or mechanical, including photocopy, recording, or any information storage and retrieval system, without permission in writing from the publisher.

Copyright © 1980 by Westview Press, Inc.

Published in 1980 in the United States of America by
    Westview Press, Inc.
    5500 Central Avenue
    Boulder, Colorado 80301
    Frederick A. Praeger, Publisher

Library of Congress Cataloging in Publication Data
Hopple, Gerald W.
    Political psychology and biopolitics.
    (Westview special studies in international relations)
    Bibliography: p.
    1. International relations--Psychological aspects.
2. International relations--Research. I. Title.
II. Series: Westview special studies on international relations and U.S. foreign policy.
JX1255.H64   327'.01'9   80-12861
ISBN 0-89158-847-7

Composition for this book was provided by the author.
Printed and bound in the United States of America.

Contents

Tables and Figures ix
Acknowledgments xi
Copyright Acknowledgments xiii

1 INTRODUCTION   1

2 THE BIOPOLITICAL FOUNDATIONS OF ELITE
   FOREIGN POLICY BEHAVIOR 13

   Biopolitics: An Overview 13
   Psychophysiology 19
   Applications to Foreign Policy Elites 30
      Voice Stress Analysis 32
      The P300 39
      Conclusions 45

3 THE PSYCHOLOGICAL FOUNDATIONS OF ELITE
   FOREIGN POLICY BEHAVIOR 51

   The Political Science/Psychology Interface . 51
      Early Reductionism 52
      Current Eclecticism 53
      Recurring Problems 56
   Pivotal Issues 59
      Relevance 60
      Clusters of Factors 61
      Maximizers of Impact 66
      Methods 69
   A Tripartite Classification Scheme 72
      Psychodynamics 73
      Personality Traits 77
      Belief Systems Phenomena 83

4	ELITE VALUES AND FOREIGN AFFAIRS: AN OVERVIEW	111
	The Rokeach Value Approach	112
	Conceptual Background	114
	Values and Empirical Foreign Policy Elite Analysis.	119
	Descriptive Data	125
	Research Design	130
	Background: Quantitative International Conflict Analysis	130
	Independent and Dependent Variable Clusters and Indicators	135
	Intervening Variable Cluster: Type of Nation.	138
	Relative Efficacy Assessment	139
5	ELITE VALUES AND FOREIGN AFFAIRS: AN EMPIRICAL TEST	147
	Empirical Findings	147
	Cluster-by-Cluster Results	148
	Relative Explanatory Power Results	159
	Interpretation	161
	Validity	165
	Discrimination Among Subgroups	165
	Prediction of Behavior	166
	Multimethod Validation	171
	Conclusion	175
6	IN SEARCH OF THE FOUNDATIONS OF ELITE FOREIGN POLICY BEHAVIOR	183

Appendix A: Variables and Clusters 193
References 197

Tables and Figures

Tables

2.1	Psychophysiology: Types of Responses Studied	22
3.1	Some "Cognitive Process" Approaches to Decision Making	54
4.1	Value Data: State Samples (1966-1970)	121
4.2	Value Data: Most Frequently Included States	122
4.3	Values for Content Analysis	124
4.4	1970: Value Frequencies	126
4.5	Value Means and Standard Deviations (1966-1970)	126
4.6	Value Means by State (1966)	127
4.7	State vs. Year: Variance Explained (1966-1970)	128
4.8	Groupings of States	139
5.1	Constructive Diplomatic Behavior as Predicted by the Psychological Cluster (Nation-Years Aggregated, 1966-1970)	149
5.2	Non-Military Conflict as Predicted by the Psychological Cluster (Nation-Years Aggregated, 1966-1970)	150
5.3	Force as Predicted by the Psychological Cluster (Nation-Years Aggregated, 1966-1970)	151
5.4	Internal Values and Foreign Behavior	154
5.5	Foreign Behavior as Predicted by the Societal Cluster (Nation-Years Aggregated, 1966-1970)	156
5.6	Foreign Behavior as Predicted by the Interstate Cluster (Nation-Years Aggregated, 1966-1970)	157

5.7   Foreign Behavior as Predicted by the
      Global Cluster (Nation-Years
      Aggregated, 1966-1970) 158
5.8   Relative Explanatory Power of Predictors of
      Foreign Policy Behavior (Nation-Years
      Aggregated, 1966-1970) 160
5.9   Significant Value-Behavior Relationships:
      Diverse Content Areas 168
5.10 Significant Value-Behavior Relationships:
      Foreign Behavior 170

Figures

2.1   Illustrative Psychological Stress Eval-
      uator (PSE) Wave Form Charts 34
2.2   Psychophysiological Indicators Considered
      as Inputs for Biocybernetic Applications. 40
2.3   Morphology of the Event-Related Potential. 42
2.4   Relationship Between Particular Biological
      Signals and Either the Determination of
      Pilot Status or Control Functions: An
      Illustrative Biocybernetic Indicator
      System 47
3.1   A Schematization of the Crisis-Stress
      Relationship 67
3.2   Components of a Belief System 84
3.3   A Comparison of Church and Other Leaders
      Along Operational Code Dimensions 93
3.4   Constructing a Cognitive Map 100
4.1   A Freedom-Equality Model of Political
      Variations 118
4.2   Coleman Analysis 134
4.3   Value Data Analysis: Research Design . . 142
6.1   Involvement in Second-Order Crises . . . 190

Acknowledgments

Like any other field of research, the study of political psychology and foreign policy is a collegial enterprise. Without the research and assistance of others, this book would not have been possible. I am indebted to a number of individuals, as the following indicates.

My research colleagues over a span of more than five years have provided encouragement and stimulating criticism; Chapters 4 and 5 draw on work conducted at the University of Maryland with Stephen J. Andriole, currently of International Information Systems, Paul J. Rossa of the International Public Policy Research Corporation (IPPRC), and Jonathan Wilkenfeld of Maryland.

University of Maryland graduate research assistants Dan Crawford, Lilymae Fountain, Cal Jillson, Robert McCauley, and Robert Stoker worked at one time or another with me and deserve thanks for their efforts. The following undergraduate research assistants also contributed to the research process reflected in this and other publications: Mark Allen; Merle Feldbaum; Bill Goodwin; Janna Itzler; Michele Lane; Stuart Perry; and Lee Ann Taylor. Thanks also to Amy Favin, a dedicated colleague at Maryland and IPPRC. I am especially indebted to Dorette Feit and Helene Rubinstein, who collected most of the decision-maker value data discussed in Chapters 4 and 5; their hard work and friendship made this an enjoyable endeavor.

My intellectual influences are numerous. I would especially like to note the importance of Emanuel Donchin of Illinois and Thomas Wiegele of Northern Illinois (Chapter 2) and Ole Holsti of Duke (Chapter 3) as well as Herman Wold of the Universities of Uppsala and Geneva and two excellent analysts of the comparative foreign policy/political psychology overlap: Lawrence Falkowski of Louisiana State and Margaret Hermann of Ohio State. My greatest debt is to Milton Rokeach of Washington State.

Institutional support was provided by IPPRC and by the U.S. Defense Advanced Research Projects Agency/Cybernetics Technology Office (DARPA/CTO). DARPA/CTO supported portions of this work through the following contracts: Contract No. N00014-76-C-0153 to Maryland (monitored by ONR); Contract No. MDA 903-78-C-0341 to IPPRC (monitored by DSSW); and Contract No. N00014-79-C-0101 to IPPRC (monitored by ONR). The views and conclusions in this book are not necessarily those of the Defense Advanced Research Projects Agency or the U.S. Government.

Most of the graphics work was done by John Correnti and his staff of the Art Department at Decisions and Designs, Incorporated, in McLean, Virginia.

I would especially like to express my gratitude to Judith Ayres Daly, Program Manager at DARPA/CTO, and Michael A. Daniels, the President of IPPRC, for their support and encouragement.

Finally, I would like to thank the following people for their special contributions: Lynne C. Rienner of Westview Press for her willingness to support this effort and helpful advice along the way; Jean Nieroski of IPPRC for a superb typing effort; and my parents Edith Comer Hopple and Woodrow Wilson Hopple for their love and encouragement.

None of the institutions or individuals above is responsible for the contents of this book; any errors are the sole responsibility of the author.

G.W.H.

1
Introduction

The psychological foundations of foreign policy behavior constitute a fascinating area of inquiry for the student of international relations. In recent years, concepts, methods, and techniques from both cognitive psychology and psychophysiology have been transferred to the study of the behavior, belief systems, and decision-making processes of foreign policy elites. These approaches have complemented and--to a considerable extent--supplanted the more "traditional" psychopolitical perspectives drawn from psychobiography and personality theory.
   Diversity and electicism characterize the conceptual and methodological armamentarium of the political psychologist who analyzes international politics. No dominant paradigm governs psychological research on foreign policy elites. While certain recurring themes can be identified and some evidence can be adduced to support the viewpoint that we can discern at least some descriptive consensus about the foreign policy decision process, there is a paucity of theoretical consensus about why the process looks as it does (Kinder and Weiss, 1978: 728). The ongoing research tends to occur within the parameters of fairly circumscribed and impermeable nuclei or research programs (operational code profiling, cognitive mapping, etc.). When the more recent work in psychophysiology is taken into account, the diversity and lack of integration become even more striking.
   Research in this area requires a series of maps. In striking contrast to the prevailing mode of inquiry in basic social scientific research, where researchers construct frameworks and models, the emphasis here is on the concept of maps. What we require are heuristic and practicable guides to

research and analysis rather than abstract schema or frameworks. Furthermore, these maps should be viewed as holistic images which ignore the artificial boundaries associated by convention with particular disciplines and research methodologies. Biology, psychophysiology, psychology, social psychology, anthropology, political science, and various subfields of these disciplines are among the sources of indicator systems, propositional networks, and theoretical perspectives for analyzing foreign policy-makers' belief systems and decision processes. Extensive research has accrued on the various subjects pertinent to a research program revolving around the core concepts of political psychology and psychophysiology. As is customary in social scientific inquiry, however, the existing work is disparate, uneven, and often ad hoc in nature. Few efforts have been undertaken to map out the terrain in more than a cursory fashion. The research is especially sparse in the psychophysiology region of the map, although there is a plethora of indicators and techniques. In the interstices between politics and psychology, the relevant literature has experienced a quantitatively impressive expansion in recent years; the proliferation of frameworks for analysis, propositional inventories, and literature reviews all illustrate the fertility of psychopolitical research. Even here, however, ad hoc and non-quantitative research products prevail.

Psychological and psychophysiological/biopolitical variable areas both restrict the focus of attention to the individual. Hermann (1977) presents research on a variety of prominent "personal characteristics" of elite decision-makers in a number of substantive policy areas; Falkowski (1979a, 1979b) provides foreign policy-relevant examples. As Hermann (1977) notes in the introduction to her collection of empirical studies, subsumed under the construct of <u>personal characteristics</u> are all aspects of the individual as an individual:

- Biographical statistics;
- Capabilities and skills;
- Training;
- Work experiences;
- Motives;
- Cognitions;
- Affectual orientations;
- Beliefs and attitudes;
- Role perceptions;

- Values.

Since major foreign policy decisions are generally the product of individuals and/or small groups, the small group subfield of social psychology is an obvious potential component of a political psychology research design.[1] The work of Janis (1972) on groupthink is the best known of the various studies of foreign policy-making and group dynamics. Research concerning the impact of small group, organizational context, bureaucratic politics, and other social psychological dimensions of the foreign policy process is not systematically reviewed in this study. The focus here is the apex of the foreign policy elite (the head of state and, in some cases, the foreign minister) in situations which minimize the potential impact of large, institutionalized decision units. Decision contexts characterized by high levels of threat, stress, and tension--international crisis, conflict, and force situations--are the central concern of this study.[2]

Given a focus on the high level decision-maker, several questions immediately arise.[3] Are psychological factors (broadly defined to include cognitive verbal and psychophysiological indicators) relevant to the task of explaining foreign behavior? How important are such variables vis-a-vis other potential determinants from different levels of analysis? How adequately do individual-level forces or elite attributes account for the external behavior of nations?

Scientific explanations of foreign behavior have featured discrete determinants and clusters of factors from various levels of analysis, ranging from the individual and the small group to the societal, external, and systemic levels. Critics of psychological approaches to the study of foreign policy often maintain that non-individual levels of analysis account for an overwhelming portion of the variance in external behavior and that individual-level determinants explain little or none of the behavior.

In the past, this question has frequently been treated in a very cursory, nonempirical fashion, with the critic simply assuming the irrelevance of elite belief systems and other psychological factors. More recently, empirical evidence has been produced which suggests quite clearly that the characteristics of foreign policy-makers impact upon external behavior--especially in certain types of countries and/or situations. This evidence will be reviewed in some detail in Chapters 3 and 5.

In the context of the kaleidoscopic character of recent and current inquiry on foreign policy and psychology, the more relevant issue concerns the differential impact of various _types_ of psychological variables. Even if the focus is limited to belief systems, the problem persists; the latter construct refers to a variety of low- and high-level beliefs and attitudes, ranging in generality from very discrete perceptives of and beliefs about a voluminous number of phenomena (actors, issues, etc.) to a smaller number of central beliefs to an even smaller set of basic "master beliefs" or values.

Assuming that psychological variables are not without significance as determinants of the actions of states in the sphere of foreign policy, the _relative_ impact of such variables emerges as a critical question. Here the evidence is less extensive, although the available work does support the tentative conclusion that psychological factors perform fairly well when compared to determinants from other levels of analysis.

In a very fundamental sense, however, the issue is not the relative effect of variable clusters but the operative causal configurations. This suggests that the focus should shift from ranking sets of factors--a pre-theoretical undertaking which is chronicled in Chapters 4 and 5--to the construction, testing, and refinement of causal models.[4] This should be regarded as a dynamic, iterative process in which a series of first-generation models provides the foundation for more sophisticated second- and third-generations.

The third basic question--the _strength_ of the linkage between psychological variables and foreign behavior--is one which requires further exploration. The available research indicates unambiguously that the personal characteristics of foreign policy elites are related strongly to external behavior, especially for certain types of international actors and in certain situational contexts. When such mediating variable clusters are taken into account, the nexus is often quite robust in magnitude for the relevant subsets of leaders and nations.

Aside from the potency of the belief-behavior nexus per se, two other considerations favor an emphasis on the beliefs and other characteristics of elites. One stems from a concern with policy-relevance; unlike systemic parameters and many other factors, the preferences, perceptions, and choices of elites are susceptible to direct and immediate modification.[5] Such modification can apply to the belief systems of incumbent elites or, as is more frequently the case, a new set of elites and therefore a new belief system can replace the incumbent policy-makers.

The second consideration is associated with the proximity of elite decision-makers to the dependent variable of foreign behavior. In the causal chain which culminates with verbal and physical behavior toward other actors in the interstate arena, the policy-maker--and his or her perceptions, attitudes, beliefs, and values--intervenes between the more remote determinants of foreign behavior and the actual outputs. Not surprisingly, most foreign policy decision-making models equate behavior in the realm of foreign affairs with the actions and decisions of the individuals who are directly responsible for formulating foreign policy: the head of state, the foreign minister, and perhaps a small group of officials and advisors. Environmental factors influence state decisions <u>indirectly</u>; the impact is always mediated by the <u>individual</u> decision-maker or the decision-making unit.[6]

To an extent, of course, this statement is true by definition; in a very trivial and tautological sense, the perceptions and beliefs of decision-makers must intervene between the environment and the decision. Nor does the posited sequence preclude instances of "environmental determinism," when decision-maker perceptions <u>and</u> the decision are both shaped by environmental <u>forces</u>.

However, there are numerous occasions when there are discrepancies between the objective and the psychological environments. These are manifested most graphically when competing actors (individual states or coalitions) perceive strikingly different versions of reality (e.g, Arab versus Israeli decision-makers, the Axis partners versus the Anglo-French alliance in 1938-1939, etc.). This phenomenon is also illustrated by changes within systems; elites may experience cognitive reorganizations because of unusual events, such as the attack on Pearl Harbor for U.S. policy-makers (see Ben-Zvi, 1978), or the elite itself may be replaced, as in Japan in October of 1940 (when General Tojo became Premier and Minister of War) and in Britain in May of 1940 (when Churchill replaced Chamberlain).[7] In all of these cases, at least two orthogonal psychological environments coexisted with a single objective environment.[8]

In unstructured, unprecedented situations, the latitude for elite belief systems is theoretically at its maximum. If the levels of stress, tension, and danger are simultaneously high, perceptual factors became even more influential. Thus, in situations of crisis, severe conflict, force, and war, the characteristics of elites can be expected to be especially influential as determinants of decisions.

Purely environmental models can produce very respectable results even in contexts saturated by stress and tension. However, explanations which exclude the psychological environment can only narrow the range of alternative choices; such models can never identify a particular decision if the degree of situational ambiguity is high. For non-routine, high threat decision contexts (i.e., crisis and potential force or war decisions), it is necessary to engage in "microanalysis" of elite beliefs and perceptions if the goal is to explain or predict a specific choice.

This distinction is analogous to the one between the sources and processes of a decision. Source analysis, exemplified by the frameworks of Rosenau (1966) and Andriole et al. (1975), attempts to identify the environmental and other sources of external behavior; empirical research in the source tradition attempts to illuminate (and perhaps rank) the causal determinants of a phenomenon. In contrast, process analysis, illustrated by the various decision-making frameworks (e.g., Brecher, 1977; Caldwell, 1977; Snyder et al., 1962), involves the tracing in detail of the processes which precede a decision.[9] Perception and definition of the situation, information processing, and the identification, evaluation, and selection of options (and the subcomponents of these elements of decision-making) comprise the core of process analysis. Psychological variables, which may or may not be introduced into a source analysis design, are absolutely essential to the process or decision-making analytical mode.

The process perspective can be contrasted with a less ambitious form of psychological analysis of foreign policy elites: the charting or empirical profiling of observable traits or states of decision-makers. As Hermann (1979a) notes in her essay on indicators of stress in policy-makers, foreign policy elites leave many traces of their behavior in the form of verbal and nonverbal indicators; the latter are discussed in Chapter 2 and the former in Chapter 3.

By restricting the focus to such verbal and nonverbal traces (i.e., to the end-products of elaborate decision processes), the observer is not constrained by the demanding requirements for data and interpretation which are imposed by the process approach. Comparative analysis (within and across decision systems) is facilitated because of the data collection task; process tracing requires extensive and elusive data on the sequences which lead up to the verbal output (e.g., a speech) or the nonverbal or psychophysiological indicator (e.g., voice stress or paralinguistic data). Such data are difficult to secure and would be prohibitively expensive in a single study of many systems.

However, the trace approach "black boxes" the internal dynamics and processes which precede and shape the observable output. In the absence of genuine process analysis, the nexus between the trace measures and the processes of perception and thought which preceded them is simply assumed. This leads to the potential danger that a verbal or nonverbal indicator will be misinterpreted or will be mistakenly treated as an index of an elaborate decision process.

Process data are certainly less accessible and more "expensive" to collect than trace data. The problem is compounded by the fact that decision-making is a complex and multifaceted phenomenon. Eventually, there will probably be theories for each of the subcomponents of the process rather than a general, inclusive theory of decision-making and choice. In the interim, it is critical that basic research be conducted on the processes of decision-making as well as on the overt manifestations of actual decisions.

Even if it is conceded that characteristics of foreign policy elites are significant determinants of foreign behavior, the formidable task of securing valid, reliable data must be confronted. Data-creation methodologies have been prolific; observation, questionnaires, interviews, simulation, and biographic statistics are among the most prominent methods for generating data about the decision processes and belief systems of foreign policy elites.

Observation, questionnaires, and interviews are frequently precluded, however. While data on age, education, and other elite attributes are relatively available and some evidence points to the impact of such traits on both attitudes and behaviors (e.g., Quandt, 1970), the use of biographical statistics seems to be more appropriate for explaining generalized phenomena (e.g., relationships between elite attributes and type of political system) than for analyzing the process or content features of a particular decision. The frequent lack of fit between simulation contexts and the real world often rules out this particular data-making strategy.

The most frequently employed methodology is content analysis of public and/or private documents (speeches, memoirs, etc.). Since private or confidential sources are available only fortuitously and sporadically, the researcher is generally compelled to rely on public sources. The pitfalls of such data sources are well known.

It would, however, be decidedly premature to conclude that public source data are invariably useless. Especially if the concern is with patterns and trends rather than with specific beliefs or decisions, content analysis data from public sources "work" surprisingly well, as extensive research on the U.S., Israel, and other countries demonstrates. Even for closed systems, public source data have been used to map the belief systems of the foreign policy elite, with results that are credible and permit at least some valid predictive inferences to actual behavior; the work of Bobrow, Chan, and Kringen (1979) on China is a pertinent example.

The central premise of the latter study is that the behavior of decision systems in the arena of world politics is patterned and nonrandom in nature. This hypothesis reinforces the image of international politics as a giant communications network in which states (and their policy-makers) send a stream of verbal and physical "messages" to other actors. Deception and image projection are both present in the communications channels, but the bulk of the volume consists of directly interpretable cues and messages. This implies that public source data can be employed to explain, monitor, and forecast elite behavior in the realm of foreign affairs, especially if such data are longitudinal and if the focus is trends and patterns.

Several cross-national public source foreign policy elite data bases are available. One, discussed in Chapter 3, features data on elite beliefs and personality traits (see also Hermann, 1979b); the second, the subject of Chapters 4 and 5, consists of data on elite values. Both display respectable relationships with foreign behavior, especially for certain types of states and situations.

The work of Falkowski (1978) on U.S. foreign

policy elites and flexibility also illustrates the potential utility of public source data.[10] Essentially, Falkowski posits that a decision-maker's response to feedback from the environment is indicative of his or her flexibility. Flexibility is linked to behavior and crisis decision-making via the leader's ability to handle and respond to feedback information. Incoming information can reinforce or alter an individual's policies, goals, or both. Differences among individuals are at least partly a function of memory; the degree of difference in individual memory can be expected to predict differences in the intensity and direction of behavior.

Memory is comprised of referents and themes, according to Falkowski (1978). Referents consist of perceived cognitive objects (e.g., events); a referent can be defined in terms of several dimensions:

- Temporal (past, present, future);
- Location (foreign, domestic);
- Affect (positive, negative).

Leaders who use present, foreign referents are hypothesized to be most likely to display consistent patterns of flexible behavior in foreign policy crises.

Theme is the second major element of memory. Theme involves the attitudes associated with a referent; themes can be subdivided into goal ("what") and policy ("how") types.

Falkowski's (1978) data source is the <u>New York Times Index</u>. Failure in crisis, the intervening variable, is measured by coding newspaper editorials; failure is defined by the presence of negative affect in the editorials. Referents, goal themes, and policy themes comprise the independent variables; the public speeches and news conferences of U.S. presidents and secretaries of state (selected crisis cases, 1948-1978) constitute the data base. The dependent variable--level of flexibility--is determined by the difference in the direction and intensity of referents and goal and policy themes after a crisis has occurred.

Five incidents were used to represent crisis/failures: Czechoslovakia (Truman); Lebanon (Eisenhower); Berlin (Kennedy); Tet (Johnson); and the 1973 Middle East war (Nixon). An overall indicator of change was developed by assigning weights of five to goal change, three to policy change, and one to referents. The rank order correlation between use of present referents and overall behavior change was .74; the correlation between past referents and overall behavior change was .16. Both results supported the expectations. Congruence (a measure of fit along six dimensions of referents and goals during the pre-crisis period) showed a rank order correlation of .80 with behavior. Both type of referent and overall congruence, then, predicted flexibility (i.e., change of goals, policies, and referents after experiencing a crisis failure).

The Falkowski findings, although they should be regarded as tentative given the low number of cases, do nevertheless converge with other research to suggest that foreign behavior can be explained by the personal characteristics of foreign policy elites. Furthermore, all of the relevant research has utilized public data sources, such as the <u>New York Times</u> or the Foreign Broadcast Information Service (FBIS) <u>Daily Reports</u>.

As critics charge, the observed belief-behavior linkages do not demonstrate directly and unequivocally that beliefs precede behavioral outputs. Post-decision justification or rationalization could clearly be operating, with decisions dictating the expressed beliefs rather than the reverse. As Kinder and Weiss (1978: 727) point out, converging evidence from pre- and post-decisional data makes the problem less vexing. The common use of documentary evidence and content analysis, however, means that most of the empirical evidence will be of the post-decisional variant. International relations data, as Jervis (1976) emphasizes, are rarely in such a a form that perceptual and behavioral variables can be manipulated as directly or as clearly as in the social psychological laboratory.

The complexity and difficulty of conducting process analysis, the problems of inferring from data sources to the intentions and perceptions of decision-makers, and the necessary caveats about interpreting belief-behavior linkages suggest the array of obstacles which confronts the psychological study of foreign policy. Concurrently, however, the progress in the past decade clearly implies that the empirical and--increasingly--comparative analysis of beliefs and other characteristics of foreign policy-makers is sufficiently productive to counterbalance the inevitable roadblocks and frustrations. A host of theoretical and methodological issues--some of which are discussed in the concluding chapter--awaits resolution; recent work, however, has

clearly provided the necessary foundation for
launching a subfield which blends political psychology with foreign policy analysis.

NOTES

1. On recent trends in small group research, see McGrath (1978). National security-related work is summarized in two useful literature reviews: Kirk (1976) and Shapiro and Gilbert (1975). See also Semmel and Minix (1979) and Shapiro and Cummings (1976); on social psychology and international relations in general, see especially Druckman (1977a, 1977b, 1979).
2. On crises and decision units, see especially Smart and Vertinsky (1977).
3. These issues are discussed in the concluding chapter of Falkowski (1979b) and in Chapters 3 and 5 below.
4. See Hopple (1979c) and Hermann and Hermann (1979).
5. See p. 61.
6. This proposition is central to the decision-making approaches of Snyder et al. (1962) and many others; see, e.g., the interesting review and critique by Gold (1978).
7. Dissensus within a decision unit (i.e., bureaucratic politics) also exemplifies this syndrome; perceptions of the environment may vary within an elite, with decision variations reflecting changes in the internal balance of power. Evidence relating to the impact of intra-unit bureaucratic politics factors is presented in Snyder and Diesing (1977).
8. This assumes that there is a "knowable" objective environment for a given set of actors, issues, and time parameters; such consensus is almost invariably restricted to hindsight rather than foresight contexts.
9. This is similar to George's (1979) distinction between congruence and process tracing approaches to belief systems analysis.
10. See also the relevant chapters in Falkowski (1979a, 1979b).

2
The Biopolitical Foundations of Elite Foreign Policy Behavior

Currently, biopolitics and psychophysiology are "growth industries" in political science. The upsurge in interest is reflected by the numerous panels devoted to the topic at recent International Political Science Association (IPSA), American Political Science Association (APSA), and International Society of Political Psychology (ISPP) conferences.[1] The Paris Conference on Biology and Politics (sponsored by the IPSA) was held in January of 1975; a landmark collection of essays which resulted from this conference was subsequently published (Somit, 1976a). A recent literature survey in the nascent "subfield" of biopolitics identified about 200 relevant studies in the period from 1963 to 1977 (Somit et al., 1978).[2] Also noteworthy is the establishment of research centers and programs devoted specifically to the study of psychophysiological and/or biopolitical aspects of political science.[3]

BIOPOLITICS: AN OVERVIEW

Biopolitics is an amorphous area of inquiry, as is the case for most new subdisciplines in political science. The subfield "emerged" a little over a decade ago and much of the early work consisted of exhortatory appeals designed to demonstrate that the concepts, theories, and research tools of the life sciences were or could be made relevant to political science generally or political philosophy specifically.[4]

According to Somit (1976b), the first modern political science panel on the subject of "biology and politics" was organized at the Annual Meeting of the Southern Political Science Association in 1967.

While the published literature has proliferated since then, much of the relevant work is contained in unpublished conference papers and manuscripts which circulate among the members of an "invisible college" of political scientists interested in biopolitics. The Notes of the Center for Biopolitical Research at Northern Illinois University provides a centralized mechanism for the diffusion of information about the professional activities of and the publications of interest to "biopoliticists."

While in some respects this is an oversimplification, the literature on biopolitics can be dichotomized into studies which treat biological factors (broadly defined) as independent variables and those which employ biological research methods.[5] The former will be discussed briefly; the latter will be the subject of the following section of the chapter.

Theoretically, psychophysiological and other biological explanations of human behavior can be viewed as one significant set of causal influences, along with other clusters of determinants. The theoretical argument is strengthened immeasurably if it can be demonstrated that somatic (and other biopolitical) variables significantly influence the dependent variable (political behavior) and also the psychosocial processes which are conventionally posited to be the independent variables in empirical political research (Schwartz, 1976: 21). Such processes include political socialization, personality, specific political predispositions, and exposure to political stimuli. In addition, if it is shown that biopolitical factors exert a direct impact (independently of psychosocial processes), then the case for a subdiscipline of biopolitics is even more compelling (Schwartz, 1976: 27-28). The two conditions can be depicted as:

Biopolitical factors ⟶ psychosocial processes ⟶ political behavior;

Biopolitical factors ⟶ political behavior.

Examples are provided by the work of Schwartz (1976), who presents evidence that health status and other biological factors indirectly (through psychosocial processes) and directly explain political behavior. Others have employed ethology (the scientific study of animal behavior) as well as sociobiology (the study of the genetic bases of social behavior) in theoretical analyses of human

attitudes of journalists.
   Theoretically, psychophysiological and biopolitical phenomena have thus been posited to be determinants of political behavior or precursors of processes which produce political behavior. This suggests that research designs which seek to account for elite behavior and decision-making processes should explicitly introduce variables from this domain. Corning (1978: 4) identifies three general theoretical applications in biopolitical research:

- Applications of systems theory and cybernetics to the modeling of political phenomena at individual and systemic levels;

- Applications of ethological concepts to the analysis of political behavior;

- Analyses of the impact of biological variables on individual and collective behavior.

   Corning (1971) and Scott (1978) provide examples of the first perspective. Masters (1976, 1978c, 1978d, 1978e), Schubert (1973), Somit (1968), and Willhoite (1971, 1977, 1978) exemplify the work which has been reported in the areas of ethology, sociobiology, and evolutionary theory more generally. Finally, extensive research has accrued on an array of physiological, biological, and pharmacological influences on human behavior; examples include the work of Wiegele (1973) on fatigue and stress, the research of Jaros (1972) on drugs, the previously noted study of health and political behavior (Schwartz, 1976), and the analysis of pharmacological factors (Somit, 1968).
   Biopolitically-oriented theories of political behavior have been subjected to a barrage of epistemological, theoretical, methodological, and ideological criticisms. Genetic (and other biological) theories are not necessarily reductionistic or deterministic.[6] However, the methodological difficulties (in both the narrow, technical and broad research strategy senses of "methodology") are extraordinarily problematic, as a recent review essay by two advocates of a biopolitical approach clearly recognizes (see Peterson and Somit, 1978). Especially troublesome is the generalization problem which confronts ethologically-oriented biopoliticists.

Generalization barriers, in fact, constitute a potentially immobilizing obstacle; the enthusiastic introduction of genetic and similar theoretical perspectives into mainstream political science would be decidedly premature. The simultaneous impact of genetic endownment, learning-related and experiential factors, and cultural determinants injects into biopolitics methodological problems "far more complex than those encountered in the study of any other species [Peterson and Somit, 1978: 18]."

The very nature of comparative analysis--the heart of ethological approaches in biopolitics--underlines the gravity of this problem. Again, Peterson and Somit (1978: 20) provide a brief but very relevant discussion. Analogy (resemblance in some trait across two or more different species) is a typical mode of comparison in ethological research; homology, the other form of comparative analysis, is resemblance between two or more species which can be explained by their evolutionary descent from a common ancestor who possessed that particular trait. Frequently, analogies are interesting but far from compelling in nature; Greenstein's (1975: 18) apt characterization of psychobiographical case studies in political psychology as research which produces "undemonstrated--and possibly undemonstrable--half-insights" can also be applied to "political ethology."

The inference or generalization problem plagues the ethologist (or ethologically-oriented political scientist) who attempts to "travel" from non-human species to humans. The controversial nature of theoretical biopolitics also emerges as a key problem area. Attacks on sociobiology and other biological approaches to the study of human behavior often reflect considerable animus; the criticisms levelled at the sociobiologist E. O. Wilson are particularly illustrative.[7]

This controversy is beyond the scope of the discussion in this chapter. However, there is impressive evidence that other clusters of factors exert more impact on individual and social behavior. Clearly, the burden of proof is on the advocate of biopolitics (especially given the ad hoc nature of theoretical research in biopolitics). The fact that this is characteristic of any adolescent subfield does not exempt its practitioners from the need to design their research more carefully, become more aware of major lacunae, and consciously strive to meet standards of rigorous empirical inquiry and cumulativeness. The latter is especially critical since the point has been reached at which a moratorium should be imposed on <u>general</u> exhortations for a greater emphasis on the nexus between the life sciences and the study of politics; advocates of a general science of biopolitics should begin to pursue systematic empirical research.

A caveat about biopolitical "imperialism" should also be offered. The life sciences should not be related to political processes in an isolated fashion:

> ...unless contained in a comprehensive theory which includes social, political, and psychological variables, biologically oriented theories of conflict and aggression (although sometimes valid within their domain) offer at best severely limited and at worst highly misleading explanations of complex human events [Nelson, 1975: 735].

Finally, many of the theories and concepts of biopolitics are not directly applicable to the study of foreign policy elites, where the focus is on the individual decision-maker or the small, high level decision-making group. Wiegele (1979a, 1979b) shows convincingly that evolutionary and other system-level biopolitical theories are relevant to the study of international politics at the nation and systemic levels. At the elite or individual level of analysis, certain biologically-oriented individual-level factors are undoubtedly pertinent (e.g., age, health status, circadian and other body rhythms, etc.); more macrocosmic biological processes are distal and not directly relevant. What Easton (1976: 244) refers to as <u>biopolimetrics</u>, in contrast, which is the focus of the following section, is an area of undeniable but primarily potential relevance to the analysis of the decision processes and belief systems of foreign policy elites.

PSYCHOPHYSIOLOGY

<u>Biopolimetrics</u> subsumes all of the discernible and measurable manifestations of activity within the human organism conceived as an information processing and decision-making system. Technically, of course, the explicit content which constitutes verbal behavior comprises part of the foreign policy elite's repertoire of indicators of cognitive activity (defined as a process which extends from the

definition of the situation to the final response to a stimulus). In reality, however, linguistic verbal output (as opposed to paralinguistic output) is always separated from the array of detectable indicators which collectively represents the cumbersome concept of biopolimetrics.

Essentially, biopolimetrics includes a number of discrete nonverbal and psychophysiological indicators. In contrast to theoretical biopolitics, methodological biopolitics generally posits political behavior to be the independent variable and the physical and physiological manifestations to be the effect indicators or dependent variables. For example, Hermann's (1979a) comprehensive review essay catalogues a number of overt verbal and nonverbal indicators of stress in foreign policy-makers.[8]

Generally, nonverbal behavior is directly observable whereas fairly elaborate equipment is required to measure the internal bodily processes which are indexed by such psychophysiological indicators as sweat gland activity, muscular movements, or brain electrical activity. Speech disturbances (e.g., stuttering, omissions, the "ah" sound), which are often used to measure anxiety, are typical nonverbal indicators.[9]

The extensive research on nonverbal indicators is summarized in Druckman and Slater (1979) and in Harper et al. (1978). The empirical work is typically organized in terms of five distinct channels of nonverbal communication:

- Paralanguage (content-free vocalizations associated with speech);

- Facial expressions;

- Kinesics (body movements);

- Visual behavior (e.g., eye contact, pupillary behavior);

- Proxemics (how people structure, use, and are affected by personal space).

Psychophysiology, which involves the observation of bodily changes to detect emotional states, is discussed in Greenfield and Sternbach (1972), Hassett (1978), and numerous other sources. In psychophysiology, the polygraph, an electronic device for recording minute electrical changes in the human body, is the standard instrument for securing empirical data.

The process of recording human physiological responses is threefold in nature. First, electrodes are placed on the body surface to <u>detect</u> the electrical activity. The signal is then electronically processed by a series of amplification circuits; after the <u>signal refinement</u> phase (i.e., amplification and filtering), the <u>signal display</u> occurs on a device used to display electrical changes (i.e., the polygraph).

The typical independent variable in psychophysiology is behavior (just as political behavior would be the independent variable in a science of political psychophysiology). The dependent variable is one or more physiological indicators. Note that physiological psychology, the mirror image of psychophysiology, manipulates an aspect of physiology while behavior is observed; physiological psychology is very intrusive and has therefore concentrated on animals lower than humans on the scale of evolution.

With the advent of electrical psychophysiological recording, the early approaches (direct observation and fairly cumbersome mechanical recording systems) have become less prominent although not quite extinct. The list in Table 2.1, adopted from Hassett (1978), features the major areas of psychophysiological research; the emphasis has been on EDA or sweat gland activity and, to a lesser extent, heart rate, blood pressure, and the electrical activity of muscles (EMG) and the brain (EEG). Overall, the cardiovascular system is more biological than psychological in nature; the respiratory and digestive systems are not studied very often in psychophysiological research, although the former is still commonly measured in the "science" of lie detection. The most common psychophysiological variable is skin resistance (SR) and its reciprocal skin conductance (SC), which are indices of sweat gland activity.

Nonverbal and psychophysiological indicators represent potential additional methods for investigating different aspects of cognitive and decisional activity and for representing elite beliefs, perceptions, and values. An exclusive reliance on the manifest content of verbal behavior is an extremely risky strategy. There are numerous problems with verbal (self-report) measures of attitudes, beliefs, and values; the primary difficulties are noted in the following discussion.

First, the individual may not know (or be able to verbalize) his or her attitude toward a given

Physical System	Response/s Studied
1. Sweat gland	Electrodermal Activity (EDA) (skin resistance or SR, skin conductance or SC, etc.)
2. Cardiovascular system	Heart Rate (electrocardiogram or EKG); Blood Pressure; Blood Flow; Skin Temperature
3. Respiratory and digestive systems	Electrogastogram (EGG)[b]
4. Eyes	Pupillary Diameter; Eye Blinks; Electrooculogram (EOG)[c]
5. Muscles	Electromyography (EMG)
6. Brain	Electroencephalogram (EEG)

[a]Source: Based on Hassett (1978).
[b]The EGG measures electrical changes at the body surface which reflect stomach muscular contractions.
[c]The EOG, which (like EDA, EKG, EGG, EMG, and EEG) is recorded on a polygraph, measures eye movement.

Table 2.1

PSYCHOPHYSIOLOGY: TYPES OF RESPONSES STUDIED[a]

object (issue, person, etc.). In certain instances, nonverbal behavior (e.g., facial expressions, direct eye contact, etc.) can be used as surrogate measures of the affect or intensity dimensions of attitudes and beliefs.[10] Certain psychophysiological measures, such as various indicators of the electrical activity of the skin or electrodermal activity (EDA), are responsive to external stimuli and stress and are not generally subject to conscious control by the subject.

Secondly, respondents in survey research and subjects in psychological experiments do not always tell the truth; elites also engage in deception in international politics--for both domestic and/or ex-external reasons. In their assessment of the potential applicability of nonverbal behavior indicators to international affairs, Druckman and Slater (1979) evaluate the potential of such measures as indices of cognitive activity (information processing) and as indicators of dissimulation and impression management. Nonverbal indicators could be employed to supplement verbal measures if it is suspected that the speaker is attempting to deceive the audience; additionally, nonverbal indicators can in certain instances be used by the target to infer deception as part of the decoding process.

Thirdly, forces unrelated to content may intrude in the verbal research setting, causing the respondent or subject to react primarily or exclusively to the non-content-relevant features of the stimulus. Various response biases (e.g., social desirability, acquiescence, etc.) can be regarded as "method" factors which can in some instances override the "content" component.[11] Among members of lower social strata, for example, attitude scales biased in the agree direction may elicit an appreciable amount of acquiescence response bias that does not necessarily reflect the true underlying attitude or belief of the respondent (see, e.g., Jackman, 1973). This suggests that, whenever possible, nonverbal or physiological indicators should be used to supplement self-report measures.

A fourth issue relates to the imprecision of verbal attitude scales, which often collapse responses into a few (2-7) categories. A considerable amount of such data is consequently nominal or ordinal. In contrast to such category scales, psychophysical (magnitude) and psychophysiological scales do not force responses to stimuli to "bunch up" and such data cover the full range of theoretically possible responses (see, e.g., Tursky, 1977; Tursky et al., 1979). This in turn makes the data interval in nature, thereby increasing its precision and facilitating the application of more powerful statistical techniques.

The work of Bernard Tursky, Milton Lodge, and their colleagues at Stony Brook, which will be discussed briefly below, exemplifies a convergent, multitrait-multimethod approach to validation. The idea of convergent and discriminant validation by the multitrait-multimethod matrix reflects an explicit desire to estimate the relative contributions of trait (e.g., content) and method variance (Campbell and Fiske, 1959). The basic idea is that measures of the same trait should correlate at a higher level with each other (across methods) than they do with measures of different traits involving separate methods.

Within the domain of verbal attitude or belief systems research, this approach to validation is certainly not unknown. Jackman (1973), for example, presents evidence which indicates that the theory of working class authoritarianism depends heavily on scales which use uniformly positively-worded items and therefore generate an education-related acquiescence response bias which is not indicative of the individual's real attitudes. She found that the anti-Semitism scale measured by method 1 correlated more with F(Fascist) and anomie scales measured by the same method than with an anti-Semitism scale measured by method 2. In a path model, education and general knowledge explained 42 percent of the variance in the "method" factor but only 3 percent of the variance in the "pure anti-Semitism" factor.

A foreign policy-relevant example is provided by the Bobrow et al. (1979) verbal cognitive model representation of the Chinese foreign policy elite's operational code.[12] Explicitly adopting a convergent-divergent validation strategy, Bobrow, Chan and Kringen (1979) start with the premises that decision processes are rarely directly accessible and that any single access mechanism or tool (i.e., research method) is probably weak and suspect. They therefore embrace an "ensemble of methods" strategy, integrating qualitative content analysis of various Chinese documents and comparing propositions across source and temporal parameters. Verbal association tests are used to infer perceptions of key political symbols. Three analytical strategies are subsequently pursued to illuminate the relationships between beliefs and patterns of behavior: the identification of actual conflict behavior in varying historical situations and events data analysis; a quasi-experimental analysis of Chinese responses to salient foreign policy events; and a multivariate analysis of the Chinese elite's image of other actors.

An array of verbal and nonverbal (psychophysiological, psychophysical, and physical) indicators could be used simultaneously in a multitrait-multimethod design. Such a strategy reflects the realization that no single method is perfect or foolproof. The weaknesses of verbal data are well known. The disadvantages of nonverbal data, on the other hand, should not be overlooked or minimized; such data are often ambiguous. The search for a consistent, across-the-board relationship between physical or physiological indicators and emotional states, psychological arousal, or attitudes and beliefs has proven to be illusory.

The simultaneous use of verbal, nonverbal, and psychophysiological indicators would presumably maximize the reliability and validity of attitude and belief measures. Another approach has involved the comparative analysis of the relative impact of verbal and nonverbal channels of communication. In a study of the impact of verbal content vis-a-vis tone (paralinguistic variations of pitch and stress), Mehrabian and Wiener (1967: 114) concluded:

> ...when an implicit communication of attitude is inconsistent with an explicit content communication of attitude, the contribution of the implicit component may be disproportionately greater than its independent effect.

While such multiple-channel research has been rare, the available evidence does suggest that in cases of disagreement, the nonverbal aspect may be more determinative of the target's inference than the verbal component.[13] In another study, Mehrabian and Ferris (1967) discovered that facial expression accounted for more of the variance in inferred attitudes than the vocal component. The following regression equation summarizes the relative contributions of combined facial-vocal attitude communications (see Mehrabian and Ferris, 1967: 251):

$$A_{Total} = 1.50 A_{Facial} \text{ and } 1.03 A_{Vocal}$$

In a second analysis of the interactive effects of two or more channels, Mehrabian (1972) reported that the relative importance of type of channel was as follows:

$$A_{Total} = .07 A_{Verbal} + .38 A_{Vocal} + .55 A_{Facial}$$

In the measurement of social attitudes, the search for non-content measures of prejudice and racism has been especially sustained. Research dating back to the 1930s has revealed a disappointingly weak linkage between verbally expressed attitudes and actual behavior in this sensitive area. Quite a few studies have employed physiological indicators (primarily skin electrical activity and pupillary dilation) in an effort to discover automatic and valid indices of attitudes.[14] While the evidence has been mixed and the standard measure (GSR or Galvanic Skin Response readings) reveals intensity but not direction, there has nevertheless been a great deal of interest in physiological and other nonverbal attitude indicators.[15]

In contrast to standard verbal self-report techniques, nonverbal indicators can be nonreactive. In many content domains other than racism and prejudice, social desirability, acquiescence response bias, and other "response sets" and confounding variables (such as demand characteristics of the situation and interviewer effects) may intrude upon and bias verbal responses. Two recent psychophysical/psychophysiological approaches to attitude measurement in political science will be briefly chronicled here. Both are designed to provide substitutes for (or at least supplements to) the verbal and behavioral (observational) response modes.

The first, which is associated with Lodge, Tursky, and their associates at the Laboratory for Behavioral Research at the State University of New York at Stony Brook, extends psychophysics from the measurement of sensory phenomena to the measurement of social and political phenomena (Tursky et al., 1979).[16] Numerous psychophysical experiments in political scaling have been completed (e.g., a support for political institutions scale). The cross-modal, biobehavioral approach can be applied to the measurement of the cognitive and evaluative components of political attitudes. The basic rationale for such a multiple indicator approach is that:

> ...verbal, physiological, and physical responses are concurrent multiple behaviors, all functionally sensitive to individual-environmental interactions but not necessarily interrelated in simple linear fashion. Therefore, a dual research strategy is proposed. First, because the sole reliance on verbal measurement of beliefs, feelings, interactions, and actions is conceptually as well as empirically untenable, there is need to incorporate, systematically, multiple measurements <u>across</u> verbal, physical, and physiological response modes. Second, multiple response measurements are required <u>within</u> each response mode [Tursky et al., 1976a:

62; emphasis in the original].

Tursky et al. (1979) provide an example of simultaneous psychophysical and psychophysiological evaluations of the direction, intensity, and meaning of social stimuli (in this study, race-related concepts). They note at the outset that the verbal response mode has dominated empirical research despite the intrusion of a number of major conceptual and methodological problems. The use of magnitude estimation and other psychophysical scaling procedures, they continue, generates more precise data, but:

> ...it does not solve the problem of multiple meanings or substantially reduce the effects of response bias. One possible solution to this problem is to utilize less voluntary response measures in conjunction with psychophysical scaling procedures to obtain maximum intensity and meaning information [Tursky et al., 1979: 453].

The first phase of the research involved psychophysical scaling and cross-modality validation. On the average, the 10 preselected black items were 21 times more black-related than the standard; the 10 preselected white stimuli were 12 times more white-related than the standard; the 12 political test items fell in between. Equally significant, the categorical data (i.e., the standard verbal response mode) were forced to cluster into a 7-category scale while the magnitude scale values displayed a range of 900 to 1.

In the second phase, Tursky et al. (1979) focus on the extent to which the race-related concepts generalize to a set of denotatively nonracial stimuli via classical conditioning. Half of the 60 student subjects were assigned to the black conditioning group and half to the white. The race-related concepts were conditioned stimuli (CS) and the unconditioned stimulus (UCS) was a loud burst of noise. Skin conductance response measures were recorded.

All 10 white items and 9 of the 10 black items were significantly different between groups in the predicted direction. The 12 test stimuli (political issues) were divided into 6 white and 6 black subsets (on the basis of previous categorical judgments regarding their race-related nature). These stimuli also produced a significant response difference in the predicted direction.

Overall, the results suggest that each of the modes (verbal, psychophysical, pyschophysiological) has utility. However, verbal category scaling collapses responses artificially. Furthermore, noteworthy instances of differential response patterns separated both of the judgmental measures (category and magnitude scaling) from the SC (skin conductance) responses.

Watts (1978) has also conducted research on physiologically-based attitude measurement techniques. He uses such indicators as skin conductance response and heart rate to measure the affective component of attitudes and to validate standard verbal scales. One particular scale focuses on violence and aggressive behavior in the milieu of children; Watts (1978: 13) hypothesizes that high scorers--those who reject violence in the presence of children--will tend to show stimulus rejection (heart rate acceleration) and greater autonomic arousal (as measured by skin conductance response or SCR).

Watts and Sumi (1979) treat verbal and psychophysiological measures as potential indicators of social attitudes in a convergent validation design. In one study, they examined the validity of the CF or Children's F scale; the subjects were 20 children (both sexes) between the ages of 11 and 14. Heart rate (HR) and skin conductance (SC) were both recorded. The visual stimulus consisted of a series of violent and non-violent episodes from television. Analysis of variance was conducted with sex, CF score, and stimuli as posited main effects; there was a significant effect for stimulus event and a significant interaction between the latter and CF, but no significant difference in arousal by sex, CF score, or sex by CF interaction. As expected, high CF (i.e., violence-accepting) subjects tended to experience heart rate (HR) deceleration and low CF subjects tended to display HR acceleration.

The second experiment in Watts and Sumi (1979) involved college students and a larger number of attitudinal measures. The same episodes were shown as in the previous experiment. There were three independent variables: sex; attitudinal dispositions regarding interpersonal tactics (measures of Machiavellianism, Violence Ideology, etc.); and the videotaped sequences from television programs. As predicted, HR was negatively correlated with all of the attitude scales, showing that aversion to violence, aggression, and manipulativeness covary with stimulus rejection. Generally, the findings were more consistent and significantly more robust in magnitude for male subjects.

The work of Tursky et al. (1979), Watts and Sumi (1979), and others clearly demonstrates that at least some psychophysical and psychophysiological indicators can reveal the direction as well as the intensity of attitudes. This contrasts sharply with Mueller's (1970) pessimism concerning the utility of nonverbal indicators for measuring the cognitive dimension of attitudes.

In the context of the multitrait-multimethod validation philosophy outlined earlier in this chapter, it is obvious that political psychology is moving ineluctably in that direction. Watts and Sumi (1979) embrace a convergent validation strategy in which verbal self-report and physiological indicators are both used to measure social attitudes, thus building redundancy into the measurement process. Tursky et al. (1976a, 1979) go beyond this in their advocacy of a cross-modal, multi-indicator approach, an orientation which facilitates both discriminant and convergent validation.

Four distinct methodologies are available for measuring attitudes and other components of belief systems:

- Verbal (category scaling, etc.);
- Psychophysical;
- Nonverbal (physical);
- Physiological or psychophysiological.

The first two are judgmental and allow for the measurement of complex attitudes as well as the identification of sophisticated and subtle patterns. Both are subject to the limitations imposed on any approach which relies on the conscious, voluntary cooperation of human subjects; dissimulation, response biases, and lack of self-knowledge are among the numerous pitfalls which pervade the judgmental tradition. While the nonverbal and psychophysiological modes are usually nonreactive (and are certainly less subject to conscious control by the subject than the verbal techniques), these approaches are often crude (for example, body movements frequently reveal global psychological states rather than discrete attitudes) and cannot yet be used to illuminate all of the dimensions of an attitude. Given the fallibility of any single method, a multimethod strategy is significantly less risky and more likely to yield reliable and valid measures.

APPLICATIONS TO FOREIGN POLICY ELITES

Nonverbal applications have been rare in the foreign policy-political psychology area. One pioneering effort will be described in detail below; a second research program, which is not directly concerned with foreign policy decision processes, nevertheless provides an example of a sustained and empirically productive psychophysiology project which could provide the foundation for future research on political psychophysiology and decision-making.

The relevant inquiry in social psychology and political behavior has usually employed college students as subjects. When the focus has been shifted beyond the confines of an experimental laboratory at a university, the subjects have usually been members of the mass public and the "samples" have typically been both small and unrepresentative. There have been some direct verbal studies of lower level and even a few high level decision-makers (via interviews, questionnaires, observation, etc.); generally, however, access has been indirect (e.g., using experts as surrogates for elites, content analysis, etc.) Political psychologists who employ nonverbal and psychophysiological methodologies have never secured direct access; no political decision-maker is known to be anxious to be hooked up to a polygraph via electrodes for the purpose of recording his or her brain electrical activity patterns or some other psychophysiological process.

Empirical inquiry on foreign policy elites consequently requires "at-a-distance" research designs. Fortunately, many of the forms of nonverbal behavior analysis are compatible with such requirements. There is a burgeoning literature in psychology on the relationship between nonverbal and paralinguistic verbal forms of behavior and stress and such stress-related states as anxiety, fear, uncertainty, and defensiveness (see Frank, 1973, 1977; Hermann, 1977: 63). Nonverbal behavior includes such subtypes as maintenance of physical distance in interpersonal interaction, posturing behavior, gesturing, and facial affect. Paralinguistic verbal behavior can be dichotomized into nonsemantic verbal data (e.g., voiceprints, speech rate, voice pitch) and such semantic but "noncommunicatively significant" data as type-token ratios and frequency of self references (see Frank, 1977: 64).

physiological approaches focus primarily on the implicit and the unintended.

Wiegele uses the Psychological Stress Evaluator (PSE), an unobtrusive measuring instrument which produces physiological data on the human voice.[19] Stimuli such as high levels of psychological stress ordinarily produce two types of vocal changes. Gross vocal change (variations in rate, volume, voice tremor, etc.) can be audibly detected and can also be controlled by the speaker. The second type of vocal change, which is inaudible and presumably unconscious, results from a slight tensing of the vocal cords and leads to the dampening of selected frequency variations.

A tape recording is used to capture the speech pattern containing the words that carry the involuntary speech components indicating stress. According to Wiegele (1979e: 81):

> Using electronic filtering and frequency discrimination techniques, the PSE processes the voice frequencies and displays the inaudible stress-related FM [frequency modulation] patterns on a moving strip chart. Utilizing interpretation criteria developed by the manufacturers of the PSE, these FM patterns indicate levels of psychological stress.

The steps in PSE or voice stress analysis consist of two distinct subprocesses: stress production and stress analysis. The <u>stress production</u> phase includes:

- External stimulus configuration (the international crisis);

- Individual decision-maker (as part of an authoritative decision unit);

- Generation of psychological stress in the individual decision-maker;

- Change in vocal characteristics (as evidenced in a recorded crisis speech).

Among the discrete aspects of <u>stress analysis</u> are:

- Tape recording of the crisis speech;

- Electronic analysis of the tape recording with the PSE;
- Production of PSE wave form charts for each word;
- Interpretation of word stress configurations.

Unstressed charts reflect patterns which are the product of totally relaxed vocal cords and display an undulating wave form. Tensed vocal cords are characterized by tight "squarish" configurations. Typical of extreme stress is an almost rectangular pattern. Illustrative charts appear in Figure 2.1.

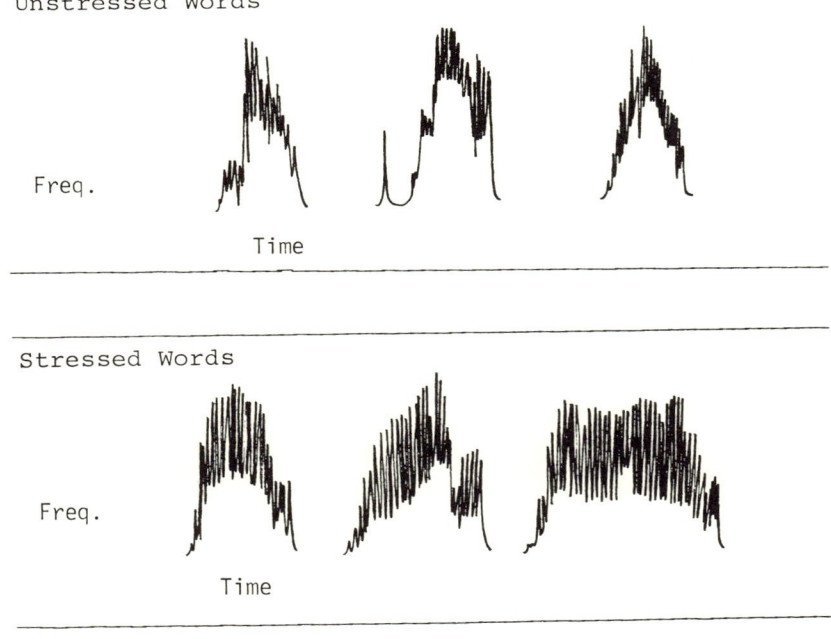

Figure 2.1

ILLUSTRATIVE PSYCHOLOGICAL STRESS EVALUATOR (PSE) WAVE FORM CHARTS

Considerable nonpolitical PSE research--some of which is alluded to below--has been produced (see also Wiegele, 1979e: 82-86). In a study which explored the effectiveness of the PSE as a tool for measuring anxiety and the effectiveness of anti-anxiety drugs, Borgen and Goodman (1976) conducted an experiment on eight paid male prisoners.

They examined the responses of the subjects to a Stroop Test, which produces a presumably stress-inducing conflict situation. Along with PSE measurements, blood flow, skin potential, and EKG readings were taken. Subjects also received either 10 milligrams of a tranquilizer or a placebo two hours prior to the experiment.

The Stroop Test elicited an arousal state, as indexed by significant increases in blood flow and the other indicators. Although the results showed movement in the expected directions (e.g., the tranquilizer reduced the degree of stress reflected by the traditional measures and the PSE), the small subgroup N's mitigated against acceptable levels of statistical significance.

In a political study not related to foreign policy, Wiegele (1978a) used the PSE to analyze two extemporaneous speeches by Richard Nixon during periods of presumptive high stress: the 1962 California gubernatorial concession speech and the 1974 farewell to his staff speech after his resignation from the presidency. The themes which reflected the highest PSE levels revolved around personal concerns in both cases, indicating that Nixon viewed political crises in highly personal terms.

In his research on the five international crises, Wiegele (1978b) examined the text of each paragraph to determine the dominant substantive themes. A count was then made of the total number of words in each paragraph and a standardized score of high-stress words per paragraph was produced by dividing the total into the number of high-stress measures for a decision-maker. Wiegele views the overall percentage of high stress words as a summary measure of the general state of physiological arousal in the subject at that point in time.

In the ten highest stress paragraphs in President Kennedy's quarantine speech during the Cuban missile crisis, two composite themes dominate the list. One concerns the Administration's determination to see the crisis through to a conclusion which would be in the general interests of the United States; the other represents signals of encouragement for both sides to move away from direct confrontation.

In his discussions about the other cases, Wiegele (1978b) provides several interesting examples of the use of PSE evidence. In Truman's speech on the North Korean invasion of South Korea, the highest stress theme in the entire document is one associated with the role of the United Nations and the fact that Communist authorities never permitted U.N. observers to visit North Korea. Wiegele infers that the amount of stress was related to Truman's knowledge that previously articulated U.S. defense policy was more responsible for North Korean aggression than the failure to admit U.N. observers.

In Johnson's Tonkin Gulf speech, the highest stress theme concerned the announcement that U.S. air strikes against naval vessels and supporting facilities in North Vietnam had been launched. The extremely high stress is understandable in the context of subsequent disclosures about the doubts concerning the guilt of North Vietnam; there was the additional factor of the precise timing of the announcement in order to maximize the achievement of the goals of the air strike and simultaneously reassure decision-makers in Peking.

The _Pueblo_ speech contained a paragraph with a stress level of 37.93 (the _mean_ stress level for the speech was 20.57); the theme of "precautionary measures being taken in the Korean area" characterized this paragraph. Wiegele offers the interpretation that the high stress for this theme was attributable to the fact that Johnson knew he was overstating his case.

The absence of objective base rate data precludes the identification of invariant generalizations concerning the impact of _situation_ (variations in stress), _personality_ (variations in susceptibility to stress), or _context_ (variations in spatial and/or temporal context factors). Some tentative judgments, however, may be possible on the basis of the comparative information which is contained in the overall stress levels reported in Wiegele (1978b), which vary from Pueblo/Johnson (20.57) to Cuba/Kennedy (5.12), with Berlin/Kennedy (9.49), Tonkin/Johnson (10.66), and Korea/Truman (10.66) falling between.

The largest overall mean stress level is the _Pueblo_ crisis; the mean of 20.57 is almost twice as large as the mean of 10.66 for Korea and the Gulf of Tonkin episodes and significantly higher in magnitude than either of the Kennedy crises. A plausible inference for the unusually high level of stress concerns the characteristics of this particular situation.

In each of the other crises--Korea, Berlin, Cuba, and the Gulf of Tonkin--it was in all likelihood perceived by each president that an American response in the crisis could credibly influence the course of events. But with regard to the U.S.S. Pueblo, seized as the United States found itself enmeshed in the Vietnam War, nothing could realistically be done by the U.S. which would cause the release of the ship. Hence, it is suggested as a plausible explanation that an action-oriented president such as Johnson would find himself under strong stress because of his inability to act credibly or to act at all [Wiegele, 1978b: 500].

Given the paucity of research with the voice stress analysis technique, generalizations are hazardous. However, one of the findings suggests the possibilities for PSE analysis from the perspectives of elite-based crisis warning and management. Wiegele speculates that when the percentage of high stress words in precipitating act statements (i.e., identifications of the stress-producing external stimulus configurations) rises above the mean for the speech, the observer should be alerted. Generally, precipitating act statements express low stress facts about which there is virtually no ambiguity or uncertainty. Significantly, the mean for the precipitating act statement in the Gulf of Tonkin address deviated from the "normal" stress pattern for such statements. Such deviations could signal doubt or ambiguity or, in some cases, deception.

Further research has been conducted, with additional cases being analyzed (e.g., Cambodia in 1970, the Dominican intervention in 1965, etc.). Furthermore, longitudinal analyses of all public vocalizations of a head of state relating to a single crisis are being done for Berlin (1961), Cambodia (1970), and the Dominican Republic (1965). Preliminary results for the latter are reported in Wiegele (1979c).

While the empirical results have been extremely encouraging, several serious methodological problems regarding the PSE have surfaced.[20] The most general and significant of these concerns the validity of the Psychological Stress Evaluator.

Originally designed and currently marketed commercially as a lie detector, the Psychological Stress Evaluator (PSE) has a mixed record in independent validation studies, especially in experimental contexts. Quite a few of the lie detection studies have yielded negative or unimpressive results, as Wiegele's (1978d) summary notes. Horvath (1978), for example, instructed subjects to select and then try to conceal a number; the PSE detected only 20 percent of the cases correctly whereas the GSR was successful with 70 percent of the subjects.

There is some supportive evidence, however. With a variety of subjects and in various real world contexts, the PSE has been shown to be valid. Wiegele (1978d) and Brenner et al. (1979) cite the major positive as well as negative studies.

Overall, the validity studies suggest that the PSE is weakest in experimental situations which do not offer the subject genuine challenges and performs most impressively in real world contexts and at higher stress levels. Brenner and his colleagues (1979) provide evidence which reinforces this position.

In one experiment, Brenner et al. (1979) offered subjects a reward to conceal successfully the correct answers to a series of innocuous personal questions about the subject. The PSE variation patterns were unrelated to the experimental manipulation.

The second experiment employed a mental arithmetic task involving problems of varying difficulty which had to be executed under a fixed pacing schedule. PSE scores varied significantly across the arithmetic-operation instructions; 15 out of 16 subjects displayed a positive linear trend in response to the magnitude of the required operation.

Brenner et al. (1979: 356) conclude that "some aspects of the PSE analysis of stress are valid" and that the instrument may not be useful for low stress tasks. This suggests unequivocally that Wiegele's use of the PSE to measure vocal stress in presidential crisis speeches was valid, since the level of "objective" or situational stress in such situations is undoubtedly high and the "task" is "ego-involving" and "relevant" to the "subject."

A second problem concerns the ambiguity about the physiological dynamics underlying the PSE patterns. Originally, it was assumed that the instrument reflected involuntary vocal change. However, it has since been discovered that subjects provided

with knowledge about the PSE could conceal lies from
the analyst. This could be attributable to the fact
that the PSE can only tap stress at the time of
vocalization; by taking a deep breath or coughing,
a subject may interfere with the procedure (Weigele,
1979d: 21).

More problematic is the fact that the posited
underlying basis of the PSE--the microtremor--has
not been independently found in the vocal mechanisms (Brenner et al., 1979: 352; Wiegele, 1979: 6).
Several attempts to test this explanation have failed. However, this criticism is less devasting in
the light of Brenner and his colleague's (1979a:
352) contention that:

> ...a disallowance of the microtremor
> explanation would not necessarily dis-
> count the entire explanation offered
> by the manufacturer [of the PSE]. A
> relationship between FM perturbation
> in the voice and psychological stress
> has been previously noted...and this
> relationship might be caused by several
> physiological mechanisms other than
> microtremor.

Regardless of the litany of methodological problems, it is clear that the PSE, when used in higher
stress and nonartificial situations, is measuring
something and that that something is important. The
PSE and voice stress analysis, along with the underlying decision-maker stress model articulated by
Wiegele (1977, 1978b), provide a firm foundation for
conducting future research on the nature and significance of PSE-based patterns of elite signals.

The P300

While the criticism could be made that Wiegele's application of the PSE to a real world problem area may be premature, that kind of charge
would not be applicable to the research of Emanuel
Donchin of the Cognitive Psychophysiology Laboratory
at the University of Illinois. Donchin's research
program has evolved incrementally and painstakingly,
providing the basis for an avalanche of experimental
research on a brain electrical wave pattern called
the P300.

Figure 2.2 distinguishes between two very general categories of psychophysiological indicators:
brain electrical activity and peripheral activity.

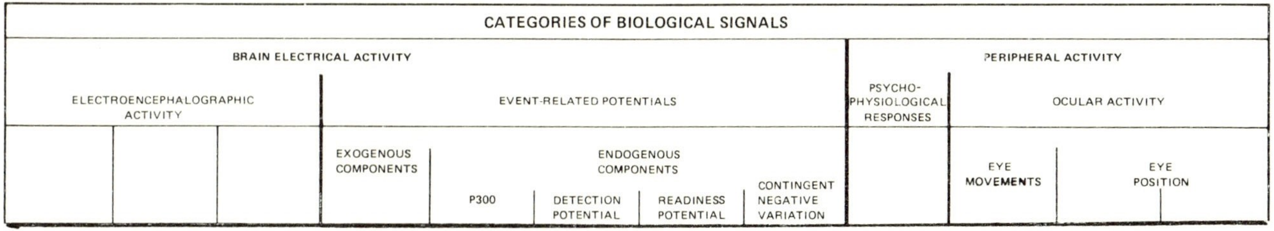

CATEGORIES OF BIOLOGICAL SIGNALS							
BRAIN ELECTRICAL ACTIVITY						PERIPHERAL ACTIVITY	
ELECTROENCEPHALOGRAPHIC ACTIVITY	EVENT-RELATED POTENTIALS					PSYCHO- PHYSIOLOGICAL RESPONSES	OCULAR ACTIVITY	
	EXOGENOUS COMPONENTS	ENDOGENOUS COMPONENTS					
		P300	DETECTION POTENTIAL	READINESS POTENTIAL	CONTINGENT NEGATIVE VARIATION		EYE MOVEMENTS	EYE POSITION

[a]Source: Gomer et al. (1979: 108).

Figure 2.2

PSYCHOPHYSIOLOGICAL INDICATORS
CONSIDERED AS INPUTS FOR BIOCYBERNETIC APPLICATIONS[a]

The former includes the P300 and a variety of other discrete EEG-based indicators; the latter includes non-brain electrical activity (EMG, EDA, EKG, etc.) and such other standard measures as heart rate, blood pressure, and blood flow.

For monitoring brain electrical activity, electrophysiological techniques are used to "observe the underlying interactions within and between populations of cortical cells [Gomer et al., 1979: 109]."[21] Donchin and others maintain that cognitive operations can be conceived in terms of coherent activity patterns within distributed cell groups.

The electrical activity of the brain of an animal was first recorded in the 1870s. While physiological psychology electrically records from isolated neurons, human-oriented psychophysiology is less intrusive and must record from the surface of the scalp. Electroencephalographic (EEG) activity consists of spontaneous or ongoing voltage fluctuations; these brain waves vary in frequency and are so grouped.

Event-related potentials (ERPs), in contrast, are "transient voltage fluctuations which are associated with a critical inducing event (i.e., a sensory stimulus or a cognitive operation) [Gomer et al., 1979: 109]." ERPs or AERs (average evoked responses) are averaged EEG responses to repeated stimulation. Sophisticated methods (including signal averaging or specialized digital computers) are employed to measure and display ERPs.

If a visual, auditory, or other stimulus is presented to a subject who must classify it and respond behaviorally, the resultant ERP consists of successive positive and negative deflections which continue for up to 750 msec after the stimulus. Figure 2.3 depicts a typical waveform. The components are labelled as to polarity (P = positive, N = negative) and temporal delay between the eliciting event and the component's peak voltage. Thus, the P300 is a positive potential with a peak at 300 msec.

Contrary to the early research on evoked potentials, the structure is not an amorphous representation of the state of the cortical tissue. As Donchin (1979) notes in his overview of ERP research and the P300, the ERP is a sequence of overlapping components.

The physical attributes of the evoking stimulus determine the components occurring within 200 msec after stimulus onset. These are the early or exogenous components. As Figure 2.3 indicates, includ-

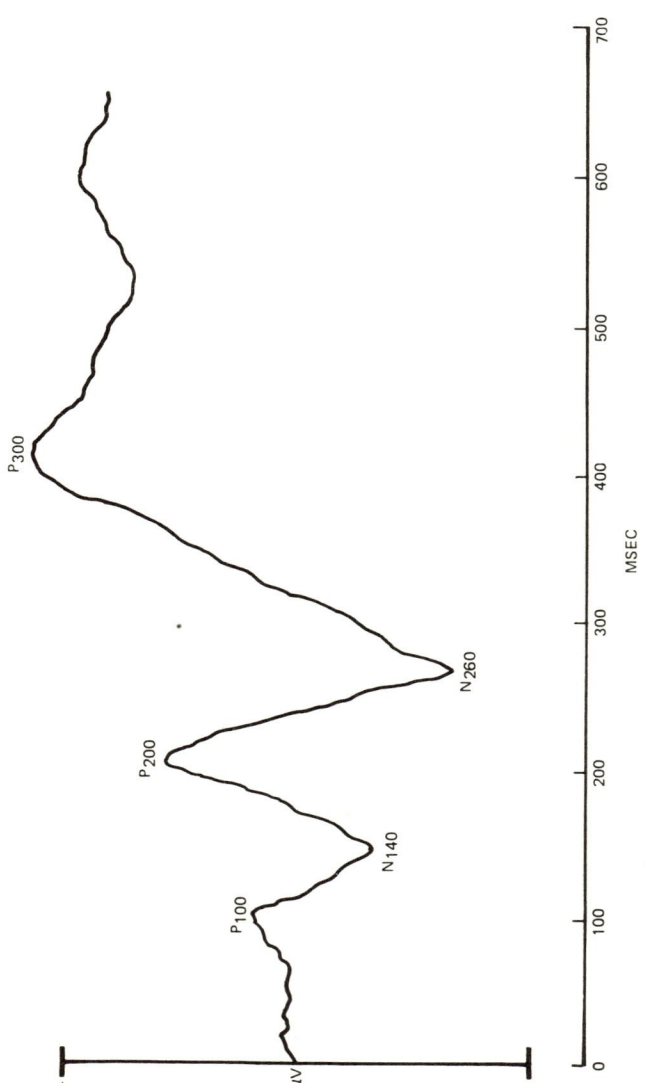

Source: Gomer et al. (1979: 112).

Figure 2.3
MORPHOLOGY OF THE EVENT-RELATED POTENTIAL[a]

ed in this realm are the P100 and N140, which are obligatory responses.

The later, endogenous components reflect differences of a more psychological nature. In this series of peaks and troughs, the amplitude of a given component depends on psychological circumstances.[22] The P300 component appears in ERPs elicited by unpredicted stimuli. The CNV or Contingent Negative Variation is a large, slow negative potential which has been called the "expectancy wave;" quicker reaction-times covary with large-amplitude CNV's. The detection potential (DP) is a transient change in EEG activity which was discovered during studies of vigilance performance; among pilots, DP is associated with the detection of dynamic target events. Readiness potential (RP) is a slow, negative potential shift which occurs prior to voluntary movements; it is an "early warning" indicator of the intent to begin a response sequence.

Donchin and his colleagues have concentrated on the P300.[23] The P300 can be viewed as a physiological index of one significant aspect of human cognitive activity or information processing. Generally, it has been verified in a variety of experimental contexts that the amplitude of the P300 wave elicited by task-relevant events is inversely proportional to the subjective probability which the subject assigns to the stimulus. In other words, the more surprising the event, the larger the P300.

In an expectancy model used to account for the variance of the P300 amplitude, expectancy was posited to be proportional to a combination of:

- The prior probability of the event;

- A memory factor (i.e., the expectation that a given tone will repeat);

- An alternation factor (i.e., subjects tend to "chunk" alternating pairs into single units when the sequence is ABAB<u>A</u> or BABA<u>A</u>).

Overall, the model accounted for 78 percent of the variance (see Donchin, 1979).

In addition to subjective probability or surprise, task relevance is also a necessary and sufficient condition. In the performance of an explicitly unrelated task during an experiment, no P300 is elicited.

Extensive research has also accrued on P300

latency (i.e., the interval in msec from the occurrence of an event to the peak of the component). The P300 label has been applied to peaks whose latency ranges from 250 to 700 msec.

Some studies have shown a positive correlation between P300 latency and reaction time (RT); others have revealed dissociation between P300 latency and RT. P300 latency depends on <u>stimulus evaluation</u> processes and is largely unrelated to response selection and execution time. The overt response of the subject indexes the latter process. Confirmatory speed-accuracy tradeoff experiments demonstrate that the RT-P300 correlation is lower during the <u>speed</u> regime (i.e., the subject's response tends to be generated before a full evaluation of the response is completed).

The P300 and other endogenous components have "performed" impressively in a number of experiments in psychophysiological laboratories. However, the political psychologist searching for a set of indicators which is simultaneously empirically potent and theoretically primitive should be cautioned that the P300 and similar phenomena do not conform to the criterion of simplicity. It seems that any theory of the decision process will be complex.

This is illustrated very well by Donchin's (1979) discussion of the causal role of ERP components. A psychophysiological index, he points out, is quite properly viewed as a (potential) correlate of a psychological process. But this does not mean that correlations must always hold between the component and a specific, overt behavioral index.

As a typical case, Donchin (1979) refers to the CNV-reaction time (RT) correlation. Within a series of trials, he notes, the amplitude of the CNV is only weakly related to RT. If the CNV is an index of preparation, then a robust CNV-RT correlation can be expected--but only in the context of a crude S-R or stimulus-response model in which the organism is conceptualized as inert and passive.

Donchin (1979) offers a cognitive model which is more complex and more consistent with such "discrepancies" as the imperfect CNV-RT relationship and the fact that a subject can respond <u>before</u> P300 is elicited. According to the cognitive <u>model</u>, the subject brings a belief system (including expectations, strategies, or plans, to use Donchin's terms) into the trial.

The subject goes on processing data from past "trials" and continues to deal with old, unsolved problems, the stimuli presented impinge on this stream of ongoing activity and lead to a number of parallel processes. Not all of the latter culminate with overt responses--at least during the current trial. An ERP component in this more complex model is not a "correlate" of some global psychological state variable but is rather:

> ...a manifestation, at the scalp, of neural activity which plays a certain role in the informational transactions of the brain. Our task is to determine the functional role of the component rather than to seek preconceived correlations between the component and ill-defined psychological constructs [Donchin, 1979: 20].

Conclusions

Both the voice stress and the P300 research programs are relevant to exploring the foundations of foreign policy elite behavior. The former work, unfortunately, is directly pertinent to the realm of international affairs but has a disturbingly weak psychophysiological substructure. The P300 research has never been applied to foreign policy-makers or even to real world political decision-makers, but the empirical and theoretical psychophysiological foundation is impressive. Perhaps the two types of approaches will become less divergent in the future.

Several very basic problems limit the utility of one or both studies; the first and second points apply to the Donchin work and the third is pertinent to both. First, the extensive reliance on the artificial laboratory environment mitigates against making generalizations to the real world. The low N's and the overreliance on unrepresentative university students should both induce caution about extrapolating too far beyond the ivory tower. For research on foreign policy (and other) decision processes, a future generation of political psychophysiologists should consider human and human-machine simulations rather than experiments; the former sacrifice some internal validity but compensate for it with higher external (real world) validity.

Secondly, the EEG is an intrusive instrument. While there have been applied or on-line applications with pilots (see Gomer et al., 1979), it is difficult to envision any kind of "on-line" or even parallel application with political decision-makers or even lower level analysts.

Thirdly, both the P300 and the voice stress research have almost completely neglected the domain of individual differences. Donchin and Isreal (n.d.: 28) concluded a review of ERP and P300 research with a call for such inquiry, noting that the same sequential effects may characterize all subjects but with possibly significant variations. Other differences could also be uncovered. Wiegele has also recognized this problem; his recent work has focused on analyzing speeches within crises for a single leader as well as across crisis and role incumbent boundaries. But we know little about the "average" PSE patterns or about possible subgroup variations (e.g., by sex, race, culture, etc.).

The P300 research program at Illinois has begun to probe the intricacies of the decision process. In political psychology, the emphasis has been on a melange of overt "traces." The "below-the-surface" aspects of decision-making--initial perceptual processes, information processing and stimulus evaluation dynamics, response selection and execution sequences--have not been studied intensively or rigorously. Aside from the use of psychophysiological measures as indicators of overt preferences and predispositions (i.e., as measures of beliefs and attitudes), the promise for cognitive psychophysiology as applied to the analysis of political elites is its potential payoff in terms of a theory (or theories) of the unseen individual decision process.

An applied science of political psychophysiology is not inconceivable. Real time, on-line applications would of course not be feasible--politically or practically. But the use of surrogates as subjects (e.g., academics, area specialists, etc.) is certainly not out of the question. Even more desirable would be a subject pool of actual decision-makers or policy analysts, perhaps culled from the National Defense University and similar institutions. Alternatively, lower level officials and analysts from one or more agencies might be induced to participate.

Figure 2.4 illustrates the relationship between EEG-based and other psychophysiological indicators and biocybernetic applications with respect to pilots. Biocybernetics is designed to enhance pilot performance; perhaps bipolimetrics could eventually be employed in an analogous fashion to enhance the performance of decision-makers.

method (the speaker reads a standard passage) is used most frequently. However, equipment is also used in some instances (e.g., electronic filtering which masks the high-frequency sounds of the voice which enable people to correctly identify words or randomized splicing of recording tape); see Harper et al. (1978: 23-26) for a discussion of the methodology of paralinguistic analysis.

10. Mueller (1970) points out that physiological measures may measure the affect component of attitudes (if the level of arousal or activation is sufficient) but not the cognitive element (e.g., positive or negative direction). But see Watts and Sumi (1979) and Tursky et al. (1979); both are discussed below. Both Mueller (1970) and Hassett (1978) refer to the controversial evidence about pupil size change and direction of affect; the pupils of the eyes clearly dilate in response to strong emotional stimuli. There is less firm evidence that dilation signifies positive affect and constriction indexes negative affect.

11. Method variance, which attenuates the validity of content variables, is the product of variegated factors, ranging from lexically ambiguous items and idiosyncratic "sets" to vague instructions and generalized response styles and biases.

12. This study is discussed in Chapter 3; see pp. 85-87.

13. See Druckman and Slater (1979) for details.

14. See Mueller (1970) for a review of the literature and an assessment of the results of and prospects for physiological attitude research.

15. The term GSR, which refers to the electrical activity of the skin, has since been superseded by EDA (electrodermal activity) and other terms (see Hassett, 1978); the research in the 1950s, however, invariably refers to Galvanic Skin Response or GSR.

16. See also: Lodge and Tursky (1979); Lodge et al. (1975, 1976); Tursky (1977); Tursky et al. (1976a, 1976b). Psychophysical scaling was initially used to generate ratio scales of physical continua; it has since been adapted to the scaling of political and social stimuli. Both involve making judgments about the intensity of attributes. For an application to international relations, see Shinn (1969).

17. See Druckman and Slater (1979) for other examples and for a tentative research design for the nonverbal assessment of elite decision processes and belief patterns.

18. See also Wiegele (1977, 1979a, 1979b), Center for Biopolitical Research (1978a, 1978b), and the additional sources cited below in this section of the chapter.

19. See the sources cited in note 18 and especially Center for Biopolitical Research (1978a) for detailed discussions of the PSE.

20. See, e.g., Wiegele (1979d).

21. The discussion in this and the following several paragraphs is drawn from Gomer et al. (1979) and Hassett (1972).

22. Duncan-Johnson and Donchin (1979), in a study which demonstrates that both a priori probability and sequential constraints determine the amplitude of the P300, conclude that the <u>specific physical stimulus</u> does not affect P300: "Different stimuli, equally unexpected, yield the same P300 complex; while the same stimuli, differentially unexpected, yield different P300 complexes [Duncan-Johnson and Donchin, 1979: 466]."

23. This review of P300 is based on Donchin (1979), Donchin and Israel (n.d.), and McCarthy and Donchin (1978); for a variety of interesting but primarily speculative inferences about the relationships between P300 and numerous nonverbal indicators, see Druckman and Slater (1979).

3
The Psychological Foundations of Elite Foreign Policy Behavior

At least implicitly, such classical political philosophers as Plato, Aristotle, Machiavelli, Locke, Hobbes, Rousseau, and Marx were all "psycho-politicists." Theories from political philosophy incorporated a number of assumptions about human nature, national character, the impact of personality characteristics, and other phenomena which would be housed within the domain of political psychology. In contrast, Thucydides, one of the earliest students of foreign policy strategy, can be viewed as an embryonic rational choice theorist (Hernes, 1977).

This tension between psychologistic interpretations of statecraft and rationalistic postulates has recurred in discourse about international relations and foreign policy. Rational actor presuppositions have coexisted with Freudian and other depth-psychological models of world politics. In modern political science, Lasswell's (1930, 1948) seminal work has provided the foundation for a series of subsequent explorations of the nexus between psychology and politics. This chapter will illuminate the linkage from the perspective of foreign policy elites and international politics.

THE POLITICAL SCIENCE/PSYCHOLOGY INTERFACE

Along with a cadre of "microempiricists" who were active in the 1920s and 1930s (including Graham Wallas and Charles Merriam), Harold Lasswell can be regarded as the progenitor of modern political psychology. Although the roots of the subfield are depth-psychological (and primarily Freudian), Lasswell and other pioneers did attempt to shift the focus to the confluence of the three streams of political science, psychology, and sociology. Culturalist/psychoanalytical Freudians (Erich Fromm, Harry Stack Sullivan, etc.) also sought to incorporate social psychological and sociological perspectives into their theories of human personality and behavior.

Early Reductionism

The "psychologizing" tendencies and reductionism fallacies of the 1930s and 1940s discredited psychological approaches for a considerable period. After World War II, behavioral scientists launched a bandwagon which was designed to transfer their findings, methods, and theories to the study of international conflict and thereby avoid nuclear war, reduce the dangers of conventional war, and provide an environment which would be conducive to peace.

The fervor of the behavioral science onslaught was not accompanied by the necessary amounts of caution and rigor. Interstate conflict was attributed to misperception, misleading mirror images, and other psychological processes (see, e.g., White, 1970). The slogan that "war begins in the minds of men" provided a rallying cry for the psychologists and other new students of world politics but simultaneously provoked ridicule from more traditional students of the subject. The latter tended to emphasize such non-psychological factors as the inexorable balance of power mechanism or the rationally-based interests of sovereign actors in the decentralized, chaotic international "system."

The flavor of work during the "infancy" and "adolescence" of "international political psychology" can be intuited by examining some examples. Much of the early research flowed from the implicit a priori premise that war and conflict were the products of individual aggressiveness (Durban and Bowlby, 1939; Eysenck, 1950; Tolman, 1942). Also advanced as prominent themes were the more general role of intrapsychic variables and the causal relevance of psychological defense mechanisms (Farber, 1955; McNeil, 1959; Stagner, 1965; Strachey, 1957; Whitey and Katz, 1957). The psychology of international conflict emerged as a dominant motif during and after the 1940s and the "discipline" of conflict-resolution appeared (see, e.g., Bramson and Goethals, 1964; Cantril, 1950; Fisher, 1964; Frank, 1964; Pear, 1950; and Stanton and Perry, 1951).

Current Eclecticism

In chronicling the history of the nexus between psychology and political science generally or international relations specifically, it becomes obvious that reductionism, the almost exclusive focus on aberrational or pathological aspects of behavior, and the excessive preoccupation with normative issues have all been abandoned or downgraded. The early hegemony of Freudian and other depth-psychological theoretical frames of reference has been superseded by theoretical eclecticism.

Diversity is the rule, as Holsti (1976: 129) contends.[1] This variety applies to theory, scope, concepts, data, and analytic procedures. Table 3.1 provides a synopsis of research completed by 1976 in the area of cognitive studies of foreign policy elites.

No single theoretical perspective dominates inquiry. Models and theories from political philosophy and other subfields of political science, psychology, and other disciplines infuse the studies which are listed in Table 3.1. An eventual integration of the theoretical fragments may be the preferred long-range strategy. Both rational premise theories (decision theory, game theory) and theories from psychology are presumably pertinent to the analysis of the process of decision-making.

Case studies are prolific in the literature, although research based on larger samples of elites has also been conducted (e.g., Burgess, 1968; Etheredge, 1978b; Mennis, 1972). Some works focus on one concept (e.g., Rokeach [1973] on values or Abelson [1971] on search capacity) or stage (e.g., Pool and Kessler [1965] on information processing or Hermann [1974, 1978, 1979b] on the decision-maker as believer). Other efforts deal with the entire process of decision-making; the cognitive mapping work described later in this chapter is a salient example.

Analytical concepts vary considerably. Even the basic unit is referred to as a mind set, image, operational code, world view, or belief system. Some researchers employ inductively-derived, "common sense" conceptual systems (e.g., George, 1969); others construct an elaborate, abstract conceptual scheme (e.g., Bonham, et al., 1976).

The diversity in sources of data is striking (see also Hermann, 1977). Some studies rely on one source (e.g., simulation or content analysis); others combine data sources (e.g., Jervis, 1976).

DECISION MAKER AS[b]	STAGE OF DECISION MAKING[c]	THEORETICAL LITERATURE[b]	ILLUSTRATIVE CONSTRUCTS AND CONCEPTS	ILLUSTRATIVE STUDIES OF POLITICAL LEADERS
Believer	Sources of belief system	Political socialization Personality & politics Political philosophy Ideology	First independent political success	Barber (1972) Glad (1966) George and George (1956)
(Pre-decision: conceptual baggage that DM bring to decision-making tasks)	Content of belief system		Mind Set Image Operational code World view Decision premises Cognitive balance/congruity	Operational code studies Brecher (1968) Cummins (1973) Stupak (1971) Axelrod (1972)
	Structure of belief system	Cognitive psychology	Cognitive complexity Cognitive rigidity/dogmatism	M. Hermann (1972a) Osgood (1959)
			Cognitive "maps"/style	Scheidman (1961, 1963, 1969) Axelrod (1972a, 1972b); Bonham and Shapiro
Perceiver	Identification of a problem	Psychology of perception Cognitive psychology	Definition of situation Perception/misperception Cognitive "set" Selective perception Focus on attention Stereotyping	Jervis (1968) Jervis (1976) Zinnes (1966) Zinnes et al. (1972)

Table 3.1

SOME "COGNITIVE PROCESS" APPROACHES TO DECISION MAKING

DECISION MAKER AS[b]	STAGE OF DECISION MAKING[c]	THEORETICAL LITERATURE[b]	ILLUSTRATIVE CONSTRUCTS AND CONCEPTS	ILLUSTRATIVE STUDIES OF POLITICAL LEADERS
				(1976); Shapiro and Bonham (1973); Steinbruner (1968, 1974)
Information Processor	Obtain information	Cognitive consistency theories	Search capacity	Abelson (1971)
		Theories of attitude change	Selective exposure	Holsti (1967, 1972)
	Production of solutions	Information theory	Psycho-logic	Jervis (1976)
	Evaluation of solutions	Communication theory	Tolerance of ambiguity	
			Strategies for coping with discrepant information (various)	
			Information overload	
			Information processing capacity	
			Satisficing/maximizing	
			Tolerance of inconsistency	
Decision Maker/Strategist	Selection of a strategy	Game theory	Utility	Jervis (1970)
			Risk taking	Jervis (1976)
		Decision theory	Decision rules	Stassen (1972)
		Deterrence theory	Manipulation of images	Burgess (1967)
			End-means links	
			Bounded rationality	
Learner	Subsequent learning and revisions (post-decision)	Learning theory	Feedback	Jervis (1976)
		Cognitive dissonance theory	"Lessons of history"	Lampton (1973)
				May (1973)

[a]Source: Adapted from Holsti (1976: 131).

[b]Columns one and three were suggested by, but differ greatly from, the framework provided by Axelrod (1972a).

[c]Column two was drawn from Brim et al. (1962: 1).

Table 3.1

(Continued)

Variety in the domain of analytic procedures is also the norm. In the realm of content analysis, which is the method for acquiring and analyzing much of the pertinent data, there is a staggering number of coding systems and procedures. Holsti (1976) discusses the relevant alternatives in some detail.

In contemporary psychological approaches to the study of foreign affairs, efforts are made to avoid two extremes (see d'Amato, 1967: 264). One is the postulation of simplistic psychological premises, an egregious error which characterizes the realist theory of international relations as it was promulgated by Hans Morgenthau and others. The other is the construction of frameworks or the specification of research designs of inordinate complexity, a defect of some of the early decision-making schema.

Also pervasive is an emphasis on specifying the situations or conditions which maximize the impact of personality and other individual-level forces.[2] Related to this is the concern with the aggregative effects of psychological variables and the concomitant avoidance of the specter of reductionism (Greenstein, 1975). An awareness of the <u>interaction</u> of psychological with other clusters of <u>determinants</u> pervades current perspectives.

Recurring Problems

Numerous theoretical and methodological problems confront the analyst who attempts to conduct psychological investigations of foreign policy behavior. The focus here will be on clusters of methodological problems. Methodology is defined broadly and includes both data-generation operations and data analysis strategies. Problems include operationalization, access to data, inference from documentary data, authorship issues, and general data analysis approaches and related empirical research concerns (see also Holsti, 1976).

Operationalization emerges as an especially serious obstacle in psychodynamic analyses of foreign policy elites (see Glad, 1973; Rogow, 1969). From a causal perspective, this is the most "remote" form of inquiry in political pyschology in terms of "distance" from actual behavior. Psychodynamic hypotheses refer to determinants which operate at a deep level within the policy-maker's personality system; the etiology or genesis of these factors must often be traced to experiences and influences which occurred at a relatively early state in the life history of the individual.

The psychodynamic approach can produce brilliant insights; the work of George and George (1964) on Woodrow Wilson is the major example of depth-psychological case analysis. The Georges provide illuminating examples of the phenomenology, dynamics, and genesis of Wilson's belief system and political behavior (see Greenstein, 1975).

Phenomenology entails the identification of observed patterns of behavior and surface traits in the context of varying environmental conditions. George and George offer detailed reconstructions of the "phenomena" of Wilson's political life in two contrasting contexts: attaining power and exercising power.

Analysis of the dynamics of depth-psychological forces involves the derivation of hypotheses which account for patterns of behavior. Here the central focus is the elucidation of pertinent ego-defense mechanisms. Wilson's reliance on both denial and reaction-formation is demonstrated convincingly.

Genetic analysis entails the specification of causal antecedents of a personality syndrome or pattern. Research on the childhood sources of adult authoritarian tendencies is perhaps the most prominent example (Greenstein, 1975: 110-114). In the Wilson work, the Georges conducted a detailed study of the subject's early life and made inferences about the nature and intensity of the father-son relationship. The stern, mocking father implanted both the repressed rage and the compulsiveness which permeated Wilson's personality, governed the "choice" of defense mechanisms, and explained recurring patterns in subsequent behavior. The link between the young Wilson and Wilson as president was forged in a lucid and masterful fashion in later chapters of the work.

Aside from the monumental Wilson study, qualitatively impressive psychodynamic research has been rare. Generally, psychobiographical case studies produce "undemonstrated--and possibly undemonstrable--half-insights [Greenstein, 1975: 18]." Almost insurmountable operationalization and data access problems are prominent among the bewildering array of theoretical ambiguities and methodological nightmares in psychodynamic research (see, e.g., Glad, 1973; Greenstein, 1975: 86-92).

Selection of the specific research strategy will determine the magnitude of operationalization problems. Holistic analysis, which involves the entire tripartite conceptual scheme of phenomenology, dynamics, and genesis, is obviously less prac-

ticable than more circumscribed analyses which
simply attempt to elucidate central patterns and
trends in the psychic structure of the subject. An
example is the Holsti (1962; 1967: 38-39, 94) research on Secretary of State John Foster Dulles.
Holsti portrayed a personality syndrome in which a
theological world view, dogmatism, and rigidity interacted to influence perceptions and shape reactions to stimuli; no effort was made to trace the
genesis of the Dulles syndrome.

Both the availability and the quality of data
are relevant issues. In most cases, data are nonexistent, inaccessible, ambiguous, or contradictory.
Sometimes simple facts about an individual's early
life are unavailable or in dispute; Mazlish (1972:
20), for example, reports that it is difficult to
determine when Richard Nixon's brothers were ill.
The quality of the George and George (1964) study
can be attributed--at least in part--to the unusual
availability of reliable data and to the opportun-
ities to validate the data by consulting several
sources.

Operationalization and data access problems are
only relatively less immobilizing in research on
other, more proximate dimensions of the decision-
maker's personality. Direct access is rare, especially with high level officials in larger polities.
Consequently, most researchers utilize documentary
material as a source of data.

As Holsti (1976: 132) points out, documentary
materials may be contaminated in one way or another.
Intentional dissembling is certainly not unknown;
image projection is often present in available
sources. Both data scarcity and biases in available
sources recur with alarming frequency. Biases may
be of two types; one involves skewed samples (e.g.,
the overrepresentation of formal documents and the
underrepresentation of verbatim materials) and the
other concerns unrepresentative samples of foreign
policy decisions (e.g., the probable overrepresentation of documents for "successful" decisions and
the concomitant underrepresentation of materials
concerning fiascoes or disasters).

Ingenuity and eclecticism have characterized
solutions to the access problem. While content
analysis has been the undisputed "monarch," interviews, observation, and simulation have also been
employed. Axelrod (1972b, 1976) constructed cognitive maps on the basis of verbatim transcripts and
referred to analogous sets of documents, including
Madison's notes on the secret debates in the Ameri-

can Constitutional Convention and captured documents from Nazi Germany and Japan. Verbatim materials, however, are rarely preserved and become available in a haphazard fashion (primarily when a nation loses a war).

Inference from documentary data poses a special set of problems. Many documents are public and are thus automatically suspect. Even private documents may be problematic if there is evidence for suspecting that the author was seeking to project an image or provide self-serving justifications and explanations. This issue will be discussed later in Chapter 5.

Establishing authorship is critical. The preparation of collegial documents and the frequent use of ghost writers are obvious pitfalls for the psychologically-oriented analyst. Data from interviews and press conferences may be preferable, but such material is not necessarily available on a regular basis and may not be available at all during non-routine periods.

Data analysis is frequently based on some form of content analysis, a technique which will be discussed in more detail below. Questions of reliability and validity inevitably arise. Perhaps the single most problematic issue concerns the demonstration that simulation results are externally valid. Given the maze of analytical strategies, few firm generalizations can be offered. There is an obvious need, however, to provide a common frame of reference for case studies and to attempt to explicitly forge links between the latter and more quantitative research. In a more basic sense, Holsti (1976: 136) notes that few studies examine the same body of data with two or more methods; this is important for research on both the content and the structure of elite belief systems.

PIVOTAL ISSUES

Three overarching questions recur in discussions about the psychological roots of elite foreign policy behavior. Are psychological variables relevant? That is, do psychological (and other individual-level) factors really account for an appreciable variance of state behavior in world politics?[3] Secondly, which types of psychological variables are relevant? Thirdly, when are such forces relevant? The issue of research methods, which was introduced in the preceding section of the chapter, constitutes a fourth area of dialogue and controversy

Relevance

As noted, early critics of the "war begins in the minds of men" conflict-resolution school questioned the relevance of psychology to the study of international relations. The most common criticism invokes the criteria of "theoretical parsimony and research economy" (Holsti, 1976: 125; see also Bonham, 1975). More of the variance in international behavior can allegedly be accounted for by employing other clusters of determinants; psychological factors are thus superfluous.

A more reasonable question is not are psychological variables relevant but <u>how successfully</u> do such factors explain behavior <u>compared to</u> other clusters? Advocates of "relative potency" testing (e.g., Rosenau, 1966; Hopple 1979c; Hopple et al., 1977, 1980) attempt to ascertain the explanatory contributions of sets of determinants. An early example of this genre of research juxtaposed role against individual-level variables (Rosenau, 1968; Stassen, 1972).

The other dominant theme in empirical research involves efforts to specify the <u>interaction</u> patterns of clusters of factors (East et al., 1978; Hermann and Hermann, 1979; Powell et al., 1974). The ultimate manifestation of this strategy entails the construction and testing of causal models of foreign policy behavior. Psychological variables would be among the sources of independent variables of such a causal model, although the paucity of cross-national, individual-level data has generally precluded this approach. Chapters 4 and 5, however, present an analytical scheme and preliminary empirical tests which provide a foundation for implementing this strategy.

To a considerable extent, the question of the relevance or explanatory strength of elite-level or psychological data is open, although the available results are quite encouraging.[4] Nevertheless, proponents of action-reaction process interpretations and advocates of systemic determinism are among those who often aver that we can simply "black box" the national decision system. Psychological factors are consequently viewed as "luxuries" which are essentially "excess baggage." Why introduce such esoteric indicators when we can account for 70 or more percent of the variance with more easily measured phenomena?

Aside from the retort that psychological and social psychological forces are more than mere epiphenomena and can be expected to play roles of direct significance in indicator systems which are designed to monitor, forecast, and explain international affairs, an additional and very compelling justificatory argument can be offered. Psychological factors become especially crucial from an applied vantage point. Given a concern with policy-relevance, such variables emerge as an essential focus of inquiry:

> It may be the case that structural variables can provide a theory that is a better predictor, more parsimonious, and more comprehensive in coverage than thinking or decision-making variables can provide....How, then, does one justify choosing an approach that may account for less variance than other approaches, particularly when the data for such an approach (the thinking process of decision-makers) are more difficult to obtain than for approaches with higher variance payoff? To answer this question we must consider the pragmatic or extrinsic norms which govern theory construction.... The pragmatic or extra-scientific criteria one would employ to select an approach to the explanation of foreign policy outcomes would have to do with the kinds of constituencies one wished to serve and the ways one might wish to serve them. The best theory or explanation on scientific grounds may not be one that features variables within the control of the persons or groups in whose behalf the explanation is constructed. To the extent that the theory-building enterprise is to have more than merely academic significance, one must select potential users of the explanation and the kind of use to which the explanation may be put before an approach can be chosen [Bonham and Shapiro, 1977: 2-3; emphasis added].

Clusters of Factors

Across-the-board relevance becomes a sterile question when it is recognized that the psychological domain features distinct sets of phenomena. Hermann (1978) groups the phenomena into four basic clusters. The types include:

- Beliefs;
- Motives;
- Decision style; and
- Interpersonal style.

Beliefs constitute the decision-maker's basic assumptions about the world and various aspects of it. Motives refer to the reasons for action; motives analysis is described in some detail in Winter and Stewart (1977). Decision style features preferred methods of making decisions. Confidence, preference for certain levels of risk, and preference for compromise exemplify typical variables from the decision style realm. Interpersonal style refers to characteristic modes of dealing with others. Paranoia and Machiavellianism are two personality constructs which represent ways of interacting with others.

According to Hermann (1978), beliefs and motives constitute the foundation for the leader's view of the world; the latter affects strategy choices. Decision and interpersonal styles influence personal political style. The two influences are filtered through level of interest in foreign affairs, training, and sensitivity to the environment.

The Hermann scheme neglects certain types of variables and provides no criteria for distinguishing unambiguously among some of the categories. A more inclusive scheme posits three distinct types of factors: (1) psychodynamic analysis; (2) the personality trait approach; and (3) belief systems. This typology will be used to organize the extant foreign policy-and-psychology literature in the latter half of this chapter; each element in the scheme will be briefly described here.

Psychodynamic reconstructions of personality and behavioral patterns were discussed briefly in the context of the comments above on data access and operationalization problems. Aside from the George and George (1964) study, other research includes a series of case studies of leaders, primarily in the U.S.[5] A partial list would include:

- Senator William Borah (Glad, 1969);

- Boss Cermak of Chicago (Gottfield, 1962);

has also been employed: Brecher (1968) refers to the decision-maker's world view; George (1969, 1979), McLellan (1969), and others reconstruct operational codes; Burgess (1968) examines elite images and strategic images; Winham (1970) focuses on the decision-maker's image of the situation; Axelrod (1976) and those in the cognitive mapping tradition simply discuss beliefs.

In general terms, a <u>belief system</u> consists of affective, cognitive, and conative concepts (Bonham and Shapiro, 1973: 57). Affective concepts are propositions with valences; Bonham and Shapiro classify policy objectives here. Cognitive concepts consist of beliefs about reality. Conative or "behavioral" concepts consist of the alternatives from which a decision-maker selects a policy recommendation.

Any belief system consists of a potentially infinite number of discrete elements. By definition, a <u>belief</u> system contains a set of propostions (statements about reality, predictions about the future, preferred events and outcomes, basic goals); the set ranges from specific beliefs ("The United States is allied with Britain") to higher-order end-states ("National security is essential").

A belief <u>system</u> is also an organized entity. An ideological belief system is tightly and coherently organized or constrained; the structuring is deductive in the sense that knowledge of higher-level elements (such as a preference for liberalism or conservatism) permits the observer to infer lower-level phenomena (such as specific policy preferences) a degree of accuracy that departs very significantly from chance expectations.

Ideological belief systems have been described in considerable detail (see Converse, 1964; Satori, 1969). As noted, such a belief system is characterized by <u>constraint</u> (clearly delineated patterns) and <u>economy</u> (hierarchy or the ability to predict the entire ideological belief system from central elements). The juxtaposition of elite ideological belief systems with mass "non-ideological" belief systems is based on the erroneous assumption that some individuals do not actually have "belief systems." In other words, some actors may possess beliefs but lack the system attribute of organization. As Rokeach (1960: 33) maintains, in all belief systems the elements are interrelated. However, the principles for organizing or structuring belief systems may vary significantly across sociopolitical strata and other cleavage lines.

The representation or "mapping" of belief systems generally occurs via some form of content analysis. Alternatives include: computer simulation (Abelson and Carroll, 1965; Bonham et al., 1976); in-depth interviews (Lane, 1962); direct interviews and questionnaires (Semmel, 1975, 1976).

Maximizers of Impact

In addition to questions relating to relevance per se and to types of psychological influences, much of the conceptual literature on the psychology-politics nexus focuses on the forces which inhibit or maximize the impact of psychological phenomena. Hermann's (1978) framework assumes that individual-level factors exert a differential impact, depending on aspects of the situation and other forces.[7]

The influence of the individual actor in generating and processing foreign policy behavior is inhibited by a variety of factors. Among these are various bureaucratic and role constraints. The need to respond to inputs from other states constitutes a restraint of undeniable impact. Systemic realities may limit the role of the individual foreign policy-maker.

One factor which has been singled out as an especially potent determinant of actor influence is <u>position in the hierarchy</u>. It is generally recognized that top echelon elites face the fewest constraints from role and other structural or systemic parameters (Katz, 1973: 213; Kelman and Bloom, 1973: 269; and Hermann, 1974: 202). Members of the foreign policy elite (i.e., the head of state and foreign minister) comprise the decision-makers for whom psychological data are thus presumably most relevant.

Correspondingly, the psychological characteristics of lower level officials need not be introduced into research designs on foreign policy behavior. Bureaucratic politics processes provide much more adequate frames of reference for research which does not involve the foreign policy elite. The latitude which an anonymous member of the foreign policy bureauracy is permitted is obviously circumscribed; role parameters and organizational interests presumably predominate over idiosyncratic or actor-specific determinants.

<u>The nature of the situation</u> also influences the impact of psychological characteristics of decision-makers. <u>Routine</u> decisions are analogous to very simple computer programming or information retrieval

operations. A foreign policy-maker simply "searches" for and invokes the relevant precedent. Little expenditure of time or effort is necessary.

Crisis decisions contrast sharply with routine cases.[8] According to the standard definition, a foreign policy crisis is high in threat-saturation and low in time for response; such an event also elicits very high awareness (C. Hermann, 1969). In a perceptual sense, a crisis is often viewed as an unprecedented situation. The precedent-search operation may certainly be activated (as in the frequent allusions to the "lessons of Munich" in the case of the outbreak of war in Korea in 1950). But crises--or situations characterized by very high stress--evoke levels of attention and emotion which are never equalled by routine situations.

The high stress and other features which characterize a crisis situation represent intervening variables which modify the relationship between actor attributes and foreign policy behavior. A crisis intensifies the probability that a foreign policy-maker will exert an independent effect. Not unexpectedly, crisis situations tend to involve actors from the highest level of the hierarchy (Paige, 1968).

The preceding chapter provides a summary of Wiegele's extensive work on the psychophysiology of elite stress in international crises. As Figure 3.1 illustrates, political psychologists have also emphasized the relationship between crisis and stress.

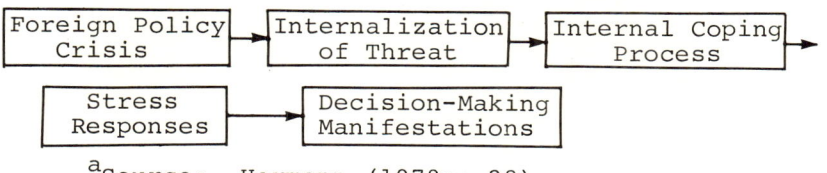

[a]Source: Hermann (1979a: 28).

Figure 3.1

A SCHEMATIZATION OF THE
CRISIS-STRESS RELATIONSHIP

In her review of the extensive literature on stress in policy-makers during foreign policy crises, Hermann (1979a) posits that the perception of a threat (crisis) situation generates feelings of distress, fear, uncertainty, or anxiety. This negative affect indicates that the foreign policy threat has been internalized. Coping behavior is then activated. Together, the internalization and coping processes represent the psychological process component of stress. Signs of a decision-maker's coping strategy are revealed by observable responses during a crisis. The entire framework is depicted in Figure 3.1.

As Hermann (1979a) demonstrates, various verbal and nonverbal indicators of negative affect or internalization can be conceived; these include such discrete signals as flustered or faster speech, change in voice quality, irritability (e.g., fewer positive head nods), and vigilance (e.g., increased eye contact). Also catalogued in the Hermann (1979a) review is an array of verbal and nonverbal indicators of coping behavior. Examples are presented for each general type of coping behavior (avoidance of the situation, contending with the situation, and inaction).

Indicators of disruptive manifestations of stress on decision-making constitute the third tier in the Hermann (1979a) classification scheme; again, verbal and nonverbal types are featured. Possible indicators are listed for each of seven general categories (fixation on only one reasonable option, simplification of the adversary and the adversary's limitations, fatigue, etc.).

Threat, stress, and crisis are central concepts in international political analysis. A threat, according to McClelland (1975: 19) is the "anticipation of approaching harm that triggers a characteristic response called 'stress.'" Stress connotes the idea that the individual is "beset by powerful pressures which greatly tax the adaptive resources of the biological or psychological system [Lazarus, 1966: 10]." According to Janis and Mann (1977: 50):

> Psychological stress is used as a generic term to designate unpleasant emotional states evoked by threatening environmental events or stimuli. A "stressful" event is any change in the environment that typically induces a high degree of unpleasant emotion (such as anxiety, guilt, or shame) and affects normal patterns of information-processing.

During international crises, situations of heightened threat produce stress; such decision contexts maximize the actual and psychological involvement of high level elites and/or ad hoc small groups, thus increasing the potential impact of the beliefs and perceptions of elites. Not surprisingly, most of the research on political psychology and foreign policy, including the pioneering studies of the Stanford group and the more recent work of Brecher and his colleagues, focuses on situations permeated by threat and stress (i.e., international crises).

In addition to positional and situational factors, <u>the type of state</u> apparently determines the extent to which individual-level variables exert an influence. If the accountability or open-closed dimension is considered, it could be predicted that decision-makers in closed regimes would impact upon foreign policy behavior to a greater extent than is the case for position incumbents in more accountable regimes. The latter face an array of expectations and demands from an institutionalized and autonomous bureaucracy, a competitive party system, public opinion, and other centers of influence which transmit inputs in a pluralistic system. Both theory and case studies tend to affirm this plausible proposition (Aspaturian, 1967; Zimmerman, 1970).

Generally, decision-maker characteristics can also be expected to display more efficacy as predictor variables in developing and revolutionary polities (Quandt, 1970: 198; and Strauss, 1973). In such systems, power is concentrated in a charismatic leader or ruling clique; roles are less clearly delineated and are comparatively uninstitutionalized.

Thus, there are three general sets of conditions which maximize the impact of psychological factors:

- <u>Level in the hierarchy</u>. High level elites exert the most impact.

- <u>Type of situation</u>. Crises maximize the impact; routine situations minimize the impact.

- <u>Type of state</u>. Individuals exert the most impact in closed and developing states.

<u>Methods</u>

Research methods and techniques, as has been emphasized earlier, represent an area of special concern for the analyst. This section will focus on the most frequently used method--content analysis. Content analysis has been a basic tool of social scientific research for decades (see Berelson, 1952; George, 1959; Gerbner et al., 1969; Holsti, 1969; Pool, 1959, 1970). Originally employed in journalism research, content analysis has been adopted for personality research and clinical psychology, small group research and social psychology, and cross-cultural research (see Stone et al., 1966). In international relations, content analysis was initially utilized in the massive RADIR (Revolution and the Development of International Relations) Project from 1947 to 1952 (see Pool, 1970).[9]

Definitions of content analysis have proliferated. Krippendorff (1969: 11) defines content analysis as "the use of replicable and valid methods for making specific inferences from text to other states or properties of its source." Stone and his colleagues (1966: 5) apply the term to any research technique for making inferences by systematically and objectively identifying specified characteristics within a text. Holsti (1969: 5) more succinctly characterizes content analysis as the application of scientific methods to documentary evidence. Holsti's unrestrictive definition will be adopted here; content analysis is thus posited to be a broad-gauged research orientation.

Much of the international relations content analytic research has involved the media (e.g., Singer, 1964; Pool, 1970) or has generated case studies of particular decision-makers, countries, or issues. Examples include Brecher (1968) on Krishna Menon of India, Burgess (1968) on Norway, and Winham (1970) on the Marshall Plan. Holsti (1976: 135) provides a sample of fairly recent studies and cross-classifies the system of enumeration (appearance, frequency counts, intensity, and contingency analysis) with the type of recording unit (word/symbol, theme/sentence, logical idiosyncracy, causal assertion, sentence, paragraph item). In addition to the selection of an enumeration system and recording unit, the analyst must also make a fundamental preliminary choice between <u>qualitative</u> and <u>quantitative</u> analysis.

While the case study literature is fairly voluminous (albeit ad hoc), the explicity comparative work is virtually nonexistent. Few comparisons have been made of <u>methods</u> or <u>subjects</u>. An exception to the latter is the Stanford Project, which analyzed diplomatic documents in the prewar crisis of 1914 and produced an avalanche of studies on this case and several more recent ones, including Sino-Soviet relations and the Cuban missile crisis (see

Holsti, 1972; Hoole and Zinnes, 1976).

Perhaps the fundamental issue for the researcher to consider is whether the method being employed is direct or indirect (remote) and reactive or nonreactive. Content analysis, the most frequently employed technique for measuring both personality traits and belief systems phenomena, is clearly remote or indirect. However, elite decision-makers are often "guilty" of projecting images and misleading and deceiving adversaries (not to mention their own publics); these tendencies are exacerbated in international affairs since distortion and deception are accepted (or expected) elements in the rules of the game. Private, confidential sources are preferable when available; obviously, however, such sources are rarely accessible and are in any case not always reliable.

Content analysis is not reactive in the same sense that interviews are; however, elites may try to manage impressions, obfuscate, and deceive. There are some instances when variables of interest are not susceptible to conscious manipulation (or decision-makers are unaware of the particular indicator); integrative complexity, which tends to decrease prior to war (see Suedfeld and Tetlock, 1977; Suedfeld et al., 1977) is one example.

Hermann's (1977) collection of landmark studies illustrates the range and diversity of data-generation methods. In addition to content analysis, political psychologists have utilized:

- Questionnaires;
- Interviews;
- Observations;
- Biographical statistics; and
- Simulation.

Two or more examples of each are provided in the chapters in Hermann (1977).

In a summary table in Hermann (1977: 459), the studies are displayed in a chart which associates each with one or more of the techniques. For example, Johnson's (1977) case study of Senator Frank Church--summarized later in this chapter--relied on three of the basic measurement techniques (interview, observation, and content analysis). Other information provided in the table includes:

- The nature of the source of data (self, judge, observable behavior);

- Whether or not the subject's cooperation was necessary (obtrusive, unobtrusive);
- Public or private access;
- The degree of inference necessary (little, some, much).

In addition to these basic techniques, researchers have resorted to such strategies as: extrapolating from history or the psychological laboratory; single and comparative case studies; surrogate analysis (e.g., interviews or experiments with students or refugees); expert-generated data; and various other techniques. The eclecticism of recent research is illustrated by the work of Bobrow and his colleagues (1979) on China--which involves the application of a melange of methods to a specific system --and by the array of data-making and analysis strategies featured in Bonham and Shapiro (1977) and Falkowski (1979a, 1979b).

A TRIPARTITE CLASSIFICATION SCHEME

Of a total of 118 comparative, empirical generalizations about foreign policy behavior identified in the course of amassing a propositional inventory (see McGowan and Shapiro, 1973), only 7 (5.9 percent of the total) refer to individual or elite variables (McGowan, 1976: 223). In contrast, 23 propositions (19.5 percent) concern political and governmental variables; linkage variables, others' policies, systemic factors, decision-making variables, and the feeedback process account for 60 (50.8 percent) of the 118 discrete propositions. As McGowan concludes:

> Research on individual characteristics of leaders which relate to foreign policy behavior is technically very sophisticated but limited to the work of the Stanford group of Robert North and his associates on the outbreak of World War I. Thus, what we know about how idiosyncratic features of leaders relate to their policies is mainly limited to one crisis situation. What about other leaders in different situations, including noncrises? [McGowan, 1976: 223-224].

In a detailed literature review which focused

on 22 major political science, international relations, and other journals, over 70 recent books and articles in the area of political psychology and foreign policy were abstracted.[10] Many of these were empirical, although few were genuinely comparative or cross-national. However, the number of published studies and other indicators--such as the appearance of edited volumes on the subject (e.g., Falkowski, 1979a, 1979b)--clearly suggests that this is an emerging area of research and analysis. This landscape is surveyed in some detail here.

The remainder of this chapter focuses on each of the three general variable clusters delineated above: psychodynamics; personality traits; and belief systems. Illustrative studies are discussed and salient problems noted. This section provides the context for the specific research presented in Chapters 4 and 5.

Psychodynamics

Psychodynamics is the most "remote" (and currently the least "popular") form of inquiry in political psychology. Psychodynamic approaches attribute elite political behavior to intra-individual, idiosyncratic processes and predispositions. The "visible" processes and predispositions reflect "below-the-surface" forces. For example, according to Lasswell's (1930, 1948) famous formula, the political type displaces private motives onto public objects; the motives are then rationalized in terms of the public interest. The power-seeker is driven by a need to overcome a low estimate of the self.[11]

Most of the psychodynamic inquiry in the foreign policy realm, as indicated earlier in this chapter, has been case-specific, scrutinizing such prominent leaders as Wilson, Hitler, and Stalin. Accompanying this emphasis has been a concern with psychopathology. Unconscious forces and irrational determinants have been central concepts in the psychodynamic literature.

This outlook pervades a recent collection of case studies on depth-psychology and leadership. In his introductory essay in the volume, Robins (1977: 14-26) notes that the inquiry can be organized in terms of a temporally-based framework which features the topics recruitment, behavior in office, and removal from office. Both medical/physiological and psychoanalytic explanations have been invoked to account for the political behavior of "deviant" leaders, ranging historically from Ivan the Terrible, Henry VIII, and Joan of Arc to Wilson, Stalin, and former Louisiana Governor Earl Long.

As was pointed out earlier in the chapter, the psychodynamic approach includes three components:[12]

- Phenomenology;
- Dynamics;
- Genesis.

Phenomenology concerns the observable patterns of behavior and surface traits; these patterns remain relatively constant in the face of fluctuating environmental stimuli. The dynamics of the personality consist of the operative ego-defense mechanisms in a given case. Does the actor rely on projection or reaction-formation? Or does the individual exhibit tendencies toward denial or rationalization (or some combination of the two)? Securing access to data which permit the analyst to sketch out a definitive phenomenological profile is difficult enough; reliable evidence concerning the dynamics of depth-psychological forces is even more elusive. Genetic analysis, which entails the illumination of the causal antecedents of a personality syndrome or pattern, is the most problematic of the three components in terms of evidence and inference considerations.

One of the few psychodynamically-based studies which has been published in the political science literature since 1974 is Friedlander and Cohen (1975). This particular article attempts to determine the etiology and dynamics of the belligerent personality syndrome. As in most psychodynamic research, the authors assume that the subject's early life is crucial for explaining the appearance of a syndrome. A constellation of family environment characteristics (female dominance, authoritarian family practices, etc.) predicts to a consistent preference for belligerent options in foreign affairs.

Another recent example is Etheredge's (1979) "hardball politics" model. Etheredge views "hardball politics" as a subculture of domestic and international political culture. The subculture consists of elites with a narcissistic personality (NP) disorder. The NP leader has two different and unintegrated self-conceptions; a depleted, insecure self coexists with a split-off "grandiose self." The two structures exist simultaneously and autonomously.

The NP manifests an "idealizing transference" to salient political institutions; the public represents a "mirror" for confirming the NP's grandiose strivings. Behind a facade of cordiality, the NP's interpersonal relations are superficial and lacking in affection and genuine warmth. He perceives others as psychological replicas of himself and views the world as competitive and Hobbesian. Other traits include defective ethics and sense of humor, aggressiveness, vanity, degenerated mental processes, and hyperactivity.

The author compares his model to a large number of other well-known personality syndromes which concern power seeking or toughness. Among these are: power compensation (Lasswell, 1948); authoritarianism (Adorno et al., 1950); tough-mindedness (Eysenck, 1954); dogmatism (Rokeach, 1960); Machiavellianism (Christie and Geis, 1968); the active-negative type (Barber, 1972); and need for power (Winter and Stewart, 1977). Similarities and differences between the Etheredge construct and these and other concepts are catalogued.

As was suggested earlier, there has been an avalanche of methodological and theoretical criticisms of psychodynamic work. Even the monumental George and George (1964) case study of Woodrow Wilson has been critiqued. Tucker (1977) contrasts the research's underlying Lasswellian assumptions about political man with Karen Horney's work on the neurotic personality.

Horney maintained that the neurotic has coexisting high and low self-estimates. When psychologically adverse experiences in childhood produce "basic anxiety," the child responds by forming a protective idealized self-image. Unless the conditions which nurture the basic anxiety are ameliorated, the individual eventually equates the idealized image with himself or herself. The constant effort to actualize the idealized self assumes a compulsive quality.

Tucker cites evidence from George and George (1964) which indicates that Wilson was a neurotic personality in Horney's sense of the term. Enormous ambition and unusual political talents interacted to produce an impressive series of successes; Wilson's career was simultaneously marred by recurring personal conflicts. Horney proposed a threefold typology of neurotic personalities: those who seek "expansive," "self-effacing," or "resignation" solutions. The three types correspond, respectively, to the goals of mastery, love, and aloofness or freedom. Tucker asserts that Wilson combined a need for mastery with a need for love, although the dominant solution was the former.

Tucker views Wilson as a "classic case" of the neurotic personality as defined by Horney. As a child, he undoubtedly experienced the required basic anxiety. The young Wilson offered sufficient evidence of the self-idealization syndrome. A search for glory emerges as the driving force of Wilson's life. Further, the neurotic personality reacts with vindictive hostility to critics--as Wilson did repeatedly--because attacks threaten to expose his or her own suppressed self-critical tendencies.

The George's distinction between Wilson the successful power-seeker and Wilson the dysfunctional power-holder does not really penetrate to the core of the problem, according to Tucker. What has to be explained is Wilson's opposition-provoking behavior in office and the politically self-defeating vindictiveness elicited by opposition. Horney's theory suggests that Wilson's motivation was not power per se but the search for glory and the more basic drive to confirm the idealized self-image. After initial successes, Wilson would be driven by his compulsive need for glory to press for further success. Wilson viewed opposition as evil; this rationalization was necessary in order to defend the idealized concept of the self.

In a more critical essay, Weinstein et al. (1978: 586) conclude that the Georges' (1964) study "presents an essentially incorrect interpretation of the personality of Woodrow Wilson and its effect on his career." Like Tucker (1977), Weinstein et al. (1978) charge that the psychological model in George and George (1964) is narrowly Freudian and consequently excludes such important phenomena as family values and cultural norms.

More seriously, they assert that the empirical evidence is inadequate and in some instances unsupported. According to Weinstein et al. (1978), this criticism applies a fortiori to what is undoubtedly the linchpin of the Georges' empirical theory: Wilson's relationship with his father. The facts and interpretation offered in George and George (1964) with respect to the controversy over the location and character of the graduate college--the dispute between Wilson the president of Princeton and Dean West--are also subjected to extensive criticism.

The critiques of the George and George (1964) research are especially compelling when it is recalled that data in comparable volume and quality

are almost never available for other political
leaders. Given the problems relating to data access
and quality which were briefly surveyed earlier in
this chapter, the prospects for psychodynamic research are not encouraging. The overreliance on
Freudian theory and the pervasive tendency to pursue
<u>verificationist</u> rather than <u>falsificationist</u> hypoth-
esis-testing strategies both compound the problem.[13]
Finally, the not infrequent examples of simplistic,
reductionist psychoanalytic interpretations--such as
Abrahamsen's (1977) case study of Nixon--and the
occasional appearance of biased, distorted studies--
such as Freud and Bullitt's (1967) "research" on
Wilson--have further discredited the depth-psychological approach.

On the other hand, Etheredge's (1979) hardball
politics model sensitizes us to the fact that assumptions of narrow rationality in the "positive"
sense do not always pertain to political elites.
Especially in situations of ambiguity and high
stress, assumptions of rationality may be both misleading and dangerous.[14] More fundamentally, the
question of elite pathology has never been definitively resolved. Some evidence indicates that
elites tend to be healthy self-actualizers; opposed
to this viewpoint is the Lasswellian formula which
states that leaders displace private motives onto
public objects and rationalize such motives in terms
of the public interest.[15]

Personality Traits

Considerable empirical research has accrued in
this area. Here no attempt is necessarily made to
analyze genetically or dynamically the measured
traits of leaders. The researcher simply attempts
to identify and empirically study key personality
traits or characteristics; the latter are then used
as predictors of policy preferences or decision-
making outcomes. Three troublesome issues surface
in the personality traits approach:

- The selection of variables for analysis;
- The question of items versus types;
- The access problem.

The selection of variables for analysis is an
especially problematic initial decision. As noted,
there are literally dozens of possible personality
traits. Given the potential number of traits and
the lack of criteria for "sampling" items or deter-

mining which are most central, it is not possible to conduct research on such factors--unless ad hoc, idiosyncratic selections are made.

The choice between discrete traits and more inclusive types is another fundamental decision. D'Amato (1967) provides an example of an attempt to derive a set of more general constructs. Clearly, the construction of general typing schemes would be preferable; a typology offers a parsimonious route to explaining and predicting any set of phenomena. From the vantage points of time and cost, a few inclusive typologies are obviously more attractive than a number of distinct traits.

In some cases, typing schemes are generated in an a priori or deductive fashion. A possible example is the Barber (1972) framework for classifying political actors, although the twofold activity/affect typology developed over a period of time and involved an interplay between empirical evidence and a priori conceptualization.

In contrast, many typologies are derived empirically. Factor analytic and other empirical data reduction or index construction approaches exemplify this inductive route to typologizing. Or empirical findings may uncover a typology. For example, Etheredge (1978b) studies the impact of general dominance over subordinates and extroversion on the advocacy of hard-line and conflictual policies; he concludes that it would be helpful to construct a general psychological typology of orientations toward the U.S.'s role in the international system.

The cross-classification of the introvert/extrovert and high dominance/low dominance characteristics yields a fourfold typology. The four "ideal types" consist of:

- Bloc Leaders (e.g., Secretary of State John Foster Dulles)
  * Manichaean moralism;
  * Tenacity;
  * Dominance of one central idea.

- World Leaders (e.g., Theodore Roosevelt)
  * Tendency to use military force;
  * Flexible and pragmatic;
  * Varied range and scope of initiatives;
  * Inclusion (worldwide leadership aspirations).

- Maintainers (e.g., Calvin Coolidge)
  * Status quo.

the mass public feature significant correlations of
personality traits with foreign policy preferences.
Additionally, several elite case studies and
comparative analyses support hypotheses concerning
personality influences on policy decisions; studies
of American diplomats contain significant personal-
ity-policy preference correlations among career pro-
fessionals.

Central to Etheredge's study is interpersonal
generalization theory, a theory which posits that
behavioral differences in interpersonal situations
will generalize or predict to behavioral differences
in international situations. In testing the theory,
Etheredge focuses on intraelite <u>variations</u> in personality characteristics rather than <u>shared</u> characteristics. Essential to the test is the selection
of cases of U.S. intraelite policy disagreements and
the subsequent determination that the direction of
such disagreements could be predicted from independently derived knowledge of intraelite personality
differences. The emphasis on <u>intraelite</u> disagreements automatically neutralizes the impact of the
major alternative hypothesis: fluctuations in the
domestic and/or international situational contexts.

Etheredge selected 36 men, including presidents, secretaries of state, and selected advisors,
from 1898 to 1968. He assessed two general personality dimensions: <u>general dominance over subordi-
nates</u> and <u>extroversion</u>. Two specific hypotheses
were derived from interpersonal generalization
theory.

- In cases of disagreement on the use of
  force, those scoring higher on dominance
  will advocate the threat or use of
  military force, intervention, ultimata,
  and occupation of other countries and
  will oppose disarmament and arbitration
  proposals.

- In cases involving disagreement about
  policy toward the Soviet Union or the
  Communist bloc, those scored as more
  extroverted will advocate cooperative
  policies when compared with those
  scored as more introverted.

The results show strong and statistically significant support for both hypotheses. In 78 percent
of the cases involving the use of force the difference along the dominant personality dimension is

consistent with the observed direction of policy disagreement. In almost 85 percent of the cases concerning the latter hypothesis, the difference along the extroversion dimension accounts for the observed direction of policy disagreement.

Two specific characteristics have been highlighted in recent research on personality traits: integrative complexity and the hard- versus soft-liner continuum. The former can be viewed as a situationally-based aspect of information processing rather than as a personality variable, as Suedfeld et al. (1977) point out in one study.

In one article, Suedfeld and Tetlock (1977) focus on the integrative complexity of communications in international crises. The data source is archival records of diplomatic communications. During crises which end in war (1914, Korea), integrative complexity declines; during crises which are resolved peacefully (the Morocco crisis of 1911, the Cuban missile crisis of 1962), complexity increases or does not change. In a related study, Suedfeld et al. (1977) test the same hypothesis for Arab-Israeli wars in 1948, 1956, 1967, and 1973. Israeli speeches show a marked reduction in complexity during every war year (nonwar years are used as controls); the same pattern holds for the Arabs (except in 1967). Bonham and Shapiro (1977) also consider integrative complexity in their computer simulation of decision processes in Finland and Austria; generally, the evidence supports the prediction of greater complexity for Finland, a nation with a foreign policy tradition which is much more innovative than that of Austria, a country which is otherwise similar.

The hard-liner/soft-liner trait is emphasized in Ben-Zvi (1975), Etheredge (1978a), Friedlander and Cohen (1975), Lockhart (1977), and Synder and Diesing (1977). Deterrence theorists (e.g., those who adopt the Munich model as their prototype) tend to be hard-liners; the spiral model theorists (i.e., those for whom the typical pattern is the World War I escalation/no escape configuration) are equally prone to take a soft-line position.

Snyder and Diesing (1977) describe the hard- and soft-line alternatives in terms of world views (i.e., belief systems). The hard-liner perceives a conflict-saturated environment, emphasizes military strength and firmness, and sees the adversary as a monolithic expansionist with unlimited objectives; the soft-liner stresses the potential for common interest, accommodation, and flexibility, generally imputes limited, specific goals to the other side, and is sensitive to possible internal disagreement within the adversary. The probable personality basis of this basic distinction is indicated in Etheredge (1978a) and Friedlander and Cohen (1975).

Belief Systems Phenomena

Recent research within the boundaries of the variable clusters of psychodynamics and (to a lesser extent) personality traits has been infrequent; neither is currently a "growth market" on the political psychology landscape. The situation with belief systems work is just the opposite: both the structural and process aspects of elite belief systems have been studied in various contexts (primarily but not exclusively the U.S.) and with an array of techniques.

Figure 3.2 provides an overview of the nature and components of a belief system as a generic entity. A <u>belief system</u> consists of cognitive (belief), affective (attitude), and conative (predispositional) elements (Bonham and Shapiro, 1973: 57; Meddin, 1975). Also present is an evaluative (value) dimension. These elements will be discussed in detail in the following chapter.

By definition, a belief system contains a set of ideas or propositions.[17] A belief <u>system</u> is also an organized entity. As Meddin (1975) notes, all research on subjective (belief systems) phenomena accepts the principle of hierarchy--the idea that there is a continuum from discrete to general. One plausible scheme extends from fundamental value-orientations to very specific opinions:

Value-orientations
↓
Sets of values
↓
Master attitudes
↓
Sets of attitudes
↓
Specific opinions

The discrete elements in a leader's belief system are potentially infinite in number. Much of the empirical research deals with the perceptions of the intentions and capabilities of an adversary (e.g., Ben-Zvi, 1975, 1978; Bobrow et al., 1979;

	Normative		Appetitive	
	Dominant Subcomponent(s)		Dominant Subcomponent(s)	
Value-orientation	Existential Beliefs Evaluative Beliefs	Sentiments Action Tendency	Applicable at this level of abstraction?	
Value	Existential Beliefs Evaluative Beliefs	Sentiments Action Tendency	Existential Beliefs Evaluative Beliefs	Sentiments Action Tendency
Attitude	Existential Beliefs Evaluative Beliefs	Sentiments Action Tendency	Existential Beliefs Evaluative Beliefs	Sentiments Action Tendency
Opinion	Existential Beliefs Evaluative Beliefs	Sentiments Action Tendency	Existential Beliefs Evaluative Beliefs	Sentiments Action Tendency

[a]Source: Meddin (1975: 900)

Figure 3.2

COMPONENTS OF A BELIEF SYSTEM[a]

Brownell et al., 1975; Handel, 1977; McCormick, 1975). Other studies analyze such disparate objects as general alignment policies, preferred general strategies, perceptions of the international system or the regional arena, specific actors, issues, or contexts, and additional foci.

Recent empirical research on the beliefs and perceptions of foreign policy elites is summarized in Hopple and Favin (1978) and discussed in the context of international crisis analysis in Hopple and Rossa (1980). Two specific examples will be featured here. One is an elaborate case study of the Chinese foreign policy elite; the other includes a stream of cognitive analyses of the Israeli decision-making elite in several Middle Eastern crises.

The study by Bobrow, Chan, and Kringen (1979) synthesizes a variety of research efforts which the three have conducted over the last several years.[18] Central to their research on the Chinese foreign policy elite belief system are the following assumptions: different regimes interpret the same action or statement in different ways; decision rules exist and can be discovered; an ensemble of methods is the most appropriate strategy for amassing data about the intentions, assumptions, and choice processes of "inaccessible" decision systems.

Part I of the book provides the overarching intellectual context by surveying foreign policy decision-making approaches in Western conflict research and identifying competing perspectives on the study of Chinese foreign policy. The relevance of elite belief system inquiry is demonstrated in the discussion of general approaches and the importance of comparing public statements over time and across sources is the central theme of the chapter devoted to Chinese foreign policy analysis. While both subjects are handled in a rather cursory fashion, the remainder of the book does a convincing job of demonstrating the validity of the primary assumptions.

Part II is devoted to the subject of "critical international incidents." One chapter juxtaposes alternative "lessons of history" culled from analyses of Chinese, Eastern European, and U.S. lists of critical incidents. The other two chapters compare Western and Chinese perspectives and tendencies regarding international crises. The standard U.S. image contrasts sharply with the Chinese view of crises. Especially helpful are the emphasis on dialectical reasoning in Chinese doctrine, the illumination of principles of crisis management, and the chronicling of Peking's behavior in five temporally dispersed military crises. Semantic evidence from Mainland refugees and Hong Kong subjects validates the inference that the Mainland political culture ascribes a primordial role to the economic aspect of crises. The two chapters offer stark evidence of the possibilities for mutual misperception in U.S.-Chinese interactions.

Part III--"Chinese Policy Analytics"--summarizes the central precepts in the Chinese foreign policy-making process, reviews the regime's doctrinal treatment of actor characteristics and relationships, and articulates Peking's rules for policy design. Part III provides a sketch of the foreign policy elite's belief system and thus leads logically to Part IV, which reports results for empirical tests of the relationships between beliefs and patterns of behavior.

The empirical tests concern Chinese treatment of foreign events and nations. The former involves an interrupted time-series approach in which events are posited to be quasi-experimental stimuli and the dependent variable is the magnitude, direction, and timing of changes in People's Daily new coverage. While the results are mixed (expectations about the use of the media to signal support for allies and warn adversaries, for example, are generally not borne out), first-order events without the danger of military confrontation do lead to increases in media coverage and concern with the primary enemy (the "main contradiction" from the Chinese vantage point) does shape media treatments of events.

Verbal rules for classifying nations are generally confirmed via a Q factor analysis of themes in People's Daily coverage (1972-1974). Five dimensions account for four-fifths of the variance. Friendly socialist regimes dominate the first factor; participants in "hot wars" (Vietnam and the Middle East) comprise factor 2; "lackeys" such as Cambodia and South Vietnam load on the third factor; Western, industrialized countries are represented on factor 4; the fifth dimension consists of regime enemies (the USSR, India, Taiwan, South Korea).

The work of Bobrow and his colleagues combines an operational code approach with an impressive amount of empirical evidence. The nonrandom (and therefore predictable) nature of the behavior of the Chinese decision system is skillfully established. Given the polemics and a priori interpretations which have pervaded analyses of China's foreign policy process, the research of Bobrow, Chan, and Kringen is a welcome addition to the literature in this area.

The work of Brecher (1979b) on Israeli decision-making is anchored in a stress-coping-choice model.[19] The central research question is the effects of changing crisis-induced stress on coping and choice processes. The model is applied to Israeli behavior in the 1967 and 1973 crises and the findings are compared to earlier empirical studies of the 1914, Korean War, and Cuban missile crises. Overall, more than two-thirds of the propositions are supported across spatial and temporal parameters, providing evidence for the existence of common patterns and attributes in international crisis behavior.

Content analysis is the basic data-making methodology employed in this and Brecher's other studies of Israeli precrisis and crisis decision-making. Interestingly, the sample is of publicly articulated statements and represents one or more of the following forms of content analysis (Brecher, 1979b: 461):

- Frequency and intensity of crisis perceptions;

- Analysis of attitudes (friendship/hostility and satisfaction with the status quo);

- Advocacy analysis (coding of all enunciated goals and their measurement along a nine-point advocacy statement scale).

In an early study of the prewar period in Israel in the fall of 1956, Stein and Brecher (1976) employ image-advocacy data to provide probabilistic prediction of choice among options by foreign policy decision-makers. Decisions can be dichotomized into strategic (broad policy acts) and tactical (operationalizations of policy acts) types. The assumption that elites act in accordance with their perceptions of reality per se provides the justification for a content analysis of the articulations of three key Israeli figures in the period preceding the initiation of the Sinai Campaign in the fall of 1956: David Ben-Gurion; Golda Meir; and Moshe Dayan.

Similarities and differences in terms of general foreign policy images, general advocacy, specific images (Sinai), and advocacy regarding Sinai are noted. Of the three, only Ben-Gurion showed a pluralist image of the subordinate or Middle East system. All three gave little attention to intra-Arab conflict. In terms of advocacy statements--urging a course of action or policy--none of the three advocated a policy of unilateral concessions; Meir was the most moderate and Dayan the most militant of the three. Not unexpectedly, the Sinai-relevant perceptions reflected a decline in emphasis on Third World actors and heightened attention to France and Britain.

Stein and Brecher (1976) determine the stability of images of the global system by comparing both salience and content across the two sets of image data. None of the three showed a statistically significant pattern of consistency. The decision-makers displayed a high degree of consistency in their pattern of perceptions of the regional environment. Both content and affect remained stable across the two sets of images; general images, then, predict content and direction of affect. Intensity patterns remained consistent. In general, using three major indicators--salience, content, and the intensity of advocacy--the two sets of images were consistent in the latter two and inconsistent only in the case of salience at the global level.

In their analysis of two central prewar decisional problems in Israel prior to the Yom Kippur War of 1973, Brecher and Raz (1977) posit the assumption that images of reality--not objective reality--shape the behavior of foreign policy elites.[20] The two problems (mobilization and preemption) are examined in an effort to probe the causal nexus between perceptions (or misperceptions) and decisions.

Between September 26 and October 5 at 5 P.M., Israeli intelligence had received about 400 items of information pointing to the possibility of war. Brecher and Raz (1977) argue that the underlying "conception" (Egypt would never launch a war without superior war power and Syria would not go to war without Egypt's involvement) and specific perceptions of major Israeli decision-makers account for the otherwise inexplicable lack of congruence between the evidence and elite assessments of the evidence. The conception reduced the ability to separate clear signals from noise and also accounted for the misperception of signals of the impending Arab attack.

The authors employ content analysis of public

documents to derive data on specific images of the setting for the prime minister, defense minister, and deputy prime minister. The content and range of images are described and the image systems of the three decision-makers are compared. During the pre-crisis period, all three focused on the regional arena. Prime Minister Meir perceived the military situation as excellent and viewed Egyptian President Sadat as a moderate. In striking contrast to Meir's complacency, Deputy Prime Minister Allon expressed dissatisfaction with Israel's policy of immobilism. Allon correctly perceived Arab goals but incorrectly evaluated their options. Defense Minister Dayan reflected the elite's collective serenity, although reports of the Soviet order to evacuate families of their advisors did increase his perceived probability of an attack.

More recently, Brecher's (1977, 1978) framework for foreign policy decision-making analysis has been applied to research on a variety of crisis cases in the International Crisis Behavior (ICB) Project. The various empirical researchers are all employing the common framework to study foreign policy crises in contexts ranging from Munich (1938) to Syria's response to the Lebanese civil war (1975-1976). The actor diversity is striking (the Netherlands, U.S., Guatemala, Soviet Union, Israel, etc.). The entire ICB data base features an N of 469 cases from 1938 to 1976.

The framework itself is a decision process rather than a source analytical device.[21] Thus, it can be employed to reconstruct and analyze all of the major phases and processes which characterize the decision process and precede the actual decision or behavior. The framework of structured empiricism, which is described in detail elsewhere (see Brecher, 1972; Brecher et al., 1969) is organized around the concepts of foreign policy system, input, process, output, operational environment, communication network, psychological environment, attitudinal prism, image, issue areas, formulation, implementation, and feedback.

Events within the environment--which is classified into ten components (five external and five internal)--or actions by international or subnational actors are introduced to decision-makers via a communication network. As such, they become inputs into the foreign policy system, constituting stimuli which are filtered through the attitudinal prisms of elites and specified as the images of the relevant components of the psychological environment; the latter predisposes elites to select among the perceived options. Bureaucratic and organizational processes become relevant during the formulation and implementation of decisions. From the implementation of choices/decisions, consequences will ensue in the form of feedback to one or more of the environmental components, the decision-makers, and/or their psychological environment.

Psychological phenomena are salient in Brecher's scheme. In crisis analysis, for example, the perception of crisis (as derived from the decision-maker's images of stimuli emanating from the external and/or internal environment) is the independent variable. The dependent variable is crisis behavior. The basic relationship in the model is that between image and behavior. Also, among the nine actor attributes relevant to crisis research are the unit's belief system (Christianity, Communism, etc.) and psychological environment (the attitudinal prism and specific images); the latter forms the predispositional response pattern to a crisis. Finally, coping depends to a considerable extent on various aspects of information processing.

Considerable empirical research has already been conducted and forthcoming studies will apply the framework to a number of crisis cases. In the course of testing hypotheses and assembling propositions, Brecher and his colleagues on the International Crisis Behavior Project can be expected to continue the task of illuminating the impact and nature of perceptual and other psychological phenomena and processes.

The framework has been converted into a testable model (i.e., a specification of variables and their expected interrelationships) in Brecher's (1979a, 1979b) research on the psychological dynamics and processes of Israeli decision-makers in 1967 and 1973. As noted, three variable clusters are highlighted:

- Perception of crisis (threat, time, probability of war)--the independent variables;

- Coping processes and mechanisms--the intervening variables;

- Choice or decision--the dependent variable.

A three-phase model (precrisis, crisis, postcrisis)

is specified in order to analyze the changes that occur during a "crisis."

The central research question revolves around the assessment of the impact of changing stress levels on the processes and mechanisms through which foreign policy elites cope with crisis and make choices. Like the other ICB case studies, the 1967 and 1973 Israeli cases address nine specific questions. What are the effects of changing levels of crisis-induced stress on:

- Information?
  (1) The perceived need and resulting search for information;
  (2) The receptivity and size of the information-processing group;
  (3) Cognitive performance;

- Consultation?
  (4) Type and size of consultative units;
  (5) Group participation in the process;

- Decisional forums?
  (6) Size and structure of decisional forums;
  (7) Authority patterns within decisional units;

- Alternatives?
  (8) Search for and evaluation of alternatives;
  (9) Perceived range of available alternatives.

Results are presented for the 1967 and 1973 cases for various dimensions of choice during the lowest, rising, higher, highest, and moderate/declining stress phases. For each discrete decision, core inputs (e.g., pressures from or acts by others), assessed costs, degree of importance, nature of the process (affective or rational), and presence or absence of novelty were ascertained. In the highest stress phase, for example, Israel's choices were characterized by (Brecher, 1979b: 469):

- A sharp rise in the number of decisions perceived to be crucial;

- A further increase in the perception of costs;

- A marked upsurge in novel decisions;

- Greater variety and content of inputs to choice; and

- More of a tendency in favor of affective-based over rational decisions.

The extensive inquiry of Brecher and others on one case through time--Israel--provides the foundation for exploring in a systematic fashion the perceptions, beliefs, values, and decision and choice processes of foreign policy elites in international crises. The prospects for cumulativeness and generalizability are enhanced appreciably by the existing stockpile of belief system studies (1914, the Cuban missile crisis, etc.) and the current and emerging case studies of the ICB Project.

The operational code approach. The two most popular approaches to operationalizing foreign policy elite belief systems are the operational code procedure and cognitive mapping. The former is depicted in Figure 3.3.[22] The operational code approach involves sampling from the belief system; excluded from consideration are the dozens of low-level beliefs which dot the landscape of any individual's belief system.

The focus is on central beliefs about the nature of politics and political conflict, the views about the extent to which the individual can shape historical developments, and notions about preferred or correct strategies and tactics (George, 1969: 197). The operational code consists of two kinds of beliefs.

- Philosophical beliefs refer to "fundamental assumptions" about the nature of politics.

- Instrumental beliefs reflect convictions about the styles and strategies which are appropriate to acting in the world.

According to George (1969), the answers to five philosophical and five instrumental questions encompass the primary dimensions of political beliefs. The philosophical issues include:

(1) What is the essential nature of political life? Is the political universe essentially one of harmony or conflict? What

93

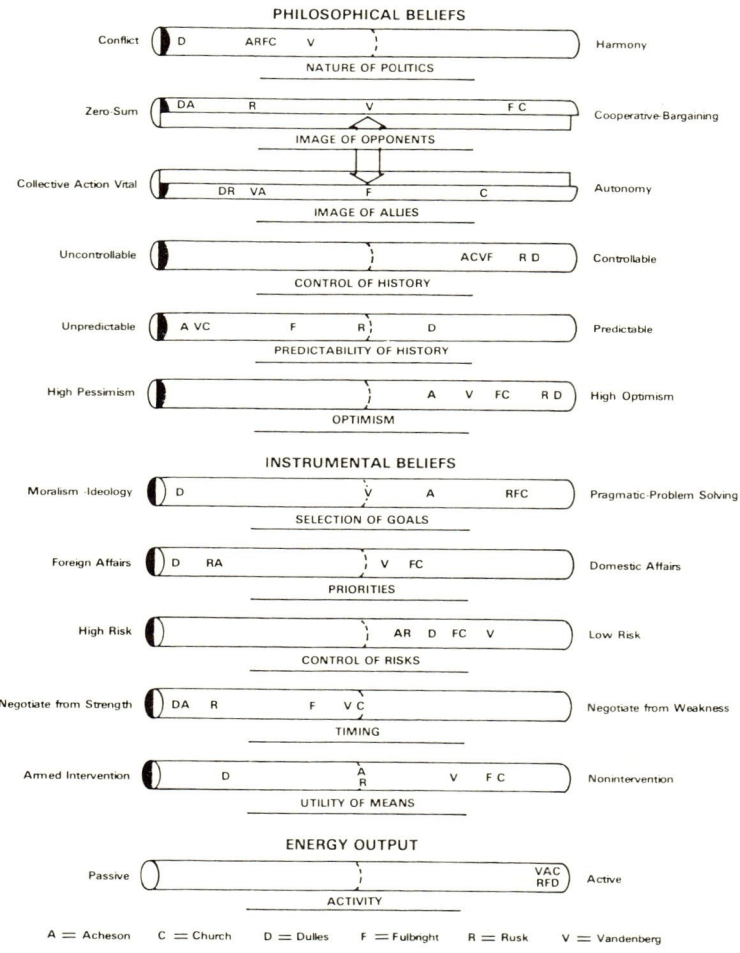

a Source: Johnson (1977: 102).

Figure 3.3

A COMPARISON OF CHURCH AND OTHER LEADERS ALONG OPERATIONAL CODE DIMENSIONS[a]

is the fundamental character of one's political opponents?

(2) What are the prospects for the eventual realization of basic goals and aspirations? Is pessimism or optimism warranted in assessing the prospects?

(3) Is the political future predictable? In what sense? To what extent?

(4) How much "control" or "mastery" can be asserted over historical development?

(5) What is the role of "chance" in human affairs and historical development?

The <u>instrumental</u> issues are:

(1) What is the best approach for selecting goals?

(2) How are the goals pursued most effectively?

(3) How does one caculate, control, and accept the risks of political action?

(4) What is the best "timing" of action?

(5) What is the utility and role of different means for advancing one's interests?

Considerable effort has been devoted to the task of developing detailed coding categories for each question (see Holsti, 1977). As the list below demonstrates, operational code case studies have appeared for a number of policy-makers:

U.S. Senator
Frank Church (Johnson, 1977)
J. William Fulbright (Tweraser, 1974)
Arthur Vandenburg (Anderson, 1973)

U.S. Secratary of State
Dean Acheson (McLellan, 1971)
John Foster Dulles (Holsti, 1970)
Henry Kissinger (Walker, 1977)
Dean Rusk (Gutierrez, 1973)

man Fulbright but deviates from Vandenburg:

- Philosophically in his images of "Opponents" and "Allies;"

- Instrumentally in his approach to the "Selection of Goals."

As Johnson (1977: 103) concludes, this comparative analysis of operational codes has implications for future work. More systematic comparisons could provide the foundation for generating explanatory and predictive typologies of political beliefs. The ultimate goal would be to account systematically for sources of variance within systems (role factors, partisan identification) and between systems (behavioral and attribute typologies, subsystem impact, etc.).

Johnson's findings about the predictive capacity of Church's operational code (with the 1956 code as a predictor of beliefs in 1972 and the 1972 code as the independent variable vis-a-vis beliefs in the following six months) indicate that the code at one point in time does predict subsequent beliefs and actions. While this generalization requires modification for the purposes of taking into consideration intervening events and experiences, the operational code is a predictive aid, at least in terms of broad parameters and in the context of basic themes. For example, the 1972 code accurately reflected Church's consistent antipathy toward U.S. foreign aid and intervention; this core belief was a central feature of Church's belief system during his political "emergence" phase in 1956.

In another major case study employing the operational code approach, Walker (1977, 1979) focuses on former U.S. Secretary of State Henry Kissinger. Specifically, Walker examines the nexus between Kissinger's operational code and his conduct of the Vietnam negotiations. The data sources consist of Kissinger's writings. The author treats the behavioral data as a varying series of stimulus-response chains with the operational code viewed as an intervening constant.

Following a detailed description of the code, Walker (1977) examines the relationships between types and sequences of U.S. and North Vietnamese behaviors (1969-1973) and the instrumental principles imputed to Kissinger. The patterns are congruent with the principles. Other variables--including bureaucratic constraints and the requirements of alliance diplomacy—occasionally intervened and account for the several discrepancies which are unearthed.

Walker's contribution is a case study which identifies the parameters of the actor's choice preferences rather than predicting their exact values; the operational code is a necessary but not sufficient condition for prediction and explanation of the subject's actual behavior. Despite these caveats, however, the article illustrates the potential utility of operational code mapping and—when considered along with the numerous other case studies of various leaders—constitutes the foundation for cumulative research in this area.

As Walker notes in the conclusion, Kissinger's operational code can be incorporated into a more general typology of decision-making strategies. As a collective set of components, his code approximates the "prisoner's dilemma" version of game theory; revolutionary leaders prefer an absolute gain solution whereas "statemen" favor a relative gain solution. A leader's operational code may reveal his "general preference relation." The value of the operational code and cognitive mapping approaches will be demonstrated conclusively when valid, predictive typologies are generated; given this work and Holsti's (1977) efforts, the preliminary aspects of this vital undertaking have already been initiated.

The proffered coding manual in Holsti (1977) is designed to foster cumulativeness in the operational code tradition of belief systems research. The large number of case studies in this area has assigned different meanings to the ten basic philosophical and instrumental questions. Furthermore, coding has tended to be qualitative. Holsti breaks the process down into four distinct stages and provides useful guidelines and detailed instructions and examples. The length and complexity of the manual are understandable, given the nature of operational code analysis.

The typology section presents a typing scheme based on the first philosophical belief; harmonious/conflictual views of political life are cross-classified with possible attributions of the sources of conflict (human nature, nation-states, the international system), yielding six cells from A to F. A preliminary empirical test involves three U.S. senators and two secretaries of state; the results are not uniform across either subjects or beliefs.

In the second empirical test, the five subjects

from the preceding test and seven others (two other U.S. secretaries of state, Bolshevik leaders, Ramsay MacDonald, Kurt Schumacher. and Willy Brandt) constitute the sample. Results for comparisons of the predicted and actual beliefs and the relationships between goodness of fit in subject classifications and support for the derived hypotheses are presented.

Generally, support for the hypotheses varies by belief. There is some tendency for the hypotheses to perform better with those in Type B (a harmonious view of political life and the attribution of conflict to the characteristics of nations). While Holsti catalogues the limits of this effort to develop a typology of belief systems, the general conclusion that the first political belief is a "master" or central belief is convincingly established.

Cognitive Mapping. The cognitive mapping approach is depicted in Figure 3.4. Axelrod (1972b, 1976) contends that in order to simplify the complexities of the external world, the decision-maker mentally fashions a representation of the world which links possible solutions to a problem with potential consequences via a network or system of beliefs. Generally, the linkage between a choice and an outcome is indirect in nature; in order to grasp the dynamics of the decision-making process, it is consequently necessary to examine the entire structure of concepts and linkages. A person links concepts with each other with beliefs that are causal in nature. The causal beliefs and the concepts which they link comprise a decision-maker's cognitive map.

Figure 3.4 illustrates the basic process of constructing a cognitive map. The concept variables are interrelated by arrows, which express the beliefs about the effect of one concept variable on another. Employing transcripts of the meetings of the Eastern Committee of the British Imperial War cabinet, Axelrod was able to construct the cognitive maps of the committee members. Figure 3.4 provides a textual example for one of the participants, lists the concept variables which were extracted from the text, and depicts the linkages among the concept variables. The conclusion is consistent with beliefs; Axelrod generally discovered an impressive level of deductive consistency in the cognitive processing patterns of Eastern Committee members.

The cognitive processing approach of Bonham and Shapiro (1973) is a holistic model which synthesizes

Text

CECIL: I was very much attracted at one time by the suggestion that it was not really justifiable for us to go on spending this amount of money in Persia, that we had very little interest in the place, that it was not at all certain that the good government of Persia really mattered to us, and further that apparently our interference had not so far, for various reasons, conduced to the improvement of the government of Persia, but that, on the contrary, the government had become decidedly worse than it was when we had relatively less to do with them. Therefore I was disposed to think that there was a good deal to be said for the "stewing in their own juice" policy.

Abbreviation	*List of concept variables* Definition
A	Amount of money spent in Persia by Britain
B	British utility
C	Quality of government in Persia
D	Existence of British interference in Persia (=opposite of policy of letting Persia "stew in her own juice")

Cause	*List of causal assertions* Connector	Effect	*List of arrows*
A	Not really justifiable	B	A — B
C	Not at all certain really matters	B	C 0 B
D	Not conduced to improvement in	C	D 0 or − C
D	Since . . . became worse	C	D − C
D	Requires	A	D + A
−D	Good deal to be said for	B	D − B

Figure 3.4

CONSTRUCTING A COGNITIVE MAP

social psychological perspectives in the areas of attitude formation and decision-making.26 The model makes three fundamental assumptions:

- Cognitive complexity is related to a range of behaviors; the decision-maker's cognitive mapping of the international environment is conceptually simple or complex.

- Decision outcomes entail a process of deduction. The degree of cognitive complexity in the perceptual system of a decision-maker is represented in terms of the number of deductive paths that may be examined in the process of explaining the significance of an event and selecting an appropriate response.

- Decision-makers use their perceptions of situations as analogues to explain and find a solution for their current decision situation.

The Bonham-Shapiro model of foreign policy decision-making consists of three interrelated components: (1) the representation of beliefs; (2) the amplification of beliefs and search for explanations; and (3) the search for options and policy choice. The model concerns the structure and process of cognition in foreign policy decision-making as well as the sequence of phases which characterizes the process.

1. <u>Representation of beliefs</u>. Beliefs represent the decision-maker's past experiences and current expectations. "In the decision-making process, beliefs act like templates for channeling information and for relating possible policy options to perceptions about the intentions and behavior of other nations, and also to the policy objectives of the decision-maker [Shapiro and Bonham, 1973: 161]."
Beliefs are represented as a map of causal linkages among three types of concepts. <u>Affective</u> concepts refer to the objectives or interests of the actors. <u>Cognitive</u> concepts index beliefs about actions that occur in the international system. <u>Conative</u> concepts include the range of options from which the decision-maker selects policy recommendations. The <u>concepts</u> and the specified <u>causal linkages</u> (represented as arrows with either <u>positive</u> or negative signs) constitute a "cognitive map" of

the individual's belief system.

2. <u>Amplification of beliefs and search for explanations</u>. Four processes ensue when a new situation requires a response: the amplification of beliefs; the search for an explanation; the search for policy options; and the choice of a policy.

During the <u>amplification of beliefs</u> phase, the decision-maker attempts to anchor the new situation in the context of his experiences. This is essentially the <u>definition of the situation</u> stage of the model. Concepts in the cognitive map that correspond to the new event are <u>highlighted</u>; the amplified set of concepts is then used in subsequent phases of the decision process.

In the <u>search for explanations</u> phase, the decision-maker seeks the arrows or <u>paths</u> connecting a set of two or more highlighted concepts. Amplification and search processes are achieved by treating cognitive maps as <u>directed graphs</u> or "digraphs" and using the rules of digraph theory for making calculations. Crucial in this context is the concept of "<u>reachability</u>." which suggests that concepts connected by paths to initially highlighted concepts will also be highlighted. If, for example, concept V_1 in digraph D is initially highlighted, then V_2, V_3, and V_4, which are reachable from V_1, would be highlighted as well.

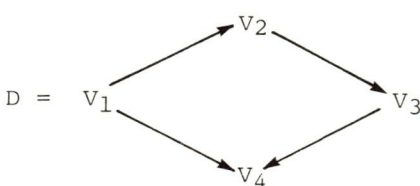

$$D = \begin{matrix} & V_2 & \\ V_1 & & V_3 \\ & V_4 & \end{matrix}$$

If there is more than one explanation, the model selects the one with the most <u>deductive support</u>. The latter can be defined as the number of logically independent reasons that reinforce an explanation; it is calculated by counting the separate paths which comprise a given explanation. Operationally, this involves the construction and manipulation of an <u>adjacency matrix</u>.[25]

If there is one explanation, it is automatically selected; if more than one is available, the adjacency matrix subroutine is pursued; if there are no explanations, the model begins searching for <u>inductive explanatory support</u>. This process involves scanning the stored events and choosing the one with the most concepts in common with the cur-

rent situation.
   3. <u>Search for options and choice</u>. At this point, the hypothetical decision-maker follows the explanatory paths from the policies which he might select (conative concepts) to the perceived objectives (affective concepts) and calculates which alternative results in the maximum net gain in objectives. The signed digraph, which indicates whether relationships are positive or negative, is converted into an adjacency matrix. This <u>valency</u> matrix enables us to determine whether there is a positive or negative path from a conative to one or more affective concepts.
   The final process is the choice of a policy option. Here, Shapiro and Bonham employ a lexicographic decision calculus which:

> ...assumes that the decision maker first uses his more important policy objective to see if the alternatives affect it differently. If this objective does not distinguish between alternatives, he then moves to his second objective, and so on, until he gets to an objective that distinguishes one alternative as better than the others [1973: 171].

This model has been applied to several cases. One, which illustrates the potential utility of the approach, concerned the Jordanian crisis of September, 1970 and the American peace initiative which culminated in an Israeli-Egyptian cease-fire accord. Extensive interviews with 15 American policy-makers concerned with the Middle East formed the basis for constructing their cognitive maps.
   In a detailed preliminary test of the model (see Bonham et al., 1976), the cognitive maps of four of the officials, a group of "Country Directors" in the Department of State's Bureau of Near Eastern and South Asian Affairs, provided the empirical basis for an aggregated cognitive map. The latter consisted of almost 100 concepts. The phases of the simulation produced the following results.
   For the simulation of the Yom Kippur War, five concepts from the aggregated map were highlighted during the initial amplification phase:

- Increase in Military Action (I 13);
- Arab-Israeli War (A 3);
- Soviet Involvement (G 8);
- War of Attrition (W 3);

- Israeli Occupation of More Arab Land (I 41).

After the initially amplified concepts are fed into the model, the search for antecedents begins. The model searches for paths which culminate in the intially amplified concepts and selects those which meet the plausibility test (i.e., were perceived to be supported by historical evidence).

The model found a total of seven antecedent paths. The first four presented slightly different explanations for the war itself. Next was the search for perceived consequences (especially for U.S. policy values). Nineteen consequent paths were identified. Interestingly, the model predicted that the war would have a positive impact on most American values, including:

- The avoidance of military confrontation with the Soviet Union;

- The containment of regional conflicts;

- Security for Israel;

- The presence of moderate governments;

- The protection of investments and trade;

- Access to oil;

- Access to air, space, and military facilities.

The basic line of reasoning here was that the war would lead to loss of control in the area, creating Soviet fears about confrontation and resulting in Soviet pressure on the Syrians. The two sides would subsequently accept a U.S. cease-fire initiative.

After generating an explanation, the model searches for relevant policy options. In this simulation, seven options were revealed on the basis of options connected to the antecedent and consequent paths.

The final step involves tracing paths from the options to the policy values and calculating whether the impact is positive, negative, or neutral. Then, taking into consideration the policy value rankings obtained in the interviews, the model calculates a preference order for the options. In the Yom Kippur

War simulations, four options tied for first place. The simulated country directors:

- Favored a combination of diplomatic moves ("diplomatic pressure on the Soviets" and "a cease-fire initiative") and military posturing;

- Ranked aid to Israel fifth;

- Ranked U.S. military intervention last.

Recent work in this area is represented in Axelrod (1976), Bonham and Shapiro (1977), and Hart (1977). Axelrod (1976) includes several introductory chapters which discuss cognitive mapping and three concluding chapters which specify the uses as well as the limitations of the approach. The heart of the book is a series of case study applications; there are five cases (three of which are directly relevant to foreign policy-making).

The chapter by Bonham and Shapiro (1977) in their edited book Thought and Action in Foreign Policy concerns computer simulations of foreign policy decision processes in Finland and Austria. The study is another example of their work on cognitive mapping and cognitive process models. Interestingly, the data for the simulation are derived from open-ended interviews with high level officials and lower-level expert advisors, indicating that direct access is not necessarily an insurmountable problem (at least in smaller political systems).

Hart (1977) constructs the cognitive maps of three Latin American policy-makers. The article contains an excellent discussion of the elements of a cognitive map and provides lucid definitions of such esoteric concepts as causal paths, path-balance, causal cycles, and density. Specific hypotheses concerning the impact of the subject's scope of political responsibility are tested.

Cognitive mapping is a general purpose approach to the task of empirically charting belief systems. Recent research provides a basis for optimism, especially if more effort is made to combine issue-specific cognitive mapping with more basic operational code profiling. Among the problems which await resolution are:

- The absence of a general framework in the realm of cognitive mapping;

- The issue-specific nature of the approach;

- The lack of empirical research concerning the stability of maps across situations (for a given actor) and decision-makers (at various levels and in varying contexts);

- The question of data access and data-making strategies (especially the contrasting documentary and expert-generated approaches);

- The possible spuriousness of the data (i.e., the criticism that decision-maker consistency reflects post-decision justification tendencies rather than pre-decision causation).

Among the advantages is that cognitive mapping can be used for both <u>descriptive</u> and <u>prescriptive</u> purposes. Hart (1977) concludes that cognitive mapping scores high on all of the standard criteria for evaluating research:

- Parsimony;
- Generality;
- Descriptive power;
- Explanatory power;
- Richness of normative implications.

At least some cumulativeness has been achieved in the realm of cognitive mapping. The various strategies for describing the content of individual belief systems are becoming increasingly well developed, although the progress concerning belief system structures and cognitive processing patterns is considerably less impressive.

<u>Conclusion</u>. The 1973 London conference on cognitive approaches to foreign policy analysis, which is the basis for Bonham and Shapiro (1977), can perhaps be singled out as a seminal event in the belief systems area of the political psychology map. The length of this section indicates that the general domain of elite belief systems work has been the most prolific of the three foreign-policy-and-psychology variable clusters. Much remains to be done; however, the progress sketched out above provides a much more solid foundation than the ones available

for the study of leadership psychodynamics or personality traits.

NOTES

1. The theme of eclecticism is illustrated later in this chapter in terms of a tripartite classification scheme (psychodynamics; personality traits; belief systems); see also Chapter 6.
2. This issue is discussed in detail later in the chapter.
3. This question is particularly relevant given the time and cost usually involved in the collection of psychological data--especially in comparison to event, attribute, and other types of data commonly employed in quantitative international politics and comparative foreign policy.
4. See especially Chapter 5 below, Falkowski (1979a, 1979b), and Hermann (1979b).
5. Especially useful is Robins (1977) and the bibliographical essay which he includes at the end of the introductory chapter.
6. Especially noteworthy is the effort to match simulation participants with the decision-makers in the 1914 crisis on the dimension of personality traits; see Hermann and Hermann (1967).
7. See also Greenstein (1975), Hermann (1976), Holsti (1976), and Walker (1979).
8. Hermann (1976) and Holsti (1976) refer to other aspects of the situation, including amount of ambiguity, long-range policy planning, unanticipated events, and situations characterized by information overload and high stress.
9. Pool (1970: vii-xiii) provides synopses of the early efforts, including RADIR, the Library of Congress project on awareness of and attitudes toward other nations, and the Foreign Broadcast Information Service's propaganda research during World War II. On the latter, see also George (1959).
10. See Hopple and Favin (1978); the literature is summarized and related to international crisis research in Hopple and Rossa (1980).
11. The psychodynamic basis of the Barber (1972) framework for classifying political types is clearly in this Lasswellian tradition. The active-negative type, for example, is motivated by a negative self-image with phenomenological roots which are similar to Lasswell's political man (see also Barber, 1977-1978). The well-known Barber framework consists of two dichotomous personality traits

(level of activity and level of affect); the <u>character</u> construct refers to the psychodynamic level; the <u>style</u> dimension is a personality trait; <u>world view</u> is a frequently employed surrogate for <u>belief system</u>.

12. See Greenstein (1975) for details.

13. The latter problem is a central one in depth-psychological inquiry; generally, the researcher ransacks the historical record for confirmatory evidence. It is notoriously difficulty to falsify (rather than verify) Freudian and similar theories; see Popper (1963: 34-37).

14. See, e.g., Snyder (1978) and Steinbruner (1974); Williams (1976) presents a defense of the concept of elite rationality in crises.

15. Barber's (1972) framework suggests that a leader may be psychopathological <u>or</u> psychically healthy. Sniderman (1975) discovers that <u>overall</u>, elites show higher levels of self-esteem than the mass public; however, a large proportion of the elite sample includes leaders who lack self-esteem and display materialistic and obsessive ambitions.

16. Professed orientation to change refers to the government's public posture regarding the need for change in the international environment; independence/interdependence of action concerns the amount of control which a nation maintains over its actions; commitment subsumes behaviors which limit a nation's future capacity to act; affect refers to the feelings ranging from friendliness to hostility which are expressed toward another nation; feedback concerns responses from other nations to one's behaviors; external consequentiality means the potential impact on other governments. For details, see Hermann (1975) and East et al. (1978).

17. Some beliefs are simple factual propositions; however, cognition and affect frequently interact, producing a tendency for one's emotional attitude toward an object to influence his or her beliefs about it. It is not possible to "fence off" cognitive, perceptual, affective, and evaluative phenomena from each other.

18. See also Bobrow et al. (1977) and Chan et al. (1979).

19. See also Brecher (1972, 1975, 1977, 1978, 1979a) as well as the studies discussed here.

20. Handel (1977) also provides a discussion of the prewar Yom Kippur crisis.

21. See the discussion of source and process models in the introductory chapter (pp. 6-7).

22. The approach was developed by Leites (1951,

1953) for the study of Bolshevism and has since been popularized by George (1969); see also George (1979) and Holsti (1977).

    23. Johnson's comparisons are based on operational code case studies from: Anderson (1973); Gutierrez (1973); Holsti (1970); McLellan (1971); and Tweraser (1974).

    24. Also relevant are Bonham (1975), Shapiro and Bonham (1973), Bonham and Shapiro (1976, 1977, 1979) and Bonham et al. (1976, 1978, 1979). On cognitive process models in general, see Axelrod (1972b, 1976); Jervis (1976); Steinbruner (1974); and Pool and Kessler (1965).

    25. An adjacency matrix of a digraph D is a square matrix with one row and one column for each point of D. For digraph D above, the adjacency matrix A (D) is:

	V1	V2	V3	V4
V1	0	1	0	1
V2	0	0	1	0
V3	0	0	0	1
V4	0	0	0	0

Each non-zero element indicates the number of paths from the row to all other elements. By raising the adjacency matrix to the nth power (i.e., from length 1 to 2, etc.), we can discover the number of paths of length n from each element to every other element. By raising the matrix to the power equal to the longest path in the reachability matrix, we can count the number of paths from each highlighted to every other highlighted concept. See also Shapiro and Bonham (1973: 167-168) and Harary et al. (1965: 408).

national research (various groups in Canada, South
Australia and Papua New Guinea, Israel, South Vietnam, Japan, and West Germany). Penner and Anh
(1977), for example, have reported results from
South Vietnamese respondents (a randomly selected
group tested shortly prior to the collapse of the
Saigon regime) and compared their value profiles
with those of one of the U.S. national samples (1428
adults, 1971). Generally, significant and intuitively meaningful differences characterized the intercultural comparisons (especially with respect to
the Vietnamese sample's lower ranking of freedom and
higher ranking of security); however, breakdowns by
educational level revealed many value system similarities between college-educated Americans and
Vietnamese.

The research literature on value, attitude, and
behavior change is voluminous and primarily supportive of the theoretical substructure articulated by
Rokeach. The latter features three central propositions:

- A special form of consistency theory--
  in which the individual is posited to
  be motivated by an attempt to maintain
  and enhance his or her self-conceptions--
  underlies the theoretical edifice.

- The method of self-confrontation (with
  the feedback of information to increase
  awareness) is the primary means for
  eliciting cognitive and behavioral
  change.

- The fundamental psychological mechanism
  which initiates change is the arousal of
  self-dissatisfaction.

Rokeach (1979c) summarizes the results of 23
experiments conducted in his and others' laboratories. Significant value changes have been brought
about regardless of variations in experimental conditions or individual characteristics. The changes
have been extended to other values, attitudes, and
behaviors (e.g., eye contact with blacks, cigarette
smoking, etc.) and other locales and samples (e.g.,
college students, adults, Air Force recruits, New
York policemen). Many of the studies have concerned
equality and freedom, which are core political
values; of the 17 appropriate studies involving
equality and freedom as target values, 15 have

exhibited long-term subject changes in one or both values.³

More recently, Rokeach has conducted research which demonstrates vividly and impressively that experimentally-induced value change has real world implications.⁴ A special film produced by Rokeach and Ball-Rokeach was shown simultaneously on the three major commercial television stations of the Tri-City area in Washington State; there were four groups (an experimental group with a six week pretest and one with a six week posttest; a control group with a six week pretest and one with a six week posttest). The film--entitled "The Great American Values Test"--featured the actors Edward Asner and Sandy Hill.

The 30-minute film featured three target terminal values: a world of beauty; equality; and freedom. Three behavioral solicitations were subsequently mailed out to each experimental and control subject:

- One to persuade Ss to financially support a black cultural group in their efforts to achieve racial equality;

- A second letter soliciting financial support for women athletes at Washington State University; and

- A third soliciting financial support for an antipollution initiative scheduled to be on the November 1979 ballot in the state of Washington.

So far, only preliminary results are available. These, however, are striking in magnitude and direction; the target behavior was significantly increased in the experimental group and the opposite behavior underwent a significant decrease. Overall, the experimental return rate of about 7 percent is much larger and statistically more significant when compared to the control return rate of about three and one-half percent.

Conceptual Background

Rokeach's conceptual framework, which will be the focus of this section, provides the basis for empirically profiling the belief systems of foreign policy elites. Content analysis will be the specific research method and the research design will be a modified "most different systems" cross-national approach.[5]

Data access obstacles invariably impose serious restrictions on the use of content analysis as a technique for the comparative study of decision-maker belief systems. Aside from the plethora of problems which plague any content analytic effort, there is the obvious limitation that only official, public documents can be employed. Private statements would undoubtedly be preferable, but such sources are unavailable to cross-national researchers.[6]

The major issue which must be resolved is the selection of specific phenomena to measure in the cross-national content analytic research context. Attempts to map the entire belief systems of dozens of foreign policy decision-makers would be excessively expensive and time-consuming. A belief system consists of at least several distinct subsystems and a potentially staggering number of discrete elements or propositions (such as statements about reality and other beliefs).

In order to avert the danger of costly and ultimately unproductive "fishing expeditions," it is necessary to adopt a coherent framework for analyzing belief systems. Such a framework is provided by the belief system and value system research of Rokeach.

Rokeach's (1960) initial emphasis on the structural properties of belief systems was an outgrowth of his interest in ideological dogmatism and authoritarianism. The Open and Closed Mind attempted to highlight the structure of beliefs; the concern was with how beliefs are held rather than with content per se. According to Rokeach, a belief system consists of interrelated beliefs. Belief and corollary disbelief systems can be compared on the basis of various criteria, including the degree of isolation of belief elements, differentiation, and comprehensiveness (Rokeach, 1960: 33-46).

In Beliefs, Attitudes, and Values, Rokeach (1968) extended his analysis of belief systems in an effort to incorporate other components. A belief system "represents the total universe of a person's beliefs about the physical world, the social world, and the self [Rokeach, 1968: 123]." An attitude is one type of subsystem of beliefs; ideology is an organization of beliefs and attitudes shared with others and derived from external authority (Rokeach,

1968: 123-124). The concept of organization or structuring is central to Rokeach's approach. Beliefs are organized within an attitude, attitudes within an attitude system, and all beliefs, attitudes, and values within a cognitive system (Rokeach, 1968: 117, 162-163).

The value concept receives primary attention in The Nature of Human Values. Rokeach (1973: 3) asserts that each individual has a fairly small number of values. Values can be subdivided into instrumental and terminal categories; terminal values are personal or social in nature while the instrumental category subsumes moral and competence values (Rokeach, 1973: 6-8). Values and value systems function as standards for action and general plans for conflict-resolution and decision-making (Rokeach, 1973: 13-14).

Each element in a cognitive system is linked to the other components. These linkages will be specified, but it is initially necessary to define each of the units of a belief system (see Rokeach, 1968: 112-114, 125).

A <u>response</u> is a verbal or other physical reaction to a stimulus on a survey or questionnaire; responses may reflect random reactions, opinions, attitudes, beliefs, or values. An <u>opinion</u> is a verbal expression of a belief, attitude, or value.

A <u>belief</u> is "any simple proposition, conscious or unconscious, inferred from what a person says or does, capable of being preceded by the phrase 'I believe that...'" Beliefs may be descriptive or existential, evaluative, or prescriptive. Beliefs have cognitive or knowledge, affective, and behavioral components.

An <u>attitude</u> can be defined as "a relatively enduring organization of beliefs around an object or situation predisposing one to respond in some preferential manner." Attitudes are often elicited operationally by assessing affective reactions to a stimulus; this procedure is satisfactory if the assumption that the responses also reflect underlying beliefs is not tenuous.

A <u>value</u> is a specific type of belief:

> A <u>value</u> is an enduring belief that a specific mode of conduct or end-state of existence is personally or socially preferable to an opposite or converse mode of conduct or end-state of existence. A value system is an enduring organization of beliefs concerning pre-

ferable modes of conduct or end-states of
existence along a continuum of relative
importance [Rokeach, 1973: 5].

These units are interrelated within a belief
system. In addition to terminal and instrumental
value systems, attitude systems, and attitudes, an
individual has cognitions about the self, one's own
behavior, the attitudes, values or needs, and behavior of significant others, and the behavior of
non-social objects (Rokeach, 1973: 220-221). The
elements are organized within each of these ten subsystems; attitudes, for example, are systems of beliefs. There are also linkages between and among
the subsystems; attitudes and beliefs are assumed
to be congruent with basic values.

Values, then, are basic <u>orientations</u> which
structure perceptions and reactions. As Rokeach
(1973: 23-24) notes, culture, institutional socialization, and personal experience shape values while
the latter determine social attitudes, ideology,
and behavior. Value differences that relate to
attitude responses in diverse content domains provide impressive support for this proposition (see
Rokeach, 1973: ch. 4). In an ingenious experiment
on long-term attitude and value change, Rokeach
(1973: 263-271) offers more direct evidence that
value change precedes attitude change.[7]

Research on mass or elite belief systems will
yield incomplete and distorted maps if the topography is not adequately described. The following
guiding generalizations can be offered at this
point.

- All individuals have belief systems;

- All belief systems include belief,
  attitude, and value subsystems;

- These subsystems are interrelated.

Rokeach (1973: 30) admits that his list of
values was selected intuitively. To what extent
does his sample of values represent the total universe? In addition to the representativeness of
the value lists in general terms, their relevance
for political analysis must also be considered.
Rokeach's terminal values include such explicitly
political end-states as equality, freedom, and
national security. But an analysis of American culture generates a somewhat different collection of

"regime moral values" (see Devine, 1972: 179-227).

The relevance of Rokeach's value analysis to political science can be determined by evaluating its efficacy in actual research. In a national survey in 1968, value differences were apparent for reactions to several different political attitudes; ten significant value differences, for example, emerged for Vietnam policy opinions (see Rokeach, 1973: 97-109). Value rankings were also related to diverse forms of political behavior, including the act of joining a civil rights organization, participation in demonstrations, and political activism in the 1968 presidential campaign (see Rokeach, 1973: 123-124, 130-131).

Rokeach (1973: 169) developed a two-value model of political ideology by concentrating on value orientations about freedom and equality. The model is depicted in Figure 4.1. Strikingly disparate relative rankings of these values, as determined by content analyses, characterized the views of diverse conservative, liberal, and left and right authoritarian leaders (Rokeach, 1973: 171-178). This typology of different combinations of freedom and equality also generated significant results within less elite strata. Mean ratings of 25 ideological concepts by five equality-freedom groups at Michigan State University showed significant differences for 18 of the concepts (Rokeach, 1973: 195-196). Rokeach's equality-freedom typology represents an undeniable improvement over earlier unidimensional approaches to political ideology.

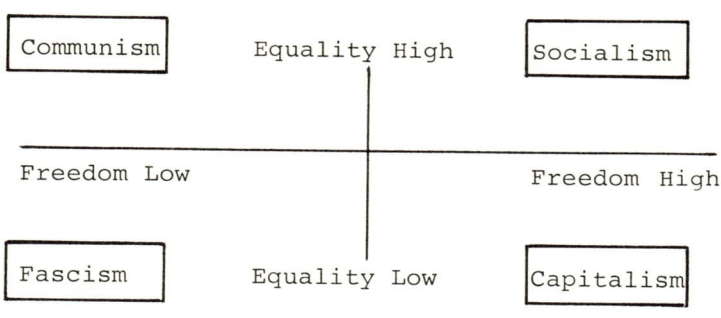

[a]Source: Rokeach (1973: 170).

Figure 4.1

A FREEDOM--
EQUALITY MODEL OF POLITICAL VARIATIONS[a]

Values and Empirical Foreign Policy Elite Analysis

Implicitly, value systems have frequently been identified as primordial forces in the literature on international political relations and bargaining. Statecraft involves the pursuit of an ordered set of end-states of existence via a hierarchy of modes of conduct. That is, interstate diplomacy and negotiation assume the existence of hierarchically arranged terminal and instrumental value systems. In addition, value systems are presumably heterogeneous within the disparate universes of countries and leaders.

The values of foreign policy-makers, however, have rarely been measured directly. Like a variety of other individual characteristics, decision-maker values have been discussed extensively but have rarely been operationalized. Recent work, however, has involved the construction of cognitive maps and the delineation of operational codes for a variety of cases.[8] Some genuinely cross-national empirical data bases have also been amassed.[9]

As the discussion up to this point suggests, the value system of a foreign policy decision-maker's belief system emerges as a logical focus for cross-national content analysis. Values can be measured fairly easily; Rokeach's list of terminal values can be applied in diverse contexts. Values and value rankings can be obtained from individuals (through questionnaires and surveys) and from institutions (through content analyses of pertinent documents and sources and via other methods as well).

As Rokeach (1979a: 58) points out, extensive research by Eckhardt (1965, 1967) and White (1949, 1951) has demonstrated that "the values contained in various historical and political documents can be reliably extracted by content analysis." The previously noted content analysis of ideological leaders uncovered distinctive value profiles for Lenin, Hitler, Goldwater, and Norman Thomas (Rokeach, 1973).[10] In another content analysis, Rokeach, Homant, and Penner (1970) concluded that the value pattern which characterizes the disputed Federalist Papers was more similar to James Madison's than Alexander Hamilton's; the evidence that Madison was probably the author of these papers has been independently confirmed by historical evidence and other research.

Rokeach (1979a: 58) notes that the material analyzed in such content analyses is typically ideological and thus exhortatory in nature. He offers three general assumptions which will also guide the research reported below:

- The purpose of any exhortatory material is advocacy of one or more means or ends values;

- It is possible to uncover the values so advocated by content analysis; and

- Exhortatory material originating with different social institutions will emphasize different values.

For measuring the value systems of foreign policy elites, the Daily Report of the U.S. Foreign Broadcast Information Service (FBIS) is the only readily available source with appropriate data for a significant number of countries.[11] The Daily Report consists of material obtained through the U.S. monitoring of foreign broadcasts; included are speeches and interviews.[12]

The countries in this analysis are a subset of a larger group of 56 nations for the period 1966 to 1970.[13] This sample of 56 included all countries which had initiated forty or more foreign policy events during the time span from 1966 to 1969, according to the World Event Interaction Survey (WEIS) events data set.

The next step involved compiling lists of heads of state (president, prime minister, etc.) and foreign ministers for all 56 states in the sample.[14] Every instance of a Daily Report speech (interview, broadcast, etc.) by one of the listed individuals was recorded. Speeches of less than 100 words were automatically excluded, as were joint communiques and purely congratulatory or ceremonial telegrams or messages.

The value subsamples were determined on an annual basis. All countries for which there were three or more "cases" or speeches by the foreign policy elite (i.e., head of state and/or foreign minister) were included. The 39 states that satisfied this criterion one or more times during the 1966 to 1970 time frame are listed in Table 4.1.

The annual state samples vary from 31 (in 1966 and 1967) to 20 (1969). Certain states appear with regularity whereas others are included rarely or not at all. States in the latter category include Canada, Brazil, some European states, Ghana, Ethiopia, and the Union of South Africa, Turkey, Lebanon

STATE	1966[b]	1967[c]	1968[d]	1968[e]	1970[f]	TOTAL
1. United States[g]	171	62	69	92	87	481
2. Cuba	20	10	6	10	11	57
3. Chile	4	9				13
4. France	13	7		8	7	35
5. West Germany	5	11	3		27	46
6. East Germany	20	15	11	22	26	94
7. Poland	4	9	11	12	14	50
8. Hungary	4	10		5	10	29
9. Czechoslovakia	7	11	41	52	19	130
10. Yugoslavia	15	19	30	20	41	125
11. Greece	12	8				20
12. Cyprus		4			4	8
13. Bulgaria					9	9
14. Rumania	9	7	16	17	26	75
15. U.S.S.R.	38	49	32	36	62	217
16. Ghana	12					12
17. Nigeria	7	21		6		34
18. Kenya	9					9
19. Algeria	8	8			6	22
20. Iran		4	3			7
21. Turkey	3	4				7
22. Iraq	21	16	11			48
23. United Arab Republic	18	16	20	14	37	105
24. Syria	10	14	5		5	34
25. Lebanon					6	6
26. Jordan	18	28	8	11	30	95
27. Israel	5	33	21	9	60	128
28. Saudi Arabia	7	3				10
29. Yemen		5				5
30. China	30	26	20	9	27	112
31. South Korea			7			7
32. Japan	4		9			13
33. India	24	4		7	4	39
34. Pakistan	27	6				33
35. Thailand			4	4		8
36. Cambodia	42	19	16	5	10	92
37. Laos					7	7
38. South Vietnam	46	4	13	10	3	76
39. Indonesia	42	3		6	4	55

[a] The figure is the number of speeches.
[b] N = 31.
[c] N = 31.
[d] N = 21.
[e] N = 20.
[f] N = 25.
[g] The source for the United States is the Department of State Bulletin

Table 4.1

VALUE DATA: STATE SAMPLES (1966-1970)[a]

and Yemen, and such Asian countries as South Korea, Japan, Malaysia, the Philippines, and Australia.

Table 4.2 highlights the states which appear with the greatest frequency. Fourteen states are in all five yearly samples; this core group will obviously yield the most useful data for such research questions as value subsystem stability across time. The 14 states include many which were of direct interest to U.S. policymakers during the 1966 to 1970 period (e.g., Cuba, Czechoslovakia, the United Arab Republic, Jordan, Israel, China, and South Vietnam).

STATE	ALL YEARS (1966–1970)	FOUR YEARS	THREE YEARS
1. United States	X		
2. Cuba	X		
3. France		X	
4. West Germany		X	
5. East Germany	X		
6. Poland	X		
7. Hungary		X	
8. Czechoslovakia	X		
9. Yugoslavia	X		
10. Rumania	X		
11. U.S.S.R.	X		
12. Nigeria			X
13. Algeria			X
14. Iraq			X
15. United Arab Republic	X		
16. Syria		X	
17. Jordan	X		
18. Israel	X		
19. China	X		
20. India		X	
21. Thailand			X
22. Cambodia	X		
23. South Vietnam	X		
24. Indonesia		X	

Table 4.2

VALUE DATA: MOST FREQUENTLY INCLUDED STATES

Generally, the states which comprise the yearly samples overrepresent the Middle East and the Communist nations. However, there is at least some variety. Third World actors such as Indonesia and India are included in four of the five samples; France and West Germany also appear on four of the five lists; such diverse states as Algeria, Indonesia, Poland, and Syria are listed three or more times. While the lists obviously reflect FBIS data collection biases and U.S. focus of attention idiosyncracies (such as the relative neglect of Western Europe and Africa in the 1966 to 1970 period), the sample does contain some heterogeneity.

As an initial training exercise, two coders content analyzed the values in 12 of the Federalist Papers. In a previous study, Rokeach et al. (1970) reported identical content analysis results. Rokeach and his colleagues were concerned specifically with the applicability of value analysis to the "disputed authorship" question (i.e., were the papers authored by Alexander Hamilton or James Madison?).

In order to assess reliability (between the foreign policy data coders and among those coders and the Rokeach coders), the rankings in Rokeach et al. (1970) were compared with those of the two coders. The Spearman's rho results were:

- .78 for the rankings reported in Rokeach et al. (1970) and coder A (statistically significant at .01);

- .89 for the rankings reported in Rokeach et al. (1970) and coder B (statistically significant at .001);

- .93 for the rankings of coders A and B (statistically significant at .001).

For the value-based content analysis of the FBIS material, the list of 13 terminal values from Rokeach et al. (1970) was employed. Exploratory content analysis work suggested the addition of five foreign policy-specific values: progress; unity; ideology; cooperation; and support of government. The 18 terminal values (and their respective definitions) are listed in Table 4.3.

In order to generate an estimate of intercoder reliability, five speeches were selected from the 1969 Daily Reports. The speeches included: Leoni of Venezuela (January 2, 1969); Pham Von Dong of North Vietnam (January 3, 1969); Svoboda of Czechoslovakia (January 19, 1969); Svoboda of Czechoslovakia (January 21, 1969); Balaguer of Venezuela (February 28, 1969). When coders A and B were compared, the resulting Spearman's rho was an adequate --albeit far from impressive--.83 (significant at the .001 level).

1. A comfortable life (a prosperous life; economic stability; economic security, raising living standards).
2. A world of peace (free of war and conflict).
3. Equality (brotherhood; equal opportunity for all; impartiality; free from extremes).
4. Freedom (democracy; independence; free choice; liberty; absence of coercion).
5. Happiness (felicity; contentedness).
6. Governmental security (stability of government; sufficient governmental control).
7. Honor (feeling honorable; having self-esteem).
8. Justice (state of just dealing or right action; people receiving their due).
9. National security (protection from attack; sovereignty; serving national interests; integrity of borders).
10. Public security (protection of the rights of the people; law and order).
11. Respect (worthy of high regard).
12. Social recognition (admiration as a result of social status).
13. Wisdom (mature understanding of life).
14. Progress (goal achievement; economic/social/cultural development).
15. Unity (absence of opposition).
16. Ideology (balance; struggle; references to Marx or Mao).
17. Cooperation (friendship; coexistence).
18. Support of government (sacrifice for government; patriotism; loyalty).

[a]The first 13 values are adopted from Rokeach et al. (1970); see also Rokeach (1973).

Table 4.3

VALUES FOR CONTENT ANALYSIS[a]

The actual coding process was very straight-forward. The speech was the initial unit of analysis; within a speech, the sentence was the coding unit. A given sentence could contain no values, 1 value, 2 values, and so on. For each speech, a frequency count was made for each of the 18 values (based on the explicit appearance of the given value or of a keyword/synonym).

DESCRIPTIVE DATA

For the purpose of providing some illustrative descriptive data, results for 1970 will be presented. The descriptive data in Table 4.4 have been aggregated across all FBIS Daily Report states with at least three speeches for 1970; frequencies are given for all 18 values.

It should be emphasized that this particular aggregation strategy is unusually crude since it simply sums the value totals across all states. Actual analyses of the data set will entail the aggregation of value totals by individual states. In other words, value profiles will consist of state A's totals for each of the 18 values, state B's totals for each of the 18 values, etc.

Table 4.4 provides absolute and relative frequencies for four categories: 0 references to the value; 1 reference; 2 references; 3 or more references. The fourth category simply combines all totals greater than 2 into one aggregate total.

The relative frequencies in the 0 column isolate the values which appear rarely; the least frequently appearing values include happiness, social recognition, and wisdom. The values a world of peace, freedom, national security, progress, and cooperation appear most often in the 1970 data set. As would be expected, different institutions (religion, science, etc.) display strikingly different value patterns (see Rokeach, 1979a). The fourth column in Table 4.4 explicitly highlights the values which were most prominent in FBIS-monitored speeches in 1970.

A summary descriptive profile of the value data set is presented in Table 4.5, where overall means for the 18 values for all of the states and years in the data set are presented. Eight values have means above 1:

- A world of peace;
- Freedom;
- National security;

	Value[b]	0		1		2		3+	
		AF[c]	RF[c]	AF[c]	RF[c]	AF[c]	RF[c]	AF[c]	RF[c]
1.	A comfortable life	377	82.9	46	10.1	12	2.6	20	4.4
2.	A world of peace	170	37.4	89	19.6	55	12.1	141	40.9
3.	Equality	364	89.0	49	10.8	15	3.3	27	5.9
4.	Freedom	232	51.0	93	20.4	47	10.3	83	18.3
5.	Happiness	396	87.0	40	8.8	12	2.6	7	1.6
6.	Governmental security	385	84.6	34	7.5	15	3.3	21	4.6
7.	Honor	365	80.2	52	11.4	14	3.1	24	5.3
8.	Justice	336	73.8	75	16.5	18	4.0	26	5.7
9.	National security	162	35.6	92	20.2	60	13.2	141	31.0
10.	Public security	286	62.9	71	15.6	29	6.4	69	15.1
11.	Respect	348	76.5	70	15.4	23	5.1	14	3.0
12.	Social recognition	421	92.5	17	3.7	7	1.5	10	2.3
13.	Wisdom	417	91.6	27	5.9	8	1.8	3	0.7
14.	Progress	132	29.0	74	16.3	55	12.1	194	42.6
15.	Unity	265	58.2	72	15.8	37	8.1	81	17.9
16.	Ideology	256	56.3	51	11.2	41	9.0	107	23.5
17.	Cooperation	147	32.3	56	12.3	39	8.6	213	46.8
18.	Support of government	371	81.5	40	8.8	23	5.1	21	4.6

[a]Total N = 457 speeches for 26 states.
[b]Results have been aggregated into the categories of 0 (no references to the value), 1, 2, and 3 or more.
[c]AF = Absolute Frequency; RF = Relative Frequency.

Table 4.4

1970: VALUE FREQUENCIES[a]

VALUE	MEAN	STANDARD DEVIATION
A comfortable life	.66	1.01
A world of peace	1.74	1.80
Equality	.34	.53
Freedom	1.60	1.36
Happiness	.47	.65
Governmental security	.65	.61
Honor	.47	.53
Justice	.63	.69
National security	2.32	1.64
Public security	1.19	1.01
Respect	.38	.36
Social recognition	.29	.43
Wisdom	.22	.51
Progress	4.54	4.16
Unity	1.52	1.30
Ideology	3.10	3.60
Cooperation	3.65	2.88
Support of government	.77	.85

Table 4.5
VALUE MEANS AND STANDARD DEVIATIONS (1966-1970)

Logically, four outcomes are possible for this state versus year comparison. If both state and year are significant, the states remain different but changes which are attributable to "systemic" factors affects states "uniformly." If neither state nor year accounts for an appreciable percentage of variance, then states change over time but the variations are the product of unmeasured internal and idiosyncratic forces. If the state variable explains more of the measurable variance, then scores by state are stable and states differ. If the year is the more potent determinant, then states are similar and vary over time as a consequence of "systemic" (i.e., supra-state temporal context) factors.

In assessing the results, both the significance of the F-values and the magnitudes of the eta^2 correlations will be employed. Both criteria show that <u>state</u> is generally a more viable predictor than <u>year</u>. Fourteen of the 18 state F-values are statistically significant while 9 of the year F-values are significant; the state eta^2's are larger than the comparable year eta^2's in 16 cases. The only exceptions to the latter configuration are happiness (equivalent eta^2's) and wisdom (.22 for state and .25 for year).

The most unambiguous supportive results are for those values for which state is significant while year is not:

- Equality;
- Honor;
- Justice;
- National security;
- Public security;
- Respect;
- Unity;
- Ideology; and
- Cooperation.

At the other extreme, there are three instances when year exerts a significant impact while state is insignificant:

- A comfortable life;
- Happiness; and
- Wisdom.

These three values fluctuate on a temporal basis and knowledge of the state is less helpful than for the other values (although the state variable explains

35 percent of the variance in a comfortable life, 25 percent in happiness, and 22 percent in wisdom).
Both variables exert significant effects in six cases:

- A world of peace;
- Freedom;
- Governmental security;
- Progress; and
- Support of government.

The third column in Table 4.7 presents the percentage of unexplained variance for each of the 18 values. When the impact of state and year is taken into account, the unexplained variance ranges from 20 percent (honor) to 55 percent (a comfortable life). The mean percentage of unexplained variance is about 40 percent on the average; knowledge of state and year accounts for 60 percent of the variance in the value data set.

RESEARCH DESIGN

Much of the empirical work on individual-level psychological and psychophysiological factors has explicitly excluded other potential determinants of foreign behavior. The research design sketched out in this section--which provides the basis for the empirical findings reported in Chapter 5--features a multicausal approach to the analysis of foreign behavior generally and conflict behavior specifically.
Progress in the study of the nature and dynamics of international conflict processes and similar phenomena has been ad hoc and uneven. Reams of data have been amassed and various discrete hypotheses have been empirically tested. No real edifice of knowledge, however, has emerged in this realm of inquiry.

Background:
Quantitative International Conflict Analysis

Several major research projects in the middle and late 1960s were launched in the then-nascent "field" of Quantitative International Politics. A tangible effect of these pioneering efforts was the collection and inductive analysis of massive data banks.[16] Since then, fairly pessimistic reassessments of the "data bank explosion" have appeared in the literature on international political analysis.[17]

The critics have frequently castigated the empiricists for "ransacking" correlation matrices for significant relationships and for generally pursuing narrowly inductive analytical strategies. A considerable amount of tension has arisen between the devotees of data base generation and the exponents of deductive and (preferably) abstract/mathematical modeling.

In the period since the late 1960s, an approach midway between the inductivists and deductivists has attracted some adherents: the route to knowledge via structured empiricism.[18] This strategy suggests a conscious effort to construct analytical frameworks or coherent "maps" to guide the researcher. Such frameworks identify relevant independent, intervening, and dependent variable clusters and thereby provide a mechanism for organizing disparate research findings. The framework is also viewed as the foundation for constructing, testing, refining, and re-testing a series of increasingly sophisticated causal models. Philosophically, the emphasis is on the fostering of a "dialogue" between (structured) inductive and deductive orientations.

Given the state of affairs in quantitative conflict analysis (the lack of theory, high complexity, the interdisciplinary nature of the research terrain, etc.)--as well as in the context of an explicit commitment to conducting research in the interstices between pure data analysis and hard modeling--the soft modeling approach emerged as a viable candidate for a preferred analytical strategy. Thus, the early data-oriented work (massive factor analyses; regression analyses involving an incredible profusion of endogeneous variables, ranging from air distance from Washington and Moscow to GNP per capita; etc.) has been succeeded by more structured research designs.

In the fall of 1975, a research program designed to construct a framework for analyzing conflict and other forms of international behavior was launched. The first product of this program was a general analytical framework which housed discrete variables in conceptual clusters (see Andriole et al., 1975). Independent variable realms were delineated, as was an intervening variable cluster. The latter grouped a large number of fairly static national attributes or characteristics into several domains via R-factor analysis and grouped the cases (56 nations, 5 years of data from 1966-1970) into statistically-based subgroups via Q-factor analysis (see Wilkenfeld, et al., 1978).[19] Finally, the dependent variable cluster was "foreign behavior," defined empirically in terms of WEIS (World Event Interaction Survey) events data and factor analytically reduced to several overarching dimensions (see Rossa et al., 1979).[20]

A series of conceptual and empirical analyses has thus provided the foundation for pursuing more sophisticated causal modeling approaches in the future. Initial conceptual and empirical research sought to establish the validity of three assumptions:

- The behavioral domain of state action in the sphere of foreign policy can be dimensionalized into distinct types (constructive diplomatic behavior, non-military conflict behavior, and force behavior).

- The determinants or "sources" of state behavior can be clustered into at least four realms (psychological, internal or societal/political, interstate, and global).

- Countries can be distinguished on the basis of four sets of structural attributes (economic structure, governmental structure, capabilities, and political stability).

The conceptual (framework-construction) and empirical (data assembly and collection) phases of the program generated an integrated data base consisting of dozens of discrete variables and indices grouped into more general variable realms.[21] Appendix A provides a comprehensive list of variables, dimensions, and conceptual clusters; Hopple (1978) presents a detailed discussion of the variables, index-construction procedures, factor analysis results, and data sources.

The next phase in the research program was to convert the analytical framework into a testable model (see Hopple et al., 1977). A "first-cut" effort in this direction involved the use of empirical data from two of the independent variable clusters (the societal and interstate) as well as the type of nation data (the intervening variable cluster) and the dependent variable (the WEIS foreign behavior measures).

The concern with the analysis of the relative

efficacy of variable clusters as determinants of external or foreign behavior outputs can be traced to the work of Rosenau (1966). A central question in the comparative study of foreign behavior has been the relative importance of different types of determinants. Much of the relevant research has juxtaposed internal and external forces.

The analytical phase of inquiry revolved around this issue of relative efficacy assessment. This question was explored via two primary analytical strategies. One, based on the Partial Least Squares (PLS) methodology, allowed for the construction of "latent" (not directly observable) variables (from manifest or measured indicators) in the realms of: foreign behavior (the dependent cluster); determinants of such behavior (the independent clusters); and the state classification scheme (the intervening clusters).[22] The use of moderators to represent static structural (contextual) factors (with and without the action-reaction element of the interstate cluster) facilitated the derivation of country-specific parameters.[23]

Coleman (1975; Coleman et al., 1966) employed a second approach in the now-famous Equality of Educational Opportunity. "Coleman analysis" assumes that the combination of indicators within a block or component should be based upon the ideal of maximizing the explanatory power of the block. The dependent variable is regressed upon the indicators of one variable realm and the (standardized) predictions serve to represent the combination of indicators; the beta weights index the effects of discrete variables. Relative explanatory efficacy between two or more indicator clusters is ascertained by regressing the dependent variable upon the set of predictions, thus providing comparative betas for variable realms.

Figure 4.2 depicts the Coleman research design in its pure form.[24] Coleman sought to explain educational achievement in terms of family background and school quality and to assess the relative potency of these two blocks of variables. As Figure 4.2 illustrates, we substitute foreign behavior for the dependent variable; variable blocks P, S, I, and G represent the four independent variable realms.

The Coleman strategy was designed to accommodate a larger number of predictive variables and to ascertain their relative efficacy in accounting for a criterion (foreign behavior). An earlier publication contains some preliminary results derived from applying this perspective (Hopple et al., 1977). We now extend that earlier effort by incorporating a variety of additional potential determinants (including elite values) and by analyzing a modified set of foreign behavior categories. The following section identifies the specific indicators and more general clusters.

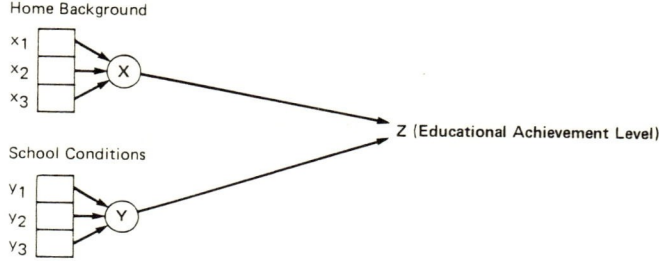

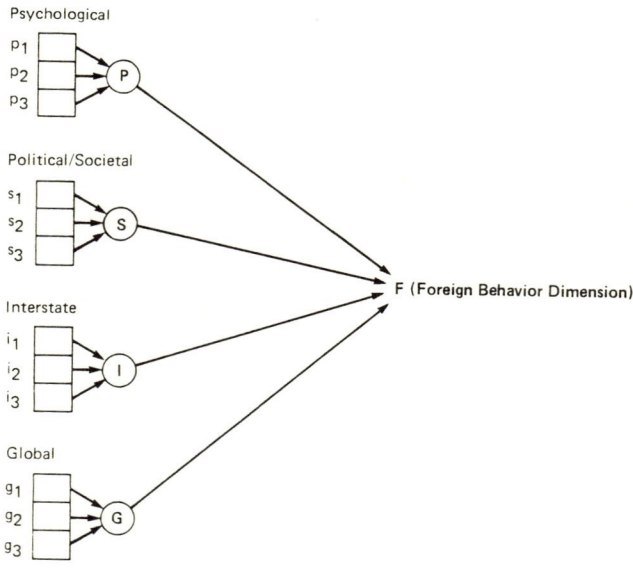

Figure 4.2
COLEMAN ANALYSIS

Independent and Dependent
Variable Clusters and Indicators

Decision-maker values are posited here to be determinants of external or foreign policy behavior. However, individual-level factors comprise only one variable realm in comparative foreign policy. A variety of additional internal and external "sources" of foreign behavior can be identified; these are often grouped into general variable clusters.

The value data set has already been described. The other variables include societal, interstate, and global factors (independent variables) and dimensions of foreign behavior (dependent variables). The latter are derived from the World Event Interaction Survey or WEIS events data set. Instead of employing the twenty-two discrete WEIS categories as dependent variables, the analysis will focus on three general dimensions that emerged in a factor analysis of the WEIS behavior sent data (see Rossa et al., 1979).

Dependent variables. The first factor--"constructive diplomatic behavior"--explained 49 percent of the total variance. Fourteen of the WEIS events loaded on this dimension: yield; comment, consult; approve; promise; grant; reward; agree; request; propose; reject; deny; warn; and impose negative sanctions (reduce relations). The second dimension, which was designated "non-military conflict," accounted for 23 percent of the total variance. Clustered here were the action categories accuse, protest, demand, threaten, demonstrate, expel, and seize. The third factor, labelled "force," explained only 9 percent of the total variance and consisted exclusively of the force category. Conflict thus bifurcated into "moderate" and "extreme" dimensions. There are three distinct dependent variables: constructive diplomatic behavior; non-military conflict; and force.

Independent variables. The societal indicator realm consists of two indices of internal unrest and instability, a measure of economic performance, and a demographic variable. The domestic conflict indicators were selected from the time-series data set collected by Banks (1971). Cross-tabulation between all possible pairs of variables identified two distinct clusters: societal unrest (riots, antigovernment demonstrations, and general strikes) and government instability (coups, changes in the executive, the cabinet, or the constitution, revolutions, and purges). General annual economic performance was assessed indirectly by the annual merchandise balance-of-payments situation within each state. Rate of population growth has also been included to represent the demographic aspect of the societal domain.

Data have been collected on a variety of measures of interstate economic involvement (see Hopple, 1978). Formulae for the variables in the interstate realm are presented below:

Interstate Energy Relationships (Indices)

1. Energy Interdependency = $\dfrac{\text{energy imports} + \text{energy exports}}{\text{energy consumption}}$

2. Energy Market Strength = $\dfrac{\text{energy exports}}{\text{energy production} + \text{imports}}$

3. Energy Dependency = $\dfrac{\text{energy imports}}{\text{energy consumption} + \text{exports/production}}$

General Trade Relationships (Indices)

4. Neo-Colonial Dependency = $\dfrac{(\text{industrial imports} + \text{unrefined exports}) - (\text{unrefined imports} + \text{industrial exports})}{\text{total imports} + \text{total exports}}$

5. Economic Involvement = total exports + total imports

Food Dependency and Advantage (Index)

6. Food Dependency = $\dfrac{\text{food imports} - \text{food exports}}{\text{food imports} + \text{food exports}}$

General Interstate Economic Relations (Indices)

7. Import Concentration = $\sqrt{\dfrac{(S_i)^2 - 1/10}{1 - 1/10}}$

Where S_i is the percentage share of import expenditures in commodity class i, where ten categories exist.

8. Export Concentration = $\sqrt{\dfrac{(T_i)^2 - 1/10}{1 - 1/10}}$

Where T_i is the percentage share of export expenditures in commodity class i, where ten categories exist.

The eight indices specified above for the purpose of empirically measuring sources of foreign behavior in the sphere of interstate economic relations incorporate the following types of information: (1) export and import flow data; (2) production and consumption within states; and (3) commodity-specific and overall relationships. Four of the indices focus on one specific commodity (energy or food); one concerns the overall relations of a state; and three attempt to combine commodity-specific information into single scales of overall relationships. The indicators describe state interdependency, dependency, and economic domination or advantage within the interstate system as reflected in dyadic or interstate relationships.

Massive conceptual and data collection problems confront researchers who attempt to analyze the impact of global determinants of foreign behavior (see East, 1978). Cross-national data have been amassed for this study in two disparate global realms: borders and intergovernmental organization (IGO) memberships.

The research of Starr and Most (1976) on the subject of borders and the occurrence of war suggests that simple contiguity may be a source of interstate conflict and violence. In order to generate data on borders, the WEIS conflictual events were dichotomized into the categories of force and other conflict (the latter includes the event types reject, accuse, protest, deny, demand, warn, threaten, demonstrate, reduce relations or send negative sanctions, and seize). The total number of events sent and received by all of the state's neighbors was recorded for each border category and for the force and conflict categories.

This yielded eight discrete variables for a given state: (1) total number of conflictual events sent and received by states with direct land borders with the state; (2) total number of force events sent and received by states with direct land borders with the state; (3) total number of conflictual events sent and received by states with colonies land-bordering the state; (4) total number of force events sent and received by states with colonies land-bordering the state; (5) total number of conflictual events sent and received by states with direct sea borders with the state; (7) total number of conflictual events sent and received by states with colonies sea-bordering the state; and (8) total number of force events sent and received by states with colonies sea-bordering the state.

IGO membership data are of two forms: the total number of inter-governmental organizations to which a state belongs and the number of new memberships for a state during a given year. The two variables tap a state's static and varying commitments to global mechanisms and provide an indirect measure of willingness to work within a global framework.

Intervening Variable Cluster: Type of Nation

In addition to the array of independent and dependent variables chronicled in the preceding section, a variety of fairly static attributes of countries can be employed to generate a typing scheme of foreign policy actors.[25] A set of 23 such variables was reduced via R-factor analysis to four major dimensions of interstate variation. These four factors are: economic structure; capability/power; governmental structure; and political stability.

Q-factor analysis was then used to identify nation clusters. For the entire 56-state sample, five groups emerged: Western; Closed; Unstable; Large Developing; Poor. The first two reflect the familiar East-West pole in world politics; the developing or Third World breaks down into three distinct clusters.

Since only 39 of the 56 countries are represented in this analysis, the nation clusters have been modified somewhat. Table 4.8 lists the groupings and the countries in each. While the Western, Closed, and Unstable clusters remain unchanged, the Large Developing and Poor groups (along with countries which had previously been unclassifiable) comprise an "Others" category; this is clearly a primarily Third World grouping and will be so labelled in subsequent discussions. Since each state-year from 1966 to 1970 constitutes a separate case for analysis, the total N is 131, broken down by cluster as follows:

- Western (N = 24);
- Closed (N = 35);

- Unstable (N = 27);
- Third World (N = 45).

WEST	THIRD WORLD
West Germany Israel Japan France United States	Large Developing India Pakistan Turkey Indonesia China South Korea
CLOSED Poland Rumania Czechoslovakia Bulgaria USSR Hungary East Germany Yugoslavia	Poor Cyprus Lebanon Cambodia Jordan Laos Yemen
UNSTABLE Syria Iraq Algeria Egypt Iran Cuba South Vietnam	Unclassifiable Thailand Ghana Kenya Greece Nigeria Saudi Arabia

[a]This list is based on Q-factor analysis groupings for the larger 56-state list; see Wilkenfeld et al. (1978) for details.

Table 4.8
GROUPINGS OF STATES

Relative Efficacy Assessment

The foreign policy analyst's concern with estimating the "relative potency" of general source clusters, which may be traced to the work of Rosenau (1966), has spawned a series of empirical studies.[26] Frequently, the question revolves around the assessment of the relative importance of internal versus external sources of behavior--or between comparative and international politics approaches to the study of the sources of external behavior or the processes of foreign policy decision-making.

The specific analysis discussed in the following chapter entails five distinct steps:

- Regress the three dependent variables (constructive diplomatic behavior, non-military conflict, and force), one at a time, on the 18 value variables, generating betas and predicted values of the dependent variables. Perform the regressions on the total group (39 states) and on the four subgroups (Western, Closed, Unstable, and Third World).

- Repeat the procedure, substituting the four societal/political variables for the 18 value variables.

- Repeat the procedure, substituting the eight interstate variables for the 18 value variables.

- Repeat the procedure, substituting the ten global variables for the 18 value variables.

- Regress the three dependent variables, one at a time, on the four sets of predicted values derived from the first four steps. Perform the regressions on the total group of 39 and on each of the four subgroups (Western, Closed, Unstable, and Third World).

In the first four steps, the three dependent variables are each regressed upon the indicators from one of the four independent variable clusters. The beta-weights index the effects of discrete variables within the cluster. For example, the impact of freedom, national security, or any of the 18 values could be assessed <u>in relation to the effects of other decision-maker values</u>. The same holds for the societal/political variables of step 2, the interstate variables of step 3, and the global variables of step 4.

In contrast to these isolated variable cluster analyses, step 5 is a direct <u>relative potency</u> test. A single indicator is developed for each of the four components; this summary measure reflects the combined effects of all variables within each cluster in terms of explaining foreign behavior. The input values for the independent variables are the predicted values for the three forms of foreign behavior that were produced in the first four stages. Relative efficacy explanatory power is directly estimated by regressing the dependent variable upon the set of predictions, thus generating comparative betas which can be viewed as <u>relative efficacy scores</u>.

Figure 4.3 presents the overall research design in summary form. There are four independent variable clusters, four subgroups (type of nation), and three dependent variables. Appendix A lists all of the specific indicators.

As the findings in Chapter 5 will demonstrate, both the overall analysis (i.e., all 39 states) and the subgroup analyses should be examined. The four subgroups represent distinct types of nations. Variables which mediate between independent and dependent variables as conditioning factors, such as the nation typological domain, are "moderators" of relationships. Moderators can be imposed upon models in two ways: through subgrouping or through moderated regression. Subgrouping is the process of dividing the sample of cases into homogeneous classes. The subgrouping technique involves model estimation for each group and the comparison of results across groups. The effects of the moderator(s) are gleaned from this comparison. Moderated regression, in contrast, entails an attempt to build assumptions of moderator effects into the model itself. While subgrouping imposes no restrictions upon the nature of the moderator effects, moderated regression involves assumptions regarding the relationship between the moderator(s), on the one hand, and the regression weight (or beta) relating independent and dependent variables, on the other. The analysis in the following chapter utilizes the subgrouping approach.

NOTES

1. For details on the background and results of this research, see Hopple (1979a, 1979b), Hopple et al. (1980), and the following chapter.

2. See Rokeach (1968, 1973) for details; the concepts are discussed in detail in the following section of this chapter.

3. On values and racism, see Penner (1971); on values and sexual equality, see Ball-Rokeach (1976).

4. Preliminary findings were presented by Rokeach at a Workshop on Belief Systems and Values at the International Public Policy Research Corporation (IPPRC) in June of 1979.

5. On the latter, see Przeworski and Teune (1970: 34-39).

142

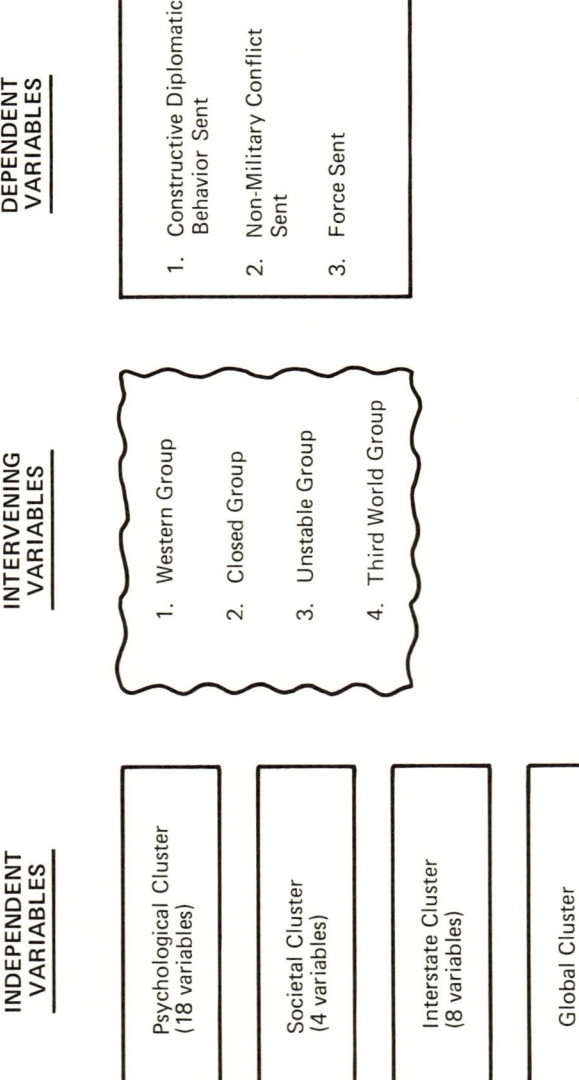

Figure 4.3   VALUE DATA ANALYSIS: RESEARCH DESIGN

47

CATEGORIES OF BIOLOGICAL SIGNALS							
BRAIN ELECTRICAL ACTIVITY						PERIPHERAL ACTIVITY	
ELECTROENCEPHALOGRAPHIC ACTIVITY	EXOGENOUS COMPONENTS	EVENT-RELATED POTENTIALS			PSYCHO-PHYSIOLOGICAL RESPONSES	OCULAR ACTIVITY	
		ENDOGENOUS COMPONENTS				EYE MOVEMENTS	EYE POSITION
		P300	DETECTION POTENTIAL	READINESS POTENTIAL	CONTINGENT NEGATIVE VARIATION		
		BIOCYBERNETIC APPLICATIONS					
ASSESS GENERAL COGNITIVE STATUS							
EVALUATE MOMENTARY ABILITY TO PROCESS INFORMATION AND MAKE APPROPRIATE DECISIONS							
					ASSESS GENERAL PHYSICAL STATUS		
						ASSESS GENERAL COGNITIVE STATUS	
ACTIVATE AND/OR CONTROL SUBSYSTEMS						ACTIVATE AND/OR CONTROL SUBSYSTEMS	
	ADJUST DISPLAY PARAMETERS						
		EVALUATE MOMENTARY ABILITY TO PROCESS INFORMATION AND MAKE APPROPRIATE DECISIONS					
			DETERMINE WHETHER TARGET HAS BEEN DETECTED				
				FIRE WEAPONS			
					EVALUATE MOMENTARY FLUCTUATIONS IN ATTENTIVENESS		
							DETERMINE WHETHER GAZE HAS BEEN DIRECTED TO APPROPRIATE LOCATION

^{a}Source: Gomer et al. (1979: 128).

Figure 2.4

RELATIONSHIP BETWEEN PARTICULAR BIOLOGICAL SIGNALS
AND EITHER THE DETERMINATION OF PILOT STATUS OR CONTROL FUNCTIONS:
AN ILLUSTRATIVE BIOCYBERNETIC INDICATOR SYSTEM^a

NOTES

1. Several significant papers on biopolitics were presented at the Conference for the Study of Political Thought at Loyola University of Chicago in April, 1978 (Masters, 1978b; Wiegele, 1978c; Willhoite, 1978).

2. See also Somit (1976c) and the comprehensive delineation of the subfield in Corning (1978); also useful is the list of references in Masters (1978a).

3. These include the Center for Biopolitical Research at Northern Illinois University under the direction of Thomas Wiegele and the experimentally oriented program in political psychology at the State University of New York at Stony Brook under the direction of Milton Lodge. Corning (1978: 72) refers to three political scientists who are participants in interdisciplinary life science/social science academic programs. Other noteworthy laboratory facilities are discussed in Center for Biopolitical Research (1978b: 60-61).

4. Favorable overviews are presented in Corning (1971), Masters (1975), and Somit (1968, 1976b); Masters (1978b, 1978d) exemplifies the biopolitics/ political philosophy perspective; critiques of biopolitical approaches are offered in Easton (1976), Nelson (1975), and Stephens (1970).

5. Somit et al. (1978) and Somit and Peterson (1978) in their literature reviews employ a classification system which organizes biopolitical research into six areas: works which deal with biopolitics as a subfield (e.g., the case for a more biologically-oriented political science, the advantages and disadvantages of biopolitics, etc.); studies which utilize an ethological, evolutionary, or sociobiological approach to political analysis; analyses concerned with the influence of physiological, somatic, and pharmacological factors on political behavior; research featuring the public policy implications of biological issues (e.g., genetic research, population policy, etc.); the application of biological techniques to political inquiry; and the metaphoric use of biological concepts.

6. See, e.g., Masters (1978c).

7. See Corning (1978: 72) for a discussion of this example.

8. This study is discussed in the following chapter; see pp. 67-68.

9. For studying paralinguistic variables, researchers often remove semantic content, which might influence judgments; the constant content

- Secretary of State John Foster Dulles (Holsti, 1962, 1967);
- Lenin, Trotsky, and Gandhi (Wolfenstein, 1967);
- Secretary of Defense James Forrestal (Rogow, 1963);
- President Richard Nixon (Mazlish, 1972);
- President Lyndon Johnson (Wolfenstein, 1974);
- Secretary of State Charles Evans Hughes (Glad, 1966);
- German Social Democrat Kurt Schumacher (Edinger, 1965);
- Soviet leader Josef Stalin (Tucker, 1973);
- President Woodrow Wilson (Brodie, 1963; Freud and Bullitt, 1967);
- Norwegian traitor/leader Vidkun Quisling (Hoberman, 1977);
- Adolf Hitler (Langer, 1972).

In addition to its case-specific bias, the psychodynamic approach has often been narrowly Freudian or neo-Freudian in orientation. A noteworthy exception is Tucker's (1977) critique of the George and George (1964) study of Wilson in terms of Karen Horney's theory of the neurotic personality. Glad (1969: 23-27) employs Horney's theory on inner conflict, denial, repression, and neurotic detachment in her case study of Idaho Senator Borah.

Furthermore, depth-psychological interpretations are generally more useful for explaining the _style_ of decision-making or _mode_ of response than for understanding the foreign policy behavior per se. Given the realities of politics and ideology, the conflict between Wilson and Senator Henry Cabot Lodge over U.S. membership in the League of Nations was undoubtedly inevitable. However, Wilson's internal conflicts and personality needs presumably determined his uniquely rigid style of response and thereby transformed a serious partisan clash into a bitter and ultimately insoluble personal conflict.

Psychodynamics deals with idiosyncratic or actor-specific psychological dispositions. Such influences relate more to the qualitative features of a decision than to the content (Kelman and Bloom, 1973: 271).

Considerable empirical research has accrued on the personality traits of decision-makers, the second general domain of inquiry. Here the concern is not with the genesis of personality processes and dispositions; the analyst simply attempts to identify and measure key personality traits or characteristics. The latter are then employed as predictors of policy preferences or behavioral choices. Examples of traits include many of the characteristics labelled as "motives" as well as a host of additional variables.

Two troublesome issues intrude here. The first concerns the selection of variables for analysis. A very partial list of discrete traits would include aggressiveness, self-confidence, nationalism, dogmatism, authoritarianism, cognitive complexity, level of self-esteem, achievement strivings, anxiety, field dependence, introversion/extroversion, and locus of control. All of these single characteristics have been examined empirically (e.g., Etheredge, 1978a, 1978b; Hermann, 1974, 1978, 1979b) or represent prominent dimensions or "traits" of personality in the field of psychology (see, e.g., London and Exner, 1978). Given the potential number of traits and the lack of criteria for "sampling" items or determining which are most central, it would be impossible to conduct comparative research on such factors.

The second difficulty concerns the impossibility of achieving direct access to most foreign policy elite members and the consequent need to make inferences of dubious validity from the available sources about personality traits. Measurement and data access problems are inescapably intertwined. Obviously, the researcher cannot ordinarily administer a battery of personality tests to members of the foreign affairs elite stratum. This approach may, however, be employed with simulation participants.[6] But the previously cited problem of establishing isomorphism between the simulational and real world contexts may preclude the formulation of valid generalizations.

The third cluster of factors can be subsumed under the belief system rubric. Consensus on the definition of this multifunctional, elastic term is far from unanimous. A panoply of competing concepts

- Conciliators (e.g., Adlai Stevenson)
  * Accommodationist style;
  * Lack of a consistent, strong will power.

The third difficulty is the access problem: how can access to high level elites be secured? If direct access is impossible, can valid "assessment at a distance" techniques be developed? This is a recurring issue in all three of the psychological variable clusters; as the preceding chapter showed, psychophysiological variables can--at least in some instances--be measured via remote and nonreactive techniques.

Obviously, the researcher is rarely in a position to administer a battery of personality tests to--or even interview--members of the foreign policy-making elite. This measurement strategy may, however, be used with participants in simulations. Simulations and gaming may of course be used for training and evaluation purposes; the envisioned application in this context is to hypothesis-testing and theory development. For example, Crow and Noel (in Hermann, 1977) and Driver (also in Hermann, 1977) employ simulation to determine the effects on foreign policy behavior of such personality traits as conceptual complexity, level of trust, and preference for risk-taking.

In addition to simulation, content analysis has also been used to study the personality traits of foreign policy elites. While this technique has been employed more frequently to measure aspects of decision-maker belief systems, there have been some applications in this area. The most noteworthy example--which is simultaneously perhaps the only illustration of genuinely cross-national, empirical research on foreign policy elite personality characteristics--is the work of Hermann (1974, 1975, 1978, 1979b).

Hermann and her colleagues on the CREON (Comparative Research on the Events of Nations) Project have developed a series of theoretical perspectives which are derived from the major levels of analysis in foreign policy inquiry (see East et al., 1978). In one study, Hermann (1975) considers six personal characteristics:

- Need for power;
- Conceptual complexity;
- Trust in others;
- Nationalism;
- Belief in own (internal)

ability to control events;
- Need for affiliation.

These six personal characteristics interact to form a configuration or a personal orientation to behavior; this is the basis for a general orientation to foreign affairs. The latter predicts that the head of state will be predisposed toward an independent or participative orientation to foreign affairs. To generate the data, Hermann (1974, 1975) content analyzed press interviews of 67 heads of state; the sources were the U.S. Foreign Broadcast Information Service (FBIS) <u>Daily Report</u> and the <u>New York Times</u>. At least 15 interview responses were found for 45 (67 percent) of the heads of state.

Hermann (1975) examines the relationship between the personal characteristics and specific foreign behaviors, including professed orientation to change, independence/interdependence of action, commitment, affect/environmental feedback, and external consequentiality.[16] The behaviors were taken from the CREON events data set.

Among the personal characteristics, the independent composite had the most significant or nearly significant correlations in the predicted directions with the foreign behaviors (48 percent of the correlations). For the participative composite, 40 percent of the relationships met the criterion. Among the individual characteristics, nationalism and need for power were significant predictors of behaviors in 34 percent of the cases; need for affiliation and distrust of others each included significant correlations in 29 percent of the total cases; for belief in internal control, only 9 percent of the correlations attained a significance level of .10 or better. Overall, 30 percent of the correlations were significant. Nine to 20 percent of the variance in behavior is explained. While this result is not striking, it should be emphasized that only six discrete characteristics (from a much larger universe) and two composite orientations were employed to explain the dependent variable of foreign actions as measured in the CREON data set.

Etheredge (1978a, 1978b) provides a recent example of empirical research which is oriented around the concept of personality traits. As he notes at the outset, analysts have frequently adopted a rational actor model and have assumed (implicitly or explicitly) that "nonrational" (i.e., individual-level) factors can be safely ignored. Etheredge maintains, however, that several hundred studies of

Head of State
Willy Brandt (Ashby, 1969)
Lyndon Johnson (Malone, 1971)
William Lyon Mackenzie King (Gibbons, n.d.)
Ramsay MacDonald (Kavanagh, 1970)
Mao Tse-Tung (White, 1969)
Lester Pearson (Lawrence, 1975)
Pierre Trudeau (Thordarson, 1972)
Getulio Vargas (Dye, n.d.)

The value of conducting operational code analysis via the comparative method can be illustrated with White's (1969) findings about differences in beliefs between Mao Tse-Tung and Liu Shao-ch'i about the nature of political life and image of the opponent (see George, 1979). Since the differences exerted no discernible impact for an extended period of time, Sinologists assumed that the Chinese Communist elite was characterized by unusual homogeneity in outlook and ideology.

Mao and Liu, however, eventually diverged in their diagnosis of the location and danger of the enemy. As the Chinese revolution passed through different stages, the differences surfaced and sharpened. While Liu felt that the internal enemy had declined in importance and consequently concluded that the intensity of the policy of "struggle" could be moderated, Mao continued to emphasize the persistence of contradictions and the resulting need for "struggle." This comparative analysis implicitly holds the impact of temporal and spatial parameters constant; similar designs could be envisioned (e.g., comparisons of Pearson and Trudeau or Acheson and Dulles).

In his evaluation of the operational code approach to foreign policy-maker belief systems analysis, George (1979) emphasizes that comparative case studies facilitate the process of tracing the impact of operational code beliefs in decision contexts. Ideally, he notes, the comparison should juxtapose two leaders matched in every important respect except for operational code beliefs. While perfect equivalence is unattainable, there are various sets of comparable cases (individuals or policy adviser groups) available for empirical analysis.

The case study selected for scrutiny here is Johnson's (1977) research on the operational code of Idaho Senator Frank Church. Johnson's concern is with the utility of the operational code construct as a predictive tool:

...the explanation and prediction of leadership behavior are improved by understanding the leader's political beliefs. The researcher will still be unable to predict with confidence the precise behavior of the subject in any specific circumstances, but he will have an idea of the <u>probable range of choices acceptable to the subject in a decision situation</u>. In this sense, the operational code is an independent variable helping to explain and predict leadership and policy-making behavior [1977: 85; emphasis added].

As Figure 3.3 indicates, Senator Church's operational code contains five primary "belief" dimensions in the standard content realms of the nature of politics, the image of the opponent, the control of history, predictability, and optimism. An axis which pervades all of the code dimensions is the energy or activity-passivity continuum. In other words, what counts is the substance of beliefs along with the individual's level of vigor or energy in articulating and propagating them.

For comparative purposes, the Church (C) position is juxtaposed in Figure 3.3 against positions for three former Secretaries of State (John Foster Dulles or D [1953-1959]; Dean Acheson or A [1949-1952]; and Dean Rusk or R [1961-1968]) and two former Chairmen of the Senate Foreign Relations Committee (Arthur Vandenburg or V [1946-1948]; and J. William Fulbright or F [1959-1974]).[23] Certain philosophical and instrumental patterns emerge with striking clarity. Church differs philosophically from former secretaries of state in his:

- Stronger beliefs in the possibility of cooperation with U.S. opponents;

- De-emphasis of principles of collective military action.

Instrumentally, Church differs from the secretaries in being:

- Less willing to seek situations of overwhelming strength;

- Less interested in intervening militarily.

Church is similar to former Foreign Relations Chair-

4
Elite Values and Foreign Affairs: An Overview

Human values are fundamental and enduring phenomena which structure beliefs, attitudes, and behavioral reactions. Formerly treated as presumably central but elusive components of the individual belief system, value systems have in the past decade emerged as the subject of empirically and theoretically impressive research efforts. The work of Rokeach (1973, 1979b, 1979c) and others has provided a firm foundation for conceptually analyzing and measuring values and value systems and for illuminating the conditions for long-term changes in values and related attitudinal and behavioral phenomena. Almost two dozen pertinent experiments can be cited (see Rokeach, 1979c).

Each individual possesses and implicitly or explicitly ranks a core set of values. Rokeach (1967), for example, lists 18 terminal and 18 instrumental values. Among the terminal values are <u>a comfortable life</u>, <u>equality</u>, <u>happiness</u>, and <u>national security</u>; the instrumental values include being <u>capable</u>, <u>honest</u>, <u>intellectual</u>, and <u>polite</u>.

In addition to individual value systems, values are also supraindividual (cultural, institutional, organizational) in nature. Value, in fact, is a core concept in both psychology and sociology. Recent work suggests clearly that various methodologies can be employed to measure institutional values such as science (see Rokeach, 1979a).

The values of foreign policy decision-makers are the focus of this chapter.[1] The Rokeach belief system and value system frameworks provide the conceptual foundation for a comparative, empirical study of foreign policy elite values. Following a brief overview of the Rokeach approach, the value data base will be described and the research design

111

for the empirical analysis discussed in the following chapter will be outlined.

THE ROKEACH VALUE APPROACH

The extensive work of Milton Rokeach and his colleagues on the subject of human values is well known to any social or political psychologist. This section will therefore provide a rather cursory overview of the conceptual and theoretical underpinnings and the major findings relating to validity and value, attitudinal, and behavioral change.

Rokeach (1979c) has been quite justifiably critical of the prevailing bias in social psychology in favor of attitudes and the consequent neglect of values and other components of the individual's total cognitive system. He identifies a number of substantive, methodological, and ethical limitations of the attitude approach, concluding that "...the attitude change literature [can be characterized] as a literature of short-term effects about attitudes that are typically isolated and trivial, and obtrusively measured with paper-and-pencil techniques that rarely have a demonstrable effect on socially relevant behavior [Rokeach, 1979c: 4]."

In the landmark works <u>Beliefs, Attitudes, and Values</u> (Rokeach, 1968) and <u>The Nature of Human Values</u> (Rokeach, 1973), value systems were treated as components of larger belief and cognitive systems. The terms attitude, belief, behavior, ideology, opinion, value, and value system form an interrelated cluster of concepts.[2]

The validity of the Rokeach value approach has been established in a number of national surveys of representative samples of the American people and in variegated experimental contexts (see Rokeach, 1979c). In the research literature, values have been found to be significantly and robustly correlated with various logically related:

- Attitudes;
- Personality traits;
- Behavioral responses;
- Life styles; and
- Occupations.

While the Rokeach Value Survey has been administered so far to only two national U.S. samples (see Rokeach, 1974), other studies have involved the use of the scale in varied settings and with diverse subjects. There has also been some cross-

- Public security;
- Progress;
- Unity;
- Ideology; and
- Cooperation

Especially noteworthy is the mean of 4.54 for the value progress. The values with the lowest means are wisdom, social recognition, equality, and respect.

The aggregated descriptive statistics in Table 4.5 can be compared with the individual state means. Table 4.6 highlights the state value means for one year (1966) which are greater in magnitude than the overall mean for that value. It is obvious that certain states are characterized by value patterns with an unusually high number of means above the overall "average" for the 1966 to 1970 span. Among these countries are the United States, Cuba, West Germany, East Germany, Hungary, Czechoslovakia, the Soviet Union, and the United Arab Republic.

STATE	1	2	3	4	5	6	7	8	9	10	11	12	13	14	15	16	17	18
United States	•	•	•				•	•	•		•	•				•	•	•
Cuba	•		•				•	•	•	•		•	•			•	•	•
Chile	•		•				•	•			•	•	•				•	
France																		
West Germany	•	•	•	•			•	•	•						•		•	
East Germany		•	•		•			•	•		•	•		•		•	•	•
Poland							•						•				•	
Hungary	•				•		•	•	•	•	•		•		•	•	•	•
Czechoslovakia	•	•	•	•	•			•	•	•	•		•		•	•	•	
Yugoslavia				•											•			
Greece				•		•											•	
Rumania	•		•	•	•			•	•		•	•		•		•		
U.S.S.R.		•		•							•	•		•		•		
Ghana	•		•	•										•	•			•
Nigeria				•			•		•									
Kenya																		
Algeria			•			•	•			•						•	•	
Turkey			•				•											•
Iraq	•		•	•	•		•		•				•			•		•
United Arab Republic	•		•	•	•		•	•	•		•		•	•	•	•	•	•
Syria				•	•								•	•				•
Jordan					•		•	•	•	•			•	•				•
Israel																		
Saudi Arabia			•	•	•		•	•	•							•		
China								•		•		•				•	•	
Japan		•					•										•	•
India		•																
Pakistan							•	•										
Cambodia				•	•		•	•	•						•			•
South Vietnam	•			•	•	•									•			•
Indonesia							•										•	•

^aSee Table 4.4 for the list of values (1 = a comfortable life, etc.).
•Mean is greater than the average 1966-1970 mean (see Table 4.5).

Table 4.6

VALUE MEANS BY STATE (1966)

Generally, all foreign policy elites in this particular sample emphasized the values which display high overall means. In other words, interstate variations are apparently not appreciable; instead of identifying distinct value ranking patterns, the procedure yields a single homogeneous profile for all states in the data set.[15] This suggests that the Rokeach value procedure is useful for delineating foreign policy value profiles which can be compared with patterns for other institutions within and across societies, but perhaps foreign policy elites in different states tend to emphasize (and rank) values in a very similar fasion.

This question, however, has not been definitively answered. A preliminary exploration of the issue has been undertaken; the findings are presented in Table 4.7. The analysis of variance results indicate that knowledge of the identity of the state is <u>generally</u> a more accurate predictor of values than knowledge of the year.

Value	STATE		YEAR		Unexplained Variance
	F-value	Eta^2	F-value	Eta^2	
A comfortable life	1.26	.35	3.31*	.10	.55
A world of peace	2.19*	.48	2.90*	.08	.44
Equality	2.42*	.51	1.03	.03	.46
Freedom	2.36*	.50	2.59*	.08	.42
Happiness	0.77	.25	9.87*	.24	.51
Governmental security	1.70*	.42	4.40*	.12	.46
Honor	7.87*	.77	0.91	.03	.20
Justice	2.26*	.49	0.82	.03	.48
National security	2.46*	.51	1.97	.06	.43
Public security	3.16*	.58	1.47	.04	.38
Respect	3.18*	.58	2.24	.07	.35
Social recognition	1.68*	.42	3.83*	.11	.47
Wisdom	0.67	.22	10.32*	.25	.53
Progress	2.77*	.54	2.49*	.07	.39
Unity	3.15*	.57	1.77	.05	.38
Ideology	5.94*	.72	1.70	.05	.23
Cooperation	5.70*	.71	1.11	.03	.26
Support of government	1.98*	.46	5.22*	.14	.40

*F-value significant at .05 level.

Table 4.7

STATE VS. YEAR: VARIANCE EXPLAINED (1966-1970)

6. Private sources may become available for specific leaders or systems in unusual circumstances (e.g., when a country is defeated in war). Axelrod (1976: 367-370) provides examples of currently available verbatim records of meetings held in confidence; for empirical studies using such sources, see Axelrod (1972b, 1976, 1977) and the excellent study of strategy choices of Dutch decision-makers in 1914 by Gallhofer and Saris (1979).

7. See also the references to the more recent experimental research (summarized in the preceding section).

8. See, respectively, Bonham and Shapiro (1979) and Walker (1977). On cognitive mapping, see also Axelrod (1976) and Bonham et al. (1979); on operational code analysis, see especially Holsti (1977). The major examples are discussed briefly in Hopple and Rossa (1980) and in more detail above in Chapter 3.

9. See, e.g., Falkowski (1979a, 1979b) and Hermann (1974, 1975).

10. For a similar analysis of other ideologists, see also Rous and Lee (1978).

11. This poses a problem for the case of the United States, since the United States is obviously not included in FBIS Daily Reports. As a substitute source, the Department of State Bulletin was employed to generate U.S. value data. Each weekly issue of the Bulletin generally contains one or more speeches by the head of state and/or the foreign minister (i.e., secretary of state).

12. The data set includes both speech and interview data, although for measuring purely actor-specific characteristics interview responses can be presumed to be more spontaneous and therefore preferable (see Hermann, 1974). However, the unit of analysis here is really the (foreign policy) institutional level, although the individual is the level of analysis for data collection purposes. It would, however, be interesting to compare speech and interview data.

13. The value data were originally collected as part of a larger research program in the period 1974-1977 (see Hopple, 1978, 1979c); at the time, the dates 1966-1970 were the most recent for which significant amounts of reliable data of various types were available.

14. Details are provided in Hopple (1979b).

15. This dominant profile was confirmed more systematically by intercorrelating the state rankings. For 1966, for example, the Spearman's rho

correlations ranged from the .30's and .40's to the .60's and .70's. Furthermore, there was only a handful of negative relationships in the entire set of correlations and these were infinitesimal. While <u>frequencies</u> show marked variations, <u>rankings</u> are uniform.

16. For examples, see Singer (1968), Singer and Wallace (1979), and many other studies. The projects include Charles McClelland's World Event Interaction Survey (WEIS), Rudolph Rummel's Dimensionality of Nations (DON) Project, J. David Singer's Correlates of War (COW) Project, and various other research projects dealing with events, aggregate, and--to a lesser extent--other forms of data. Massive volumes are necessary to summarize the indicator systems and propositional inventories of just one thrust (e.g., events data) or even one large project; in addition, several compendia of tested empirical propositions have been published (e.g., McGowan and Shapiro, 1973) and these consist, to a great extent, of research efforts and single-shot studies using one or more of the large data banks.

17. Such as, Zinnes (1976), several essays in Hoole and Zinnes (1976), and others.

18. See, e.g., Brecher's (1977) crisis analysis framework and his philosophical justification for the approach.

19. This contrasts with the dominant analytical approach at the time, which treated static country traits (GNP per capita, defense expenditures, long-term political stability indicators, etc.) as causal or independent rather than intervening--or, literally, control--variables.

20. On WEIS, see Burgess and Lawton (1972) and McClelland (1968). WEIS, which includes well over 100,000 specific events coded from the <u>New York Times</u> (1966 to the present) and the <u>Manchester Guardian</u> (1978 to the present), is the empirical data base for the applied Early Warning and Monitoring System, which is discussed in IPPRC (1979).

21. The emphasis was on the <u>assembly</u> of existing data sets (e.g., McClelland's <u>WEIS</u> data, the domestic conflict data collected by Arthur Banks, etc.). However, a considerable amount of new data was actually collected (including all of the elite value data).

22. PLS is described in detail in Hopple (1979c), Rossa (1979), and Wold (1978, 1979). For applications to foreign behavior, see Rossa et al. (1979) and Wilkenfeld et al. (1979, 1980).

23. The action-reaction element of the inter-

state component refers to World Event Interaction Survey or WEIS behavior received data (treated as independent variables within the interstate domain); action-reaction factors were included in the research design of Rossa et al. (1979) but excluded from the otherwise comparable model tested by Wilkenfeld et al. (1979).

24. Technically, Coleman's analytical strategy did not involve the construction of independent latent variables. Figure 4.2 thus portrays the Coleman design conceptually rather than methodologically.

25. This data set is described in detail in Hopple (1978) and Wilkenfeld et al. (1978). See also Appendix A for the specific variables and dimensions.

26. Examples include Hopple et al. (1977), Rosenau and Hoggard (1974), and Rosenau and Ramsey (1975).

5
Elite Values and Foreign Affairs: An Empirical Test

The analytical strategy for examining the nexus between foreign policy elite values and external behavior is straightforward. In order to gauge the impact of articulated values on foreign behavior, we initially determined the discrete relationships between the dependent foreign behavior variables and four predictor domains (i.e., the psychological, societal, interstate, and global clusters). Then, the predicted values which were generated by these four regression analyses were entered into a regression equation which predicted foreign behavior; this provided a direct estimate of relative explanatory power. Tests were conducted both for the entire sample (i.e., the 39 states which appear in the value state sample one or more times between 1966 and 1970) and for the clusters of states which had been identified in a Q-factor analysis of state attribute data (see Wilkenfeld et al., 1978). As noted, the state attribute data set consists of various static characteristics of states, grouped into economic, political, and power/capability clusters.

EMPIRICAL FINDINGS

Three special features of the research design should be highlighted: the removal of the WEIS behavior received variables (diplomatic behavior, force, and rewards/yields) as independent variables within the interstate component; the introduction of other interstate variables; and the addition of the global and psychological realms. This contrasts sharply with an early relative explanatory power test for all 56 states, where only the societal and interstate (i.e., behavior received) clusters were compared (see Hopple et al., 1977). There are thus four independent variable realms (psychological, societal, interstate, and global) and three dependent variables (constructive diplomatic behavior sent, non-military conflict behavior sent, and force behavior sent).

Cluster-by-Cluster Results

Regression results for each of the four variable realms are presented in Tables 5.1, 5.2, and 5.3 (psychological), 5.5 (societal), 5.6 (interstate), and 5.7 (global). In each table, the numbers in the columns are beta weights; each table also presents the proportion of variance explained (R^2) for that particular variable cluster. Beta weights and R^2's which are statistically significant at the .05 level are identified by asterisks.

Value/psychological domain. Perhaps the most striking finding for the prediction of constructive diplomatic behavior by the 18 values (Table 5.1) is that the overall R^2 of .24 conceals significant variations by group. The values explain 93 percent of the variance in diplomatic behavior for the Western group, 73 percent for the Closed group, 80 percent for the Unstable group, and only 39 percent for the fourth Third World cluster.

For the total group, 8 of the 18 values are significant; these include a world of peace, equality, honor, justice, national security, progress, ideology, and cooperation. Three of the betas are negative in direction; expressions about the values of justice, progress, and cooperation all tend to diminish acts of constructive diplomacy.

These overall results mask the kaleidoscopic patterns for the state clusters. Half of the values are significant for the Western group; especially noteworthy are the beta weights for wisdom (-2.64) and, to a lesser extent, a comfortable life (1.89).[1] In the case of the Closed states, national security is the dominant value in relation to events of a constructive diplomatic nature. Interestingly, a concern with two internal values--public security and progress--depresses foreign behavior sent. Unity, however, correlates positively with external behavior. The most noteworthy finding for the Unstable states is the negative relationship between articulations about progress and diplomatic behaviors. Few of the relationships for the fourth category are substantively meaningful or statistically significant.

	Total Group	Western Group	Closed Group	Unstable	Third World[b]
A comfortable life	.15	1.89*	.58*	.87*	−.35
A world of peace	.20*	.52*	.18*	.25	−.18
Equality	.37*	−.31	−.16	−.39	.02
Freedom	−.15	1.20*	.01	.39	.37*
Happiness	−.09	.41*	−.36	.05	−.22
Governmental security	−.09	−.35	−.59*	−.50*	−.38*
Honor	.27*	1.26*	.24	−.23	.17
Justice	−.22	—	.05	−.44	−.18
National security	.19*	−.32	1.15*	.45	−.06
Public security	.07	−.19	−.86*	.40	−.21
Respect	.02	1.06*	−.01	.10	−.01
Social recognition	−.09	.62	−.37*	1.05*	.10
Wisdom	−.03	−2.64*	−.55*	−.52	.02
Progress	−.20*	.12	−.67*	−1.32*	.53*
Unity	−.15	.11	1.01*	−.21	.47*
Ideology	.32*	−.75	−.15	1.20*	−.44*
Cooperation	−.26*	−1.24*	−.36	.48	−.26
Support of government	−.01	−1.23*	.20	−.84	−.20
R^2	.24*	.93*	.73*	.80	.39
N =	131	24	35	27	45

[a]Numbers in the first eighteen columns are beta weights.
[b]This group consists of all large developing, poor, and unclassifiable states.
*Beta or R^2 significant at the .05 level.

Table 5.1

CONSTRUCTIVE DIPLOMATIC BEHAVIOR
AS PREDICTED BY THE PSYCHOLOGICAL CLUSTER
(NATION-YEARS AGGREGATED, 1966-1970)

    For non-military conflict as predicted by the psychological data (Table 5.2), the same general finding emerges. The aggregate R^2 of .17 contrasts sharply with the fluctuating R^2's of .94 (Western group), .78 (Closed group), .53 (Unstable group), and .39 (Third World). For both the Western and the Closed states, the values are significant determinants of this particular form of foreign behavior.
    Again, half of the 18 values are significant

	Total Group	Western Group	Closed Group	Unstable Group	Third World[b]
A comfortable life	.09	3.18*	.74*	.43	.08
A world of peace	.23*	1.01*	.18	.60	−.52*
Equality	.09	−.51*	−.13	−.28	−.11
Freedom	.11	−.10	−.06	.49	.17
Happiness	−.04	.56*	−.36*	.04	−.18
Governmental security	−.14	−.46	−.58*	−.11	−.41*
Honor	.17*	.54	.18	−.21	.10
Justice	−.18*	−.23	.02	−.47	−.06
National security	.13	.80*	1.04*	.15	—
Public security	−.09	−.37	−.99*	.08	−.19
Respect	−.02	.04	.03	−.05	.02
Social recognition	.02	.17	−.29	1.19	.27
Wisdom	−.09	−3.76*	−.57*	−.01	.18
Progress	−.13	1.18*	−.74*	−.74	.46*
Unity	−.07	.12	1.18*	−.13	.41*
Ideology	−.01	−2.11*	−.14	.53	−.58*
Cooperation	−.20*	−.15	−.30	.29	−.01
Support of government	.19*	.75*	.19	−.70	−.43
R^2	.17*	.94*	.78*	.53	.39
N =	131	24	35	27	45

[a]Numbers in first eighteen columns are beta weights.

[b]This group consists of all large developing, poor, and unclassifiable states.

*Beta or R^2 significant at the .05 level.

Table 5.2

NON-MILITARY CONFLICT AS PREDICTED
BY THE PSYCHOLOGICAL CLUSTER
(NATION-YEARS AGGREGATED, 1966-1970)

for the Western states. As in Table 5.1, the largest single beta weight is wisdom (-3.76). Other large betas include a comfortable life (3.18) and ideology (-2.11). Within the Closed group, national security (1.04) and unity (1.18) are the primary determinants of non-military conflict. None of the results is significant for the Unstable states, although social recognition exerts some impact (a beta of 1.19). Five of the betas are significant within the Third World category, although the R^2 is insignificant.

Finally, we can consider the findings for force behavior (Table 5.3) Generally, the elite values are not significant predictors of this extreme form of foreign conflict. This finding conforms to the pattern which was unearthed in prior work (Hopple, 1979c; Rossa et al., 1979), where it was discovered that <u>force received</u> accounts for <u>force sent</u> whereas the other variable realms exert almost no impact.

	Total Group	Western Group	Closed Group	Unstable	Third World[b]
A comfortable life	.06	.90	.16	.11	.25
A world of peace	−.04	.15	.59*	−.44	−.30
Equality	.17*	−.29	.65*	−.03	−.23
Freedom	.02	.21	−.61*	.35	−.03
Happiness	−.10	.02	−.10	.21	−.08
Governmental security	−.09	−.14	−.28	−.26	−.20
Honor	.01	.97	−.07	−.91	−.30
Justice	−.05	−.95	.33	.71	.03
National security	.35*	.16	.60	1.13*	−.05
Public security	−.14	.95	.10	−.31	−.23
Respect	−.02	−.18	−.46	.35	.08
Social recognition	.12	−.73	−.14	.65	−.09
Wisdom	−.03	.27	−.24	−.98	.39
Progress	.04	−.01	−.16	−.78	−.18
Unity	−.08	−.48	−.23	−.50	.23
Ideology	−.04	.08	.30	.86	−.31
Cooperation	−.14	−.26	−.35	−.23	.28
Support of government	−.09	−.46	.40*	−.92	−.22
R^2	.19	.72	.76*	.50	.30
N =	131	24	35	27	45

[a]Numbers in first eighteen columns are beta weights.

[b]This group consists of all large developing, poor, and unclassifiable states.

*Beta or R^2 significant at the .05 level.

Table 5.3

FORCE AS PREDICTED BY THE PSYCHOLOGICAL CLUSTER
(NATION-YEARS AGGREGATED, 1966-1970)

The one exception to this generalization is the Closed group; the values account for a significant 76 percent of the variance in force behavior sent by the members of this cluster. The main contributors to this are:

A world of peace	.59
Equality	.65
Freedom	-.61
Support of government	.40

The positive relationship between the first two values and acts of force suggests that Closed states may emphasize these values rhetorically as justifications for and rationalizations of force behaviors.[2]

Table 5.3 contains one additional noteworthy finding: the impact of national security overall (with a beta weight of .35 for the total group, which is statistically significant at the .05 level) and within the Unstable group (where the beta weight is 1.13, also statistically significant). The effect of the national security value on the force behavior of the Closed states is a large but not significant .60; its influence within the Western and Third World clusters is negligible. Especially within the Unstable group, articulations of the national security value covary with acts of force behavior.

The relationship between values which refer to internal states of affairs and foreign behavior is of interest because of its potential relevance to the internal-external nexus question. Extensive research has accrued on the subject of linkages between external and internal conflict. In a more general sense, scholars, journalists, and other students of public policy have frequently alluded to the putative nexus between internal politics and foreign policy. The alleged propensity for diverting attention from domestic fiascoes and crises by becoming embroiled in foreign adventures and imbroglios is a popular illustration of this general hypothesis. In a more academic context, the research on linkage politics is based on a recognition

153

of the interplay (and even fusion) between domestic and foreign affairs (see Rosenau, 1969).

At least 4 of the 18 values presumably concern the internal dimension of politics: a comfortable life; happiness; public security; and progress. The relationships between these end-states and foreign behavior are depicted in Table 5.4; a P denotes a significant positive relationship and an N a significant negative relationship.

Much of the traditional conjectural speculation on the subject suggests that the relationships would be almost uniformly negative in direction, with emphasis on an internal value reflecting a diminution in foreign behavior. Alternatively, the linkage politics perspective simply predicts that there will be robust interrelationships; the advocates of a "subsystem autonomy" interpretation would expect the absence of any relationships.

With respect to the latter controversy, the results offer support for neither position; 19 of the relationships are statistically significant and the other 21 fail to attain significance. Of the 19 significant beta weights, 11 are negative in direction and 8 are positive.

The patterns in Table 5.4 can be summarized in a series of propositions. First of all, there is a clear tendency for the value of a comfortable life to co-vary with increases in both constructive and non-military conflict behaviors. Secondly, the other relationships are predominantly negative; this generalization is especially applicable to the Closed states, where rhetorical emphases on happiness, public security, and progress all presage a decrease in external behavior and a turning-inward process. Thus, articulations about prosperity and economic stability (the value of a comfortable life) predict increases in both general, primarily constructive and mildly conflictual foreign acts, undoubtedly reflecting the reality of economic interdependence in a world of sovereign states. This phenomenon, however, has not spilled over into domestic politics generally, at least for Closed and, to a lesser extent, Unstable states.

A final observation about the results for the value data is warranted. Debates about the explanatory potency of psychological factors become sterile exercises when it is recognized that the key questions concern <u>when</u> psychological forces exert an impact and <u>which</u> particular variables are relevant. Regarding the former issue, it is obvious that certain situations and variable configurations maximize

	CONSTRUCTIVE DIPLOMATIC				NON-MILITARY CONFLICT			
	Total	Western	Closed	Unstable	Third World	Total	Western	Closed	Unstable	Third World
Comfortable life		P	P	P			P	P		
Happiness			N	N	N			N		
Public security			N	N				N		
Progress	N		N	N	P		P	N		P

[a]P denotes a significant positive beta weight; N denotes a significant negative beta weight; a blank denotes a nonsignificant beta weight.

Table 5.4

INTERNAL VALUES AND FOREIGN BEHAVIOR[a]

the impact of psychological factors. Among these are the organizational context, level in the hierarchy, decisional and situational attributes, and the type of state. The available evidence suggests that psychological source factors would exert maximal impact in Closed states (because of concentration of power) and developing systems (because roles are less clearly institutionalized).

The prediction for politically closed systems is clearly supported in Tables 5.1, 5.2, and 5.3. However, the beta weights and R^2 values for the two "developing polity" categories are rarely large in size or significant. The two North clusters in terms of the North-South dimension--the Western and Closed states--feature the majority of the noteworthy findings. This issue will be confronted again in the relative explanatory power section of this chapter.

Societal domain. The results of the other three clusters can be dealt with in a more cursory fashion, since the focus here is the elite value data. The impact of the societal forces is assessed in Table 5.5. As in the case of other results for the entire state sample of 56 (see Hopple et al., 1977; Wilkenfeld et al., 1979) many of the relationships are anemic in magnitude. The principal exceptions involve societal unrest for the total group of 39 (all three forms of behavior), the Western cluster (constructive and force acts), the Closed category (all three dimensions), and the Unstable group (non-military conflict). Governmental instability shows a clear relationship to force for the Western states; population growth rate correlates negatively to force behaviors within the Third World cluster; economic performance predicts constructive diplomacy within the Western Q-group and both constructive and non-military conflict behaviors within the Unstable subset.

Interstate domain. Results for the 8 variables which comprise the interstate realm are presented in Table 5.6. As a general indicator, international involvement performs well, predicting both constructive and non-military conflict behaviors for three clusters (Closed, Unstable, and Third World) and constructive diplomacy for the Western group. Especially significant is the unusual sensitivity of the Closed states to the three energy measures.[3]

	Societal Unrest	Governmental Instability	Population Growth Rate	Ecomomic Performance	R^2
Total Group, N = 131					
Constructive Diplomatic	.55*	−.13*	—	.03	.31*
Non-Military Conflict	.17*	−.09	.09	.03	.03
Force	.14*	.10	.16*	—	.06
Western Group, N = 24					
Constructive Diplomatic	.22*	.12	.13	.80*	.87*
Non-Military Conflict	−.22	.21	.32	.27	.11
Force	.40*	.65*	.14	−.29	.63*
Closed Group, N = 35					
Constructive Diplomatic	.80*	−.10	.03	−.01	.61*
Non-Military Conflict	.76*	−.07	−.03	−.04	.55*
Force	.46*	−.23	.07	.01	.22*
Unstable Group, N = 27					
Constructive Diplomatic	.14	−.15	−.14	.63*	.62*
Non-Military Conflict	−.41*	−.04	−.26	.44*	.21
Force	.16	−.10	−.17	.17	.05
Third World, N = 45[b]					
Constructive Diplomatic	.04	−.19	—	.19	.08
Non-Military Conflict	.10	−.19	.07	.11	.05
Force	−.18	−.04	−.25*	.28	.16

[a]Numbers in first four columns are beta weights.

[b]This group consists of all large developing, poor, and unclassifiable states.

*Beta or R^2 significant at the .05 level.

Table 5.5

FOREIGN BEHAVIOR
AS PREDICTED BY THE SOCIETAL CLUSTER
(NATION-YEARS AGGREGATED, 1966-1970)[a]

Table 5.6

FOREIGN BEHAVIOR AS PREDICTED BY THE INTERSTATE CLUSTER
(NATION-YEARS AGGREGATED, 1966-1970)[a]

	INTERNATIONAL INVOLVEMENT	ENERGY DEPENDENCY	ENERGY MARKET STRENGTH	ENERGY INTERDEPENDENCY	FOOD DEPENDENCY	EXPORT CONCENTRATION	IMPORT CONCENTRATION	NEOCOLONIAL DEPENDENCY	R^2
Total Group, N = 131									
Constructive Diplomatic	.44*	−.13	−.22*	.14	−.07	−.01	.12	—	.26
Non-Military Conflict	.17*	−.19*	−.31*	.23*	−.09	−.08	−.10	.13	.13
Force	−.08	−.03	−.09	.10	−.08	−.01	.29*	−.03	.08
Western Group, N = 24									
Constructive Diplomatic	.54*	.03	.03	−.08	−.09	−.06	−.01	−.32	.39
Non-Military Conflict	−.09	−.40	−.20	−.37	−.33*	−.40*	−.31	−.14	.45
Force	−.19	.58*	.55	−.39	.03	.02	−.33	−.18	.31
Closed Group, N = 25									
Constructive Diplomatic	.36*	−31.70*	−7.31*	29.10*	−.06	.30	.02	.08	.66*
Non-Military Conflict	.35*	−33.96*	−7.86*	31.12*	.01	.19	−.03	.06	.66*
Force	.21	−18.67*	−4.25*	17.02*	−.16	−.05	.35	−.09	.37*
Unstable Group, N = 27									
Constructive Diplomatic	.65*	−.01	−.16	.03	.12	−.03	.19	.06	.49
Non-Military Conflict	.51*	−.12	−.33	.30	.08	−.31	−.40	.39	.45
Force	−.11	−.24	−.03	−.04	.10	−.01	.37	−.14	.09
Third World, N = 45[b]									
Constructive Diplomatic	.57*	.16	−.40	.41	−.17	−.12	−.19	.32	.24
Non-Military Conflict	.42*	−.10	−.53*	.47*	−.25*	−.02	−.34	.43	.23
Force	−.14	−.13	−.27	.39	−.12	.02	.53*	.04	.31

[a]Numbers in first eight columns are beta weights.
[b]This group consists of all large developing, poor, and unclassifiable states.
*Beta or R^2 significant at the .05 level.

	TOTAL IGO	NEW IGO	DLBC[b]	DLBF[b]	CLBC[b]	CLBF[b]	DSBC[b]	DSBF[b]	CSBC[b]	CSBF[b]	R^2
Total Group, N = 131											
Constructive Diplomatic	.32*	.04	.03	.09	.70*	-.29*	.44*	-.15*	-.29*	.08	.44*
Non-Military Conflict	-.05	-.01	.25*	.01	.75*	.46	.44	.11	-.12	.07	.40
Force	.15*	-.08	-.15*	.41*	.11	-.09	-.07	.24*	-.05	-.17	.22
Western Group, N = 24											
Constructive Diplomatic	-.22*	-.18	.07	-.01	.06	1.32*	.09	.21*	-.41*	-.14	.93*
Non-Military Conflict	-.41*	-.09	.26	-.23	1.45*	-.62*	.19	.26*	-.42*	.25	.83*
Force	-.14	-.04	-.42	.74*	.55	-.32	-.06	-.05	-.39	.15	.38
Closed Group, N = 35											
Constructive Diplomatic	.20	-.04	.08	-.03	2.97*	-1.55*	.51*	-.29*	-1.54*	.40*	.77*
Non-Military Conflict	-.06	-.05	.15	-.03	3.25*	-1.62*	.54*	-.33*	-1.59*	.46*	.78*
Force	.27	-.29	-.01	-.04	1.20	-.79	.29	-.25	-.46	-.03	.28
Unstable Group, N = 27[c]											
Constructive Diplomatic	.13	.06	.10*	.20*	-.18	.97*	.47*	-.25*	-.33*	.07	.96*
Non-Military Conflict	.25*	.29*	.11	.54*	1.71*	-1.39*	.65*	-.29*	-.34	-.47*	.88*
Force	.08	-.05	-.13	1.18*	-1.27*	-1.02	-.21*	-.19*	.27	.17	.91
Third World, N = 45											
Constructive Diplomatic	-.25*	-.17	.29	-.19	-.36	-.06	.73	.26	-.03	.07	.77*
Non-Military Conflict	-.30	-.17*	.28*	-.24	-.42	.19*	.43	.52*	.09	-.02	.67*
Force	-.03	-.04	-.10	.29	-.12	.05	-.33*	.80*	.12	-.61*	.43*

[a] Numbers in first ten columns are beta weights.
[b] Direct Land Borders Conflict (DLBC), Direct Land Borders Force (DLBF), Colonial Land Borders Conflict (CLBC), Colonial Land Borders Force (CLBF), Direct Sea Borders Conflict (DSBC), Direct Sea Borders Force (DSBF), Colonial Sea Borders Conflict (CSBC), Colonial Sea Borders Force (CSBF).
[c] This group consists of all large developing, poor, and unclassifiable states.
*Beta or R^2 significant at the .05 level.

Table 5.7

FOREIGN BEHAVIOR AS PREDICTED BY THE GLOBAL CLUSTER
(NATION-YEARS AGGREGATED, 1966-1970) [a]

Global domain. Table 5.7 zeroes in on the variables which have been employed to operationalize the global factors. A number of significant beta weights can be gleaned from the table. Among the more influential factors are total IGO (intergovernmental organization) memberships, colonial land borders conflict, colonial land borders force, direct sea borders conflict, direct sea borders force, and colonial sea borders conflict. The percentage of total variance explained ranges from 22 to 96. Ten of the 15 R^2's are significant, including constructive diplomatic behavior for the total group and all four of the state clusters, non-military conflict for all of the subgroups, and force behavior for the Third World.

Relative Explanatory Power Results

The assessment of relative explanatory strength in this chapter involves four distinct independent clusters. A single indicator is developed for each of the clusters; the latter is based on the combined effects of all of the variables within the cluster on the dependent variables. Whereas the test in Hopple et al. (1977) yielded a single dominant conclusion--that the interstate forces (with the action-reaction variables) account for an overwhelming portion of the variance in a direct "contest" with the societal realm--the results for this more elaborate model are much more complex. This test, of course, involves a different sample of states (a subset of the sample in Hopple et al., 1977), a drastically modified interstate cluster, and two additional sets of causal forces.

The relative explanatory power results are presented in summary form in Table 5.8. The states in the various subgroups are listed in Table 4.8 in the preceding chapter. Overall, the lowest percentage of variance explained figure is 26 (the force dimension for the Unstable states); the highest is 86 (constructive diplomatic behavior for the same cluster of states). All of the R^2's are statistically significant.

As noted, the earlier simple model test--which did not represent elite values--suggested that external forces outweigh internal determinants. This pattern clearly does not characterize the analysis reported in Table 5.8. The fact that the value or psychological data are significantly related to foreign behavior outputs in 10 of 15 cases (the total group, all three forms of behavior; the Closed states, all three forms of behavior; the Unstable

	Psychological	Societal	Interstate	Global	R^2
Total Group					
Constructive Diplomatic	.18*	.28*	.15*	.42*	.56*
Non-Military Conflict	.21*	.04	.15*	.49*	.46*
Force	.29*	.15*	.14*	.29*	.34*
Western Group					
Constructive Diplomatic	−.03	.58*	.01	.30	.61*
Non-Military Conflict	.07	−.05	.10	.72*	.61*
Force	.24	.29	.09	.31	.43*
Closed Group					
Constructive Diplomatic	.28*	.48*	.13	.20	.74*
Non-Military Conflict	.25*	.47*	.29	.15	.68*
Force	.55*	.16	.17	.07	.45*
Unstable Group					
Constructive Diplomatic	−.05	.09	−.01	.90*	.86*
Non-Military Conflict	.09	−.10	.30*	.50*	.56*
Force	.41*	.29	.04	.18	.26*
Third World Group[b]					
Constructive Diplomatic	.82*	−.09	.01	.21*	.59*
Non-Military Conflict	.62*	.11	.04	.23	.80*
Force	.21*	−.07	.05	.67*	.59*

[a]Numbers in first four columns are beta weights.

[b]This group consists of all large developing, poor, and unclassifiable states.

*Beta or R^2 significant at the .05 level.

Table 5.8

RELATIVE EXPLANATORY POWER
OF PREDICTORS OF FOREIGN POLICY BEHAVIOR
(NATION-YEARS AGGREGATED, 1966-1970)

states, force behavior; and the Third World group, all three forms of behavior) provides striking support for the proposition that all of the major source variable domains must be operationalized in foreign policy analysis. In comparison, the interstate economic beta weights are statistically significant in only 4 of 15 instances.

Note that in contrast to the results for the cluster-by-cluster tests, the psychological or value realm is important for the Third World but not the Western nation-states. The value data remain potent for determining the external behavior of the Closed actors.

Perhaps the most striking single finding in the entire table is the relationship between force acts and the psychological realm. The beta weight is statistically significant for the closed polities as well as for both of the developing groups. In each instance, in fact, the psychological forces are the sole determinants of the overall significance of the force equations. Given our previous inability to account for the domain of force behavior--aside from the pervasiveness of the action-reaction syndrome--this finding is both nontrivial and unexpected.

INTERPRETATION

The extensive literature which deals with the potential impact of psychological factors on foreign policy phenomena has generally focused on the questions of <u>when</u> psychological forces exert an impact and <u>which particular variables</u> are relevant. As was noted earlier in the chapter, the available evidence indicates unambiguously that certain situations and variable configurations maximize the impact of psychological factors. Various propositions <u>specify</u> the expected relationship between decision-maker characteristics (personality traits, values, beliefs, age, education, etc.) and external behavior. An array of factors inhibits the influence of the individual actor (or foreign policy elite). Among these are: numerous bureaucratic and role constraints; the need to respond to the verbal and physical behavior of other countries; and international systemic parameters.

Chapter 3 zeroed in on three clusters of factors which maximize the effects of psychological determinants. One is <u>position in the hierarchy</u>. Another set of modifying forces emanates from the <u>nature of the situation</u>, such as routine versus unprecedented or crisis decision contexts. A third noteworthy determinant is the type of state.

The perceptual and other individual determinants of international crises have been explored intensively. The early efforts of North, Holsti, and their colleagues on the Stanford Project and the more recent research by Brecher and his International Crisis Behavior (ICB) team have been inventoried and evaluated in a number of review pieces (e.g., Hopple and Favin, 1978; Hopple and Rossa, 1980; Parker, 1977; Tanter, 1978). International crisis monitoring and forecasting research, however, is frequently limited to systemic or interactional data.

An illustrative Defense Department-sponsored computerized crisis warning system has been tested and refined at the International Public Policy Research Corporation (see IPPRC, 1979). In his review of this Early Warning and Monitoring System crisis anticipation research, Tanter (1978) observes that the approach tends to "work" best for processes which intensify gradually. The method may forecast such crises as the 1967 Arab-Israeli War but not such cases as the 1973 conflict.[4] Tanter argues throughout his review that system-level (i.e., interactional) approaches of the McClelland (1968, 1972) genre cannot be substituted for the analysis of perception and intent and can never account for cases of surprise or deception.[5]

This suggests that perceptual and similar psychological variables exert an impact on crisis emergence and decision-maker awareness. Whether treated as idiosyncratic (e.g., George and George, 1964) or as cultural (e.g., Bobrow et al., 1979), the belief and perceptual systems of elite decision-makers function as screens which intervene between "reality" and the individual. These systems shape the acquisition, modification, and evaluation of beliefs and images, the perception of situations, information processing, decision-making/strategy selection processes, and learning.

The treatment of the foreign behavior realm in this chapter does not deal with crises per se. However, the explicit incorporation of the force dimension represents at least one aspect of the crisis sequence (i.e., most acts of force are preceded by crises). In international politics, in fact, crises are frequently defined as episodes which may eventuate in significant armed hostilities or war (e.g., Snyder and Diesing, 1977). In any case, force actions are the least routine and the most extreme form of foreign behavior; individual-level factors should be unusually influential with respect to this dimension of external behavior.

The expectations regarding type of nation are also clear. Presumably, elites in closed regimes would shape foreign behavior to a greater extent than is the case for their peers in more accountable or democratic polities. The latter confront a network of expectations, demands, and "pressures" from such relatively autonomous actors as the bureaucracy, the party system, attentive and mass public opinion, the media, and other non-elite forces. While the nexus between the foreign policy elite and the public is distant from the crude image of a simplistic stimulus-response model, the elite-mass linkage is presumably (and at least potentially) different in a qualitative sense when polyarchic and closed regimes are compared.

Generally, decision-maker characteristics can also be expected to explain more of the variance in external behavior in developing systems. Power in such states is often concentrated in a charismatic leader or ruling clique; roles are less clearly delineated and are comparatively uninstitutionalized. Rarely is there an entrenched, structurally differentiated bureaucracy. Furthermore, a constraining foreign policy "tradition" has not emerged in such polities.

Theoretically, then, there are three sets of conditions which singly or interactively maximize the impact of individual-level factors:

- Level in the hierarchy (the higher the position, the greater the impact);

- Type of situation (the less routine or more crisis-like the context, the greater the impact); and

- Type of state (the more closed or developing the state, the greater the impact).

Empirically, the findings conform impressively to the predictions. Level in the hierarchy is a constant, since all of the decision-makers are representatives of the highest stratum (head of state and foreign minister). The psychological beta weights are generally lowest for the Western (democratic or politically open) states, especially for the more routine constructive diplomatic and non-military conflict forms of behavior; the force beta is a much higher (but nonsignificant) .24.

The Closed and the two developing clusters display the significant findings in the value realm. For the Closed countries, a grouping which consists primarily of the Soviet Union and Eastern European states (see Table 4.8), the beta is highest for force, the least routine form of behavior.[6]

The force behavior of the Unstable countries is clearly determined primarily by the values of decision-makers; across the Unstable entries, the relative explanatory power scores (betas) are: .41 (values); .29 (societal); .04 (interstate); and .18 (global). However, the psychological scores for the other two behavior dimensions are very low; the global domain is the key predictor of constructive diplomatic behavior and interstate and global forces interactively determine non-military conflict outputs.

As Table 4.8 demonstrates, the states in the Third World category are basically members of the developing bloc or Third (and Fourth) Worlds. Included are such "large developing" polities as China and India and such generally "poor" (and small and weak) states as Cambodia, Jordan, and Laos. Articulated elite values are the basic determinants of both constructive diplomatic and non-military conflict behaviors. Along with the global source domain, values play a role in the force behavior sent process as well.

The findings are also relevant to the more general internal-external relative impact question. Whereas some of the earlier empirical work in comparative foreign policy identified the external realm as the more potent, these results suggest that both sets of source factors should be analyzed. In addition to the psychological domain, the societal cluster exerts an impact (on constructive diplomatic behavior within the Western and Closed groups and on non-military conflict behavior within the Closed states).

Of the two external realms, the global is the more important; it displays a very significant effect on non-military conflict within two clusters (Western and Unstable), shares influence in two other cases (with the interstate cluster for non-military conflict within the Unstable group and with the psychological cluster for constructive diplomatic behavior within the Third World group), and is the most potent source of behavior sent within the Third World category.

VALIDITY

This analysis is clearly preliminary in nature. Although it deals with the issue of validity by focusing on the value-behavior nexus, other validation strategies can and should be pursued. This section discusses three such approaches.

Two are criterion-related validation strategies. One entails the assessment of whether or not value ranking profiles discriminate among subgroups; the second involves the evaluation of the relationship between values and behaviors. A third perspective will then be introduced.

Discrimination Among Subgroups

The first approach is exemplified in a study of value rankings in the British House of Commons. Searing (1978: 75) focuses on the capacity of the value approach to differentiate among politicians from different political parties and camps. He compares a party's candidate with its parliamentary members and also juxtaposes Conservative and Labour members. The results offer striking support for the validity of the approach:

> Candidates are a faithful image of MPs from their own political camp. By contrast, Conservative and Labour members of Parliament are poles apart. They refer to one another as "the other side," and so they are: Unlike the family resemblance between candidates and MPs, every value comparison save one produces differences which are statistically significant, usually at the .001 level (Searing, 1978: 76).

The subgrouping validation strategy has not been pursued in a systematic fashion for the elite foreign policy value data. The available evidence on this point is mixed. In national surveys in the U.S. (see Rokeach, 1973, 1974) and in other relevant studies (e.g., the work of Penner and Anh [1977] on Vietnamese value systems), value hierarchies differ in intuitively meaningful and statistically significant ways across the subgroups of a population. Evidence for such subcultural as well as cross-national value ranking variations in mass and elite strata is extensive. Definitive analyses have not been conducted, however, to ascertain the uniformity or heterogeneity of cross-systemic foreign policy elite value profiles.

From the perspective of international conflict and crisis analysis, foreign policy elite value profiles may be homogeneous. This expectation conforms to the research findings of Rokeach, who has attempted to map the value systems of such <u>institutions</u> as science and religion. The theoretical literature on national security, deterrence, and strategy also suggests that a dominant profile would exist across states; in a world in which security is inevitably a scarce commodity, all decision-makers confront the same agenda and must formulate policies and engage in actions which are directed toward the goals of maximizing security and minimizing insecurity.[7] Foreign policy elites in different states, then, may tend to emphasize (and rank) values in a similar fashion.

In contrast, some of the available evidence indicates that the state value patterns differ.[8] This would be consistent with the argument that salient national security threats vary on the basis of the particular decision-maker's or elite's value screen (see Hopple et al., 1980). In addition, state and state type variations might produce divergent value profiles; such diversity across our sample of national decision systems would be analogous to the distinct tendency of subgroups within the U.S. and other populations to exhibit differing value patterns.

Prediction of Behavior

The large literature on the value-behavior relationship is reviewed in detail in Rokeach (1973, 1979c). A summary profile is provided in Table 5.9; of 360 total correlations, 134 are statistically significant. The expected specific values exhibit strong relationships with given behaviors. Equality, for example, is the value whose rankings predict various forms of behavior in the arenas of civil rights, prejudice, and sexism.

Certain values show an especially large number of significant relationships with the behavioral criteria. Among these are a comfortable life, equality, family security, national security, and salvation. The socio-economic, political, and religious values of a comfortable life, equality, and salvation may be the most powerful overall determinants of both attitudes and behaviors, as Rokeach (1973: 159) concludes.

In addition to survey research-based evidence, there have been numerous experiments dealing with value, attitude, and behavior change; the literature offers impressive support for the theoretical substructure articulated by Rokeach. Significant value (and attitude and behavior) changes have been brought about regardless of variations in experimental conditions or individual characteristics, as the review in Chapter 4 of the experimental literature demonstrates.

The empirical research thus establishes rather impressively that human values structure behaviors and that value change precedes behavior change. If this generalization applies to foreign affairs and elite values, then it can be concluded that articulated values are more than mere epiphenomena.

The evidence adduced earlier in the "relative explanatory power test" (see Table 5.8) clearly indicates that elite values are important "predictors" of external behavior--both absolutely and relatively. The value data display significant relationships with foreign behavior outputs in 10 of 15 "tests."

If we limit the focus to values alone, the results are certainly not insignificant. Table 5-10 summarizes the relevant findings. For the three forms of foreign behavior and the 18 terminal values, there are 69 significant relationships out of 270 total entries.[8] If we disregard the force results--for which only seven significant betas are observed--then there are 62 entries out of 180. The first proportion is about 25 percent and the second over one-third. It is unlikely that these results are attributable exclusively to chance.

An obvious shortcoming in this research is that the regression analyses involve pooled data for the years 1966-1970. Thus, there is no absolute guarantee that the elite values and other "independent" variables which "predict" to foreign behavior were necessarily and invariably temporally prior to the "dependent" variables. The obvious caveat is that the direction of influence may be from behavior to value rather than the reverse or that the two may be reciprocally linked. The former situation raises the not inconceivable possibility that articulated values are post-decision phenomena; the latter state of affairs is even less inconceivable.

Clearly, further work on the behavior-value linkage issue should be undertaken and time lags should be introduced. For example, the 1966-1967 data could be used to "forecast" the 1968-1969

Table 5.9

SIGNIFICANT VALUE-BEHAVIOR RELATIONSHIPS:
DIVERSE CONTENT AREAS[a]

	CIVIL RIGHTS			RELIGION		POLITICS	HONEST BEHAVIOR		
	Join NAACP	Eye Contact with Blacks	Civil Rights Participation	Church Attendance (National)	Church Attendance (College)	Partisan Activism	Return Pencils	Male Prisoners	Female Prisoners
A comfortable life									●
An exciting life									●●
A sense of accomplishment		●						●	●
A world at peace	●				●		●		
A world of beauty	●	● ●	● ●						
Equality	●	●	●	●	●				●
Family security						●			
Freedom			● ●			● ●		●	● ●
Happiness									
Inner harmony									
Mature love		●						●	
National security	● ●			● ●	● ●	● ●		● ● ●	●
Pleasure						●	●		●
Salvation								●	●
Self-respect									
Social recognition									
True friendship									
Wisdom									
Number of values	5	4	5	5	6	6	2	7	8

	INTERPERSONAL CONFLICT	ACADEMIC PURSUITS	LIFE STYLE		OCCUPATIONAL ROLES AND CHOICES						Number of Behaviors
	Compatible Roommates	College Major	Hippies	Homosexuals	Professors	Police V. White	Police V. Black	Priests Laymen	Science, Artists, Business, Writers	Small Entre-preneurs	Salesmen	
A comfortable life		●	●		●			●		●	●	13
An exciting life	●		●		●					●		9
A sense of accomplishment		●	●		●				●	●		6
A world at peace			●		●	●		●		●		9
A world of beauty	●		●		●	●				●	●	10
Equality			●		●	●	●	●		●	●	12
Family security				●	●		●	●		●	●	10
Freedom					●			●		●		5
Happiness	●				●	●	●		●		●	6
Inner harmony						●	●			●		3
Mature love	●		●		●		●	●	●	●		8
National security			●		●			●		●	●	11
Pleasure			●		●			●		●	●	9
Salvation	●		●		●			●		●	●	11
Self-respect					●			●		●	●	5
Social recognition	●			●				●				3
True friendship					●					●		4
Wisdom												0
Number of values	5	2	11	2	15	5	7	11	6	12	10	134

[a]Source: Adapted from Rokeach (1973: 160-161).

Table 5.9

(Continued)

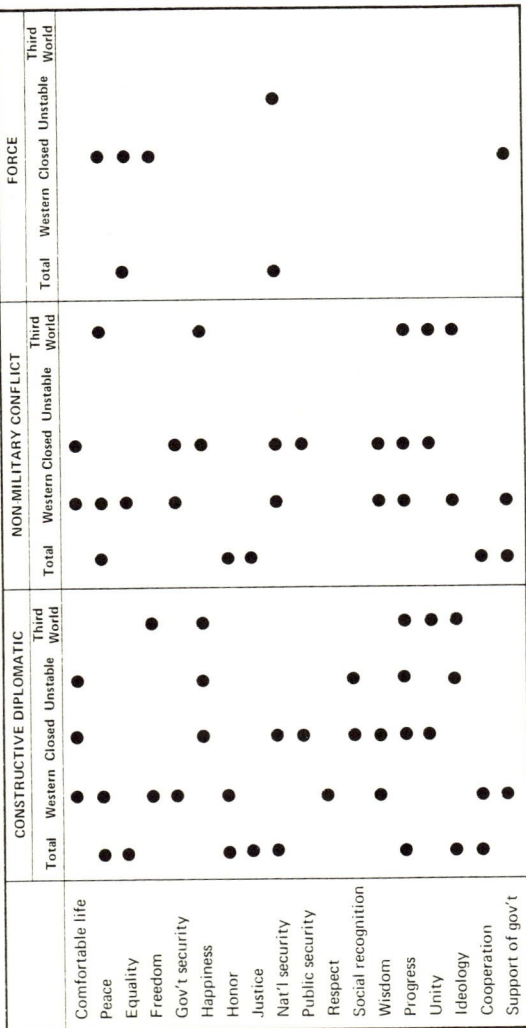

Table 5.10

SIGNIFICANT VALUE-BEHAVIOR RELATIONSHIPS: FOREIGN BEHAVIOR

behavior. More ambitiously, the 1966-1970 time frame independent variable data sets could be treated as predictors of behavior from 1971-1975.[9]

Multimethod Validation

In addition to discrimination in terms of subgroups and the value-behavior approach, a third strategy revolves around the well known convergent or multimethod route to validation. Given the fact that a single method is almost invariably imperfect, it makes sense to use an array of methods and compare their performance. This is especially desirable in the absence of an unambiguous external or behavioral criterion.

The measurement of values at the supraindividual level is not a straightforward task; institutions do not "fill out" value questionnaires. Simultaneously, however, it is obvious that different institutions can be expected to be characterized by distinctive value profiles; as Rokeach (1979a: 51) points out, social institutions can be defined as "social arrangements that provide frameworks for value specialization." The presumably divergent value patterns of business, science, religion, and the military within a given society are pertinent examples; the assumption that value hierarchies and patterns may vary systematically and even considerably across a range of national actor foreign affairs institutional contexts may also be reasonable.

Rokeach (1979a) identifies five discrete methods for measuring supraindividual values. He notes that the methods reflect several assumptions: supraindividual values are substantively identical to those manifested at the individual level of analysis; supraindividual values are primary determinants of individual values and, like the latter, can be structured in a hierarchical fashion; supraindividual values leave "value traces" that can be recovered by at least the following:

- Content analysis of organizational and institutional documents;

- Personal values of institutional gatekeepers;

- Personal values of an institution's special clients;

- Perceived values of an institution by gatekeepers; and

- Perceived values of an institution by general clients.

Rokeach (1979a) has used the five methods to attempt to reconstruct the value profile of the institution of science. As he notes, the values embedded in documentary materials can often be reliably extracted by content analysis. For example, Rokeach et al. (1970) content analyzed the disputed Federalist Papers to ascertain the authorship of the papers; the value profile evidence favored James Madison over Alexander Hamilton, a finding which was in accord with historical and other evidence. For the research on science, 80 editorials were randomly selected from the journal Science (1964-1973) and content analyzed. There were 288 mentions of values --an average of 3.6 values per editorial.

The personal values of gatekeepers can also be measured, as in Searing's (1978) previously cited study of Labour and Conservative members of the British House of Commons. Rokeach determined the personal values of scientists by administering the Value Survey to 152 science faculty members at Michigan State and Wayne State universities.

For empirically measuring the personal values of an institution's special clients (e.g., active church attenders for the value of the religion), Rokeach employed the personal values of graduate students in science. The respondents were 86 graduate students in various fields of science at Washington State University.

For ascertaining the perceived values of an institution by its gatekeepers, Rokeach obtained data on the perceived values of science by scientists (i.e., by gatekeepers of science). The respondents were 101 faculty members at Washington State University; they were instructed to "rank the values in order of their importance to the SCIENCES as a social institution [Rokeach, 1979a; emphasis in the original]."

Finally, the perceived values of science by nonscientists were measured by giving the instructions above to 122 undergraduates taking an introductory course in sociology at Washington State University. The instructions and measuring instrument were identical to those used to measure the perceived values of science by scientists.

According to the value rankings obtained with

all five methods, wisdom is the central terminal value of science; all of the methods rank it among the top three. Wisdom is followed by freedom, self-respect, a sense of accomplishment, a world at peace, and equality. Salvation is uniformly considered to be science's least important value; other values generally ranked low include pleasure, national security, mature love, true friendship, and a comfortable life.

The methods single out intellectual as the key instrumental value of the institution of science, followed by being capable, honest, responsible, imaginative, and independent. Being broadminded and logical rank seventh and eighth. Instrumental values derived from religion and those which exemplify "conventional values" dominate the roster of low importance values (obedience and being clean, polite, cheerful, forgiving, and loving).

Overall agreement among methods can be determined precisely by computing rho's (rank order correlations) between any pair of value rankings. The terminal value correlations range from .24 to .89; the mean rho is .51. For instrumental values, the range is between .30 and .80, with a mean of .64. Although the overall level of agreement is respectable, the five methods clearly vary as valid indicators of the values of science.

Generally, the least sensitive single indicator is method 3, the personal values of science graduate students (future gatekeepers); in contrast, the most sensitive indicator is method 4, perceived values of science by scientists (with a mean terminal correlation of .64 and a mean instrumental correlation of .71). Method 2--the personal values of scientists--is the second best strategy.

Interestingly, content analysis is neither the best nor the worst method. This finding has clear implications for future research on the values of foreign affairs "institutions," although it would obviously be premature to overgeneralize from a case study.

However, the presence of at least one feasible alternative method for generating data--surveying country and area experts--provides an opportunity for exploring a multimethod approach in future inquiry. In international affairs, "experts" of various kinds are frequently used as surrogate "sources" of data for a variety of reasons--and especially in contexts where "objective" data are inaccessible or suspect.[10]

Public elite articulations are notoriously

suspect in nature.[11] This problem is compounded by the fact that public source elite data are often the only form available:

> Analysts will be forced to rely on documents that are in the first instance intended to convey information to the public, to legislatures, or to foreign governments. As likely as not, they are also intended to persuade, justify, threaten, cajole, manipulate, evoke sympathy, or otherwise influence the intended audience. Words may convey explicit or implicit clues about the author's "real" beliefs, attitudes, and opinions; they may also be intended to serve his practical goals of the moment [Holsti 1976: 133].

Elite value articulations, then, may be no more than rhetorical flourishes or meaningless shibboleths or aphorisms; in more extreme instances, public statements may be used to deceive or obfuscate. While the empirical evidence above (as well as other research) suggests that this is emphatically not the case in a general sense (i.e., elite articulations in foreign affairs are often reliable and valid representations of the speaker's intentions and attitudes),[12] critics of the use of content analyses of public documents will probably not be convinced on the basis of the available data.

The existence of a large pool of sophisticated country and area experts in the academic, foreign affairs, defense, and intelligence communities suggests that it would be feasible to use experts to estimate value profiles of various foreign policy institutional elites. These data could then be compared with content analysis-based studies of the elites themselves to determine whether the "experts" agree with the actual leaders.

The strategy of utilizing country and area specialists to reconstruct elite belief systems when the actual decision-makers are inaccessible has already been applied (e.g., Kent et al., 1980). A multi-analytic expert network (e.g., CIA analysts, Department of State desk officers, Defense Intelligence Agency intelligence analysts, academic experts, etc.) could be created in order to guard against the intrusion of biases emanating from a particular institutional context. This approach pervades the extensive work on political risk analysis for corporate investment planning, with results that have been very encouraging (see, e.g., Gebelein et al., 1978). In the study of foreign affairs institutions, experts can be regarded as extra-institutional gatekeepers in the same sense in which Peterson (1979) views newsgatherers and processors as "foreign news gatekeepers."

To the extent that it is feasible, a variety of data-gathering methodologies could be employed simultaneously. These would include content analyses of institutional documents and speeches, interview data, the perceptions of various "gatekeepers" of the institution (i.e., the perceived belief system of a given country's foreign policy "institution"), and other "value trace" analyses (see, e.g., Rokeach, 1979a).

CONCLUSION

The value approach assumes that each individual has a ranked scale of preferred end-states (i.e., a value system). In a series of articulations over time, a decision-maker's basic values will presumably be revealed. Values, furthermore, are not consciously manipulated by speakers (in contrast to stated attitudes and intentions, which can be and are distorted). The foreign affairs elite speaker is not ordinarily aware that someone may eventually delineate a profile of his or her value system. All of this implies that even public articulations can be used to measure elite value preferences and hierarchies.

As the preceding section demonstrates, however, validation is clearly an open issue in the sense that several key strategies have not yet been undertaken. There is also a host of other criticisms awaiting further work. For example, more sophisticated analytical strategies could be implemented. The dependent foreign behavior realm could be conceptualized and operationalized differently (e.g., verbal versus physical behavior). Time lags should be introduced into the research design. The domain of instrumental (means) values remains unexplored; the well known operational code framework features a number of such values.

A topic to be pursued in future research is the question of <u>value change</u>. Human values, as Rokeach's work demonstrates so vividly and convincingly, are core phenomena; value change often precedes both attitude and behavior change.

At the same time, belief systems are generally

resistant to change; this can be expected to apply with special force to elite belief systems. Jervis (1976) and many others (e.g., Bonham et al., 1979) have concluded on the basis of extensive experimental and historical evidence that people tend to change as little of their attitude structure as possible.

Value change may be induced in one of two ways: as a result of rare critical events or by replacing the incumbent elite. The former process is illustrated in Ben-Zvi's (1978) research on U.S. elite beliefs about Japan in the 1941-1945 period.[13] He pinpoints the outbreak of the Pacific War as the "trigger event" which reshaped Secretary of War Henry Stimson's perceptions of the Japanese patterns of cognitive processing and acting; the attack on Pearl Harbor and the ensuing war "shattered Stimson's prewar conviction that Japanese policy makers were rational statesmen whose decisions and actions were guided by realistic calculations and assessments [Ben-Zvi 1978: 39]." Atypical, dramatic events may thus effect value change and major cognitive reorganizations; surprise attacks exemplify one probable set of such "trigger events."

More frequent as a source of foreign policy value change, however, would be the replacement of an incumbent regime with a new one. Elites are often too wedded to their values and other beliefs to change quickly or easily; the more economical--and often more effective--strategy is to replace the existing decision elite with a new one. The striking case of Czechoslovakia in 1968 is an extreme manifestation of a relatively common process.

The foreign affairs analogue to Rokeach's experimentally induced value change, then, is leadership (and thus value) change. An elite attribute data base for the 1966-1970 period already exists and includes an explicit foreign policy elite (i.e., head of state and foreign minister) change variable.[14] Consequently, it would be possible to test a model which measured the impact of change in the elite (head of state and/or foreign minister) on a country's articulated foreign policy values, treating the change as a stimulus in a quasi-experimental design.

Central to this analysis has been the explicit goal of providing a preliminary assessment of the validity of the value data set. The validation strategy which has been pursued here emphasizes the behavioral relevance of the values of foreign policy-making elites. While the results are somewhat encouraging, we must also point out the potential problems with the data set. Aside from the obvious caveat that the direction of influence may be from behavior to value rather than the reverse, perhaps the most troublesome issue revolves around the question of inferring from the source (FBIS Daily Reports based on monitoring foreign broadcasts and speeches) to the realm of behavior.

This entire issue can be reduced to one basic contrast--between the representational and instrumental models of communication (see Pool, 1959). The instrumental model involves "reading between the lines" in an attempt to determine what the message conveys, given its context and circumstance (Pool, 1959: 3). The representational model accepts articulations "at face value." As Pool (1959: 209) concludes, every act of communication has representational and instrumental aspects.

In some instances, values may be used to deceive or obfuscate, as the relationship between force behavior and the value of peace for the Closed group illustrates. To the extent that values are meaningless aphorisms, the utility of cross-national content analyses of public elite articulations is reduced to zero. Also, to the extent that elite value references are employed to confuse or mislead target(s), analysts can search for patterns of deception strategies; even a pattern of lies can be of some importance in monitoring and predicting elite behavior.

A factor which complicates this problem is the previously noted finding that the nature of the audience influences both the decision-maker's style of presentation and the substance of what is presented.[15] Generally, statements for public consumption are less "truthful" than private statements (Bonham, 1975: 8). Empirical support is provided by Gilbert's (1975: 15) research on Secretary of State John Foster Dulles's perceptions of the People's Republic of China. In his statements to the general public, Dulles gave much higher assessments of Chinese hostility and strength; statements to the press ranked between those to the public and to Congress. Since the FBIS data consist of statements directed to the public and/or the media, inescapable problems of image projection, manipulation, and distortion may intrude.

In addition, critics of content analyses of public documents undoubtedly exaggerate the amount of distortion that occurs, as was noted in the preceding section. We should recognize that manipulative (and distorting) communications, subtle cues, and direct messages are all lockstitched into the fabric of interstate interaction; instrumental and representational elements coexist. We should also distinguish between routine articulations and statements that occur during a crisis period. The value approach assumes that each individual has (at least implicitly) a ranked scale of preferred terminal end-states. In a series of articulations over time, basic values will presumably be revealed.

Decision-maker values are clearly related to other cognitive and individual-level phenomena. Ultimate (terminal) values are presumably linked to the lower-order values which are featured in cognitive mapping studies; values would be expected to relate to (and structure) the clusters of beliefs identified in the various operational code case studies; values may also be linked to personality traits such as dogmatism and cognitive complexity. The nexus between elite values and Falkowski's (1978) memory profile model is also unexplored. These various linkages should be illuminated in subsequent inquiry; eventually, an integrated model of the foreign policy elite decision-maker may be developed and tested.

Other validity criteria should be applied, but for both validation and policy-relevant purposes, the critical litmus test is the value-behavior relationship. As Marvick asserts in his review of elite research:

> Those who attempt empircally grounded work have produced ingenious and thought-provoking findings about elite perspectives. At best, these specify the distinctive ways in which elite figures plausibly behave in real-life arenas--how they analyze problems, view strategies, treat rivals, use resources and achieve results. Evidence of actual elite behavior is seldom keyed to evidence of elite beliefs [1977: 124].

This chapter has presented a preliminary assessment of that relationship; future inquiry will attempt to pursue this issue in a more systematic fashion and further ascertain the reliability, validity, and explanatory/predictive utility of the foreign policy elite value data.

NOTES

1. The result for wisdom is unusual since that particular value appears rarely in the data set generally (see Tables 4.5 and 4.6); what this finding means is that on the infrequent occasions when a reference is made to wisdom in the speeches of Western leaders, it reduces the amount of constructive diplomatic behavior sent.

2. This foreshadows a critical issue which will be discussed in the conclusion of this chapter in the context of the instrumental versus representational debate: are articulated elite values nothing more than rhetorical devices which are employed to deceive other actors and generally obfuscate reality? If we conceive of the values as a monitoring or forecasting tool rather than a scientific data set (i.e., a set of variables for explaining foreign behavioral patterns), then it is important to recognize that states may say x and do y. That is, a positive relationship between the value of a world of peace and acts of force may be expected (from an instrumental frame of reference) rather than anomalous (given a representational perspective).

3. The unusually large beta weights for Energy Dependency and Energy Interdependence mean that even an occasional fluctuation in this area exerts a large effect on external behavior. Note that the direction of the effect for energy dependency is strongly negative (resulting in decreases in all forms of behavior) while the relationship in the case of energy interdependence is equally strong but in a positive direction. The formulae for these indicators are given on page 136.

4. When a crisis erupts suddenly, the system tends to become a tracking or monitoring rather than a warning mechanism.

5. Surprise is discussed in Ben-Zvi (1976) and Handel (1977). The subject of warning, intelligence, and surprise is treated in Chan (1979) and Hopple (1978: 165-166).

6. The two exceptions (Portugal and Spain) were politically closed during the research design time frame (1966-1970). Neither country, it should be noted, is among the 39 in the value data subsample discussed in this chapter. Neither China nor Cuba loaded on the Closed factor; China was initially a Large Developing country (the Third World category in this study) and Cuba is one of the Unstable states.

7. From a game theoretic or macro perspective,

crisis, conflict, and war can occur because of the ultimate and pervasive structural factor (the anarchy of the international supergame and the consequent security dilemma); all nations pursue a basic security strategy via a number of "tactics" (acquisitions of armaments, formation of alliances, direct actions against adversaries, etc.). See Snyder and Diesing (1977) for details.

8. See, e.g., Chapter 4, pp. 128-130. This question has been explored in a very preliminary fashion. A more definitive assessment will be offered on the basis of subsequent inquiry.

9. A similar--albeit more sophisticated--strategy was pursued in a recent forecasting study of domestic conflict; see Gurr and Lichbach (1979). Such a design assumes that elite values are not susceptible to extreme temporal variation, an assumption which seems plausible in the light of research on elite belief systems (see, e.g., Putnam et al., 1979). Although this question has not been dealt with in a definitive fashion, available evidence (based on the two-way analysis of variance with state and year as independent variables and values as dependent variables) does suggest that temporal variation is generally limited; see Chapter 4 for details.

10. For recent examples of the use of expert-generated data in international relations, see Hopple and Kuhlman (1980).

11. The nature of the speaker's audience seems to influence both the style of presentation and the substance of what is presented. Although research on this issue has not been systematic, there is apparently a validity-related hierarchy ranging from elite articulations directed at the mass public to: an attentive or elite subgroup in the public, (e.g., the prestige press); other actors within the political system (e.g., the legislature); and aides and confidants within the executive branch.

12. This, however, certainly does not preclude problems of image projection, manipulation, and distortion. But the critics exaggerate the amount of distortion and lying. The real problem is more often one of interpreting the articulations; see Jervis (1976) for a sophisticated discussion of this issue.

13. The impact of a critical event and the resultant cognitive change in belief systems is analyzed from a cognitive mapping perspective in an interesting case study of Norwegian officials and a

major oil pollution accident; see Bonham et al. (1978).

14. The data are described in Hopple (1978).
15. See note 11 above.

6
In Search of the Foundations of Elite Foreign Policy Behavior

The themes of eclecticism and incrementalism pervade this "state-of-the-art" assessment of research on the roots of the behavior of foreign policy elites. As the preceding chapters have demonstrated, an impressive--and often frustrating--amount of eclecticism characterizes work at the intersection of the boundaries of psychology and the scientific study of foreign policy.

Even within a cluster like belief systems analysis, the diversity is often striking. This applies, for example, to both operational code profiling and cognitive mapping. No overarching frameworks govern research; noncomparable case studies continue to accrue.[1]

The eclecticism is especially marked with respect to research techniques and methodologies. Researchers have selected from a lengthy menu of options. As Chapters 2 and 3 show, an intentional multimethod strategy can be expected to generate the most reliable and valid data. This is a sacrosanct principle of scientific validation; in the milieu of world politics, where there are many overt and unintentional verbal, nonverbal, and even (pyscho-) physiological traces from decision-making elites, the approach becomes even more desirable. Multiple indicator systems can be expected to facilitate the elusive process of interpreting complex, ambiguous, contradictory, and even deceptive signals and indices.[2]

Incrementalism coexists with eclecticism. To the extent that there has been "cumulative" research on the psychophysiological and psychological roots of foreign policy behavior, it has conformed more to the additive than to the integrative variant of cumulation (Zinnes, 1976: 162). This, however, should not be unexpected or necessarily disconcerting.

The replication studies in the general domain of elite belief systems and international crises--a "research program" extending from the Paige (1968) work on the outbreak of the Korean War to the Stanford research on 1914 and 1962 (e.g., Holsti, 1972) and the studies of Brecher (1979a, 1979b) and his colleagues of a much larger number of cases--provide the indispensable basis for at least some descriptive consensus. In addition, a stockpile of propositions is being amassed. Both promote additive cumulation; although neither is a sufficient condition for integrative cumulation, the two can be viewed as necessary prerequisites for such cumulation.

If progress could be made in linking up the various islands of cognitive research on foreign policy elites (e.g., an integrated design which meshed operational code profiling with cognitive mapping and value analysis), perhaps a breakthrough could be achieved and more genuinely cumulative or integratively cumulative research could be produced. Compared to the state of affairs as recently as a decade ago, we are at least at a point where an integrative research design is clearly feasible.

Three themes characterize the literature on the psychophysiological, cognitive, and other psychological dimensions and foundations of foreign policy behavior. One is the question of decision system variation. The second issue, related to the first, is the theme of rationality. The third is the trace versus process distinction, a topic alluded to in the introductory chapter.

Fundamental to the pursuit of goals via power in the arena of world politics is the attempt to maximize security and cope with threat. The rational or analytic paradigm discussed in Steinbruner (1974) and elsewhere suggests that each national decision system can be viewed as a replica of all of the others; decision systems can therefore be treated as equivalent, homogeneous units of analysis.

This image of decision system uniformity contrasts sharply with the assumption of heterogeneity in Bobrow, Chan, and Kringen's (1979) study of China.[3] Actor diversity is assumed in the typical analysis of the content or structural aspects of elite belief systems. Such heterogeneity may be examined within systems (e.g., bureaucratic politics) or across systems (e.g., the comparative profiling of the perceptions of competing elites in the prewar crisis of 1914).

To an extent, the adoption of a homogeneity or heterogeneity assumption depends on the investigator's frame of reference. From a systemic vantage point or in the context of very abstract game or decision theoretic models, actor homogeneity is a useful and heuristic simplifying postulate. The concern in such analyses is with the static structure of the situation.

Decision unit heterogeneity emerges as a more plausible model for the analysis of the dynamics of bargaining or interstate interaction in general or for case studies of particular decision systems.[4] The belief system and cognitive processing characteristics of foreign policy elites intervene between the external stimulus and the system's response; discrepancies across cases (e.g., 1914 versus 1962) are often due to variations in these phenomena.

Kinder and Weiss (1978), Steinbruner (1974), and others have emphasized and reviewed the empirical and theoretical weaknesses in the edifice of the analytic or rationality paradigm. Essentially, the analytic paradigm subsumes a set of assumptions about the operation of the decision process in the context of a complex decision problem; a given decision process is analytic if there is evidence that:

- At least limited value integration occurred;
- Alternative outcomes were analyzed and evaluated; and
- New information produced appropriate subjective adjustments.

The competing cognitive theory handles the puzzling problem of decisiveness under conditions of uncertainty, which is not resolved by the analytic model. According to cognitive theorists, the mind inferentially imposes structure on ambiguous data. Under conditions of full complexity, cognitive theory posits general tendencies to conceptualize decision problems in terms of a single value, to associate a single outcome with the available alternatives, and to restrict the amount of information used.

The cognitive literature identifies a number of examples of non-analytic perception and/or information processing. If the two are simultaneously non-analytic, according to Kinder and Weiss (1978: 720), "a decision maker uses nonlogical cognitive processes to operate on a biased picture of the decision problem." Among the factors which constrain and inject into the decision process nonrational influences are (see Snyder, 1978);

- Organizational dynamics and bureaucratic politics (Janis, 1972; Janis and Mann, 1977; Snyder and Diesing, 1977);
- Idiosyncratic psychopathologies (George and George, 1964; Robins, 1977);
- Non-idiosyncratic but nonrational cognitive processes.

Snyder (1978) "revisits" the Cuban missile crisis case and concludes that it reflected the dynamics and dangers of a non-analytic, cognitive decision process. Kennedy and his advisors eschewed the war avoidance/maintenance of prestige conflict by viewing the problem in terms of "risking war now" versus "running an even greater risk of war later." Snyder (1978: 361) argues that it is Kennedy's imputation of certainty to a highly uncertain situation which provides the most convincing evidence for a cognitive model interpretation: "...he was confident that his chosen policy was not merely the right one, but the only one he could possibly adopt under the circumstances [emphasis in the original]." Fortunately, Snyder concludes, the same cognitive pressures did not govern the Soviet decision process.

While Snyder (1978) cites several mitigating factors, it is nevertheless clear that "...the mind craves certainty and will work to establish it even when it is unwarranted by objective conditions [363]." The decision-maker is likely to become locked into a strategy based on compellence; further, the cognitive model suggests that a posture favoring negotiation is improbable. The dangers of compellence are accentuated if both sides are locked into that strategy by conceptualizations which permit them to avoid explicit tradeoff considerations.

Empirical research in social psychology and behavioral decision theory complements the cognitive foreign policy work (e.g., Axelrod, 1976: 244) which emphasizes the limits on humans as information processing and decision-making systems. Hogarth (1975), in a comprehensive review, concludes that recent research on judgmental processes for assessing subjective probability distributions depicts the human as a selective, sequential information processing system with limited capacities. Extensive evidence reinforces the conclusion that humans deviate considerably from the rational actor model.[5]

Although research on probabilistic thinking has typically shown that people are oblivious to certain kinds of information that play a major role in normative models of inference (e.g., information regarding sample size, predictive validity, etc.), the prevailing pessimism may be premature. Fischhoff et al. (1979), in a recent experimental study, demonstrate that most subjects (about two-thirds) can adjust in response to base-rate and individuating information. However, subjects were generally not sufficiently sensitive (i.e., they showed the "right" kind of sensitivity but did not adjust enough).

Apparently, departures from the normative or rational choice decision model are far from unknown in the sphere of foreign policy decision-making. Interestingly, however, Kinder and Weiss (1978) note in their assessment of several major works in the study of psychology and foreign policy that the cognitive theorists marshall evidence which discredits the empirical foundation of the analytic (i.e., rational) paradigm--and then conclude by offering prescriptions which are directly tied to the allegedly bankrupt rational actor model. Similarly, throughout her essay in the Special Issue of the Jerusalem Journal of International Relations on international crisis analysis, Stein (1978) documents the extensive evidence on the relevance of nonrational models and simultaneously demonstrates that rational evaluations of crisis decision-making are inescapable. To be held responsible, Stein concludes, decision-makers must be capable of being rational.

Pure rationality is an unattainable ideal. But this does not mean that foreign policy (and other) decision-making processes cannot become less "irrational." In fact, one of the benefits of cognitive research on foreign policy elites is that it will presumably reveal common biases and highlight implicit or hidden assumptions and thereby minimize the irrational and nonrational aspects of information processing and choice behavior.

Aside from the chapter on biopolitics and psychophysiology, the focus of research has been the realm of overt traces. If international politics revolves around the analysis of power and goals (or capabilities and intentions), then means for ascertaining another actor's possible and probable behaviors entails the monitoring of the verbal and physical behavioral outputs of foreign policy-makers and state decision systems.

These outputs feature an array of words, deeds, and combinations of the two. A foreign policy decision-maker emits a number of cues and signals in the form of explicit and unintentional verbal statements and even nonverbal and psychophysiological manifestations or traces. According to Wiegele's (1979e) signal leakage perspective, the individual is constantly leaving traces of his or her behavior; Hermann's (1979a) review of trace indicators presents a number of verbal and nonverbal examples.

Traces or manifestations, however, are only the "tip of the iceberg." Elaborate decision processes (perception, information processing, choice behavior, etc.) precede the observable outputs. It is in this area that both reliable, valid data and systematic research are sparse. A comprehensive theory about the foundations of elite foreign policy behavior, however, must incorporate the pre-decision processes which culminate in an overt statement or act. Some progress (although it is only indirectly relevant at this point) has occurred in psychophysiology; the psychophysiological bases of the mentalistic phenomena which we label "information processing" and "decision-making" are being uncovered and explored.

We do not yet know whether decision systems should be regarded as fundamentally homogeneous or heterogeneous; to an extent, the issue of rational versus irrational/nonrational interpretations of elite behavior is an open question; we have identified and interpreted only some of the traces of elite behavior (both verbal and nonverbal) and have very limited knowledge about the less accessible decision process aspects of the elite-based phenomena which are constantly surfacing in the arena of world politics. An emphasis on policy-relevance, therefore, may be decidedly premature. Of all of the themes in this chapter, applied inquiry is the most tentative.

Nevertheless, many researchers who focus on the nexus between psychology and international politics are motivated by normative as well as scientific goals. The concern with improving the policy process and with avoiding or reducing the likelihood of war and conflict is a continuing theme of inquiry on the foundations of the behavior of foreign policy elites. Although the topics have changed dramatically since the 1940s and early 1950s and the contemporary "psychopoliticist" is less naive and more self-effacing, a desire to promote the values of freedom, dignity, and peace still animates many of the researchers who attempt to discover the psychological determinants of the external behavior of actors in world politics.

Especially if it can be shown that the behavior of decision systems is fundamentally nonrandom, a science of "psychology-and-foreign-policy" will be feasible. Such a science would provide the foundation for an applied program of research.

The discussion of "ordered decision rules" in Bobrow, Chan, and Kringen (1979) provides an illustration. Bobrow and his colleagues list a set of ordered decision rules for Chinese policy-making concerning the subject of intervention in "second-order crises" (i.e., crises in which the actor is initially uninvolved). The rules, which can be diagrammed in flow chart form (reproduced here as Figure 6.1), provide the necessary conditions for a crisis intervention decision.

The rules in Figure 6.1 are:

1. Identify the main enemy;

2. Assess the main enemy's level of involvement (i.e., high or low) in the crisis;

3. (a) To the extent that the main enemy is not highly involved, China should show a higher threshold for direct intervention;
(b) To the extent that the main enemy is highly involved, Chinese policies can be expected to maximize its loss or vulnerability;

4. Identify the major third-party actors;

5. Assess the prevailing current of international relations (i.e., how opposed are the actors in 4 to the policies of the main enemy?);

6. (a) To the extent that the current in 5 is unfavorable, China should abstain from direct involvement;
(b) To the extent that the current is favorable, China should pursue a more active policy;

7. Estimate the political reliability of major third-party actors;

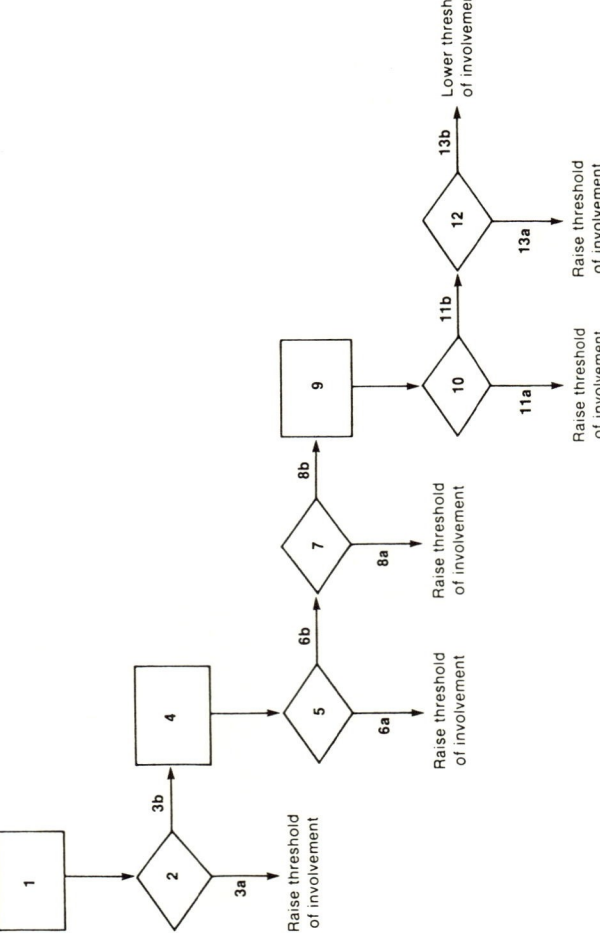

Figure 6.1

INVOLVEMENT IN SECOND-ORDER CRISES

8. (a) Discount the actor's reliability if it is domestically unstable or has a dubious ideological outlook;
   (b) To the extent the opposite conditions of (a) hold, China should consider joint actions with the actor;

9. Identify the direct conflict participants;

10. Assess the nature of relations between the actors in 9 and China's main enemy;

11. (a) If the actors in 9 are friendly toward the main enemy of Peking, China should raise its involvement threshold;
    (b) If at least one of the actors in 9 is hostile to the main enemy, China should consider supporting it;

12. Assess the internal characteristics (i.e., reactionary or progressive) of the actors in 9;

13. (a) If the "reactionary" actor is strong and stable or the "progressive" actor is weak and unstable, avoid involvement;
    (b) If the "reactionary" actor is weak and unstable or the "progressive" actor is strong and stable, China should lower its direct involvement threshold.

Bobrow et al. (1979) conclude that the flowchart decision logic sequence is confirmed by the available evidence about China's recent behavior regarding Zaire, Angola, Ethiopia, and Bangladesh. To the extent that such operational code (and other cognitive) models permit us to predict (probabilistically), the methodologies and indicator systems described in earlier chapters would contribute to the policy process.

Although there are many lacunae and the various "islands" of inquiry have not been integrated in a systematic fashion, a map to guide the analysis of foreign policy elites has been drawn. We now at least know the topography of the domain; future explorations can fill in the gaps and extend and refine our knowledge.

NOTES

1. But there has been some progress; despite the case-specific nature of the empirical work, Holsti (1977) was able to use a number of independently-conducted operational code studies in his research on generic belief system typologies. His detailed codebook may impose even more comparability on research efforts in this particular area.

2. On signals and indices, see Jervis (1970).

3. Snyder and Diesing (1977), who synthesize game theoretic rational (analytic) perspectives with frameworks from information processing and bargaining, fall between the analytic and cognitive schools.

4. See, respectively, Snyder and Diesing (1977) and Brecher (1979a).

5. In addition to the foreign policy-relevant research (e.g., Holsti, 1976; Jervis, 1976; Kinder and Weiss, 1978; Stein, 1978; Steinbruner, 1974), see the more general surveys (e.g., Manis, 1978; Slovic et al., 1977).

Appendix A: Variables and Clusters

SOURCE VARIABLES

A. Psychological Component (Decision-Maker Values)
  1. A comfortable life
  2. A world of peace
  3. Equality
  4. Freedom
  5. Happiness
  6. Governmental security
  7. Honor
  8. Justice
  9. National security
  10. Public security
  11. Respect
  12. Social recognition
  13. Wisdom
  14. Progress
  15. Unity
  16. Ideology
  17. Cooperation
  18. Support of government

B. Political/Societal Component
  1. Merchandise balance of payments (economic performance)
  2. Population growth rate
  3. Governmental instability
     • Purges
     • Revolutions
     • Number of coups
     • Number of changes in the executive
     • Number of changes in the cabinet
     • Number of changes in the constitution
  4. Societal unrest
     • General strikes
     • Riots
     • Anti-government demonstrations

C. Interstate Component[a]
  1. Interstate energy relationships
     • Energy interdependency
     • Energy market strength
     • Energy dependency
  2. General trade relationships
     • Neo-colonial dependency
     • Economic involvement (total trade)
  3. Food dependency and advantage
     • Food dependency
  4. General interstate economic relationships
     • Import concentration
     • Export concentration

D. Global Component
   1. International governmental organization (IGO) membership
      • Total IGO memberships per year
      • Total new IGO memberships per year
   2. Conflict within bordering states[b]
      • Total number of force events sent and received by nations land-bordering State X
      • Total number of force events sent and received by nations sea-bordering State X
      • Total number of force events sent and received by nations with colonies land-bordering State X
      • Total number of force events sent and received by nations with colonies sea-bordering State X
      • Total number of conflictual events (excluding force) sent and received by nations land-bordering State X
      • Total number of conflictual events sent and received by nations sea-bordering State X
      • Total number of conflictual events sent and received by nations with colonies land-bordering State X
      • Total number of conflictual events sent and received by nations with colonies sea-bordering State X

INTERVENING STATE CLASSIFICATION SCHEME DIMENSIONS AND VARIABLES[c]

A. Economic Dimension
   1. Gross National Product per capita
   2. Percent of Gross Domestic Product originating in agriculture
   3. Percent of Gross Domestic Product originating in industry
   4. Energy consumption per capita
   5. Percent of economically active male population in agricultural occupations
   6. Percent of economically active male population in professional-technical occupations

B. Capability Dimension
   Size:
   7. Total area
   8. Total population
   9. Gross National Product
   Military:
   10. Military manpower
   11. Defense expenditures
   12. Defense expenditures per capita
   Resource Base:
   13. Percent of energy consumed domestically produced

C. Political Dimension
   Development:
   14. Number of political parties
   15. Horizontal power distribution
   16. Local government autonomy
   Structure:
   17. Selection of effective executive
   18. Legislative effectiveness
   19. Legislative selection
   Stability (1946–1965)
   20. Average number of coups per year
   21. Average number of constitutional changes per year
   22. Average number of major cabinet changes per year
   23. Average number of changes in effective executive per year

DEPENDENT (FOREIGN BEHAVIOR SENT) VARIABLES[d]
1. Constructive diplomatic behavior sent
    - yield
    - comment
    - consult
    - approve
    - promise
    - grant
    - reward
    - agree
    - request
    - propose
    - reject
    - deny
    - warn
    - negative sanctions
2. Non-military conflict behavior sent
    - accuse
    - protest
    - demand
    - threaten
    - demonstrate
    - expel
    - seize
3. Force acts sent
    - force

[a] See Hopple (1978) for a discussion of data sources and other pertinent details.
[b] See pp. 136-137 for formulae.
[c] This is based on the WEIS classification of conflictual and force events. The borders data consist of aggregated neighboring conflict scores for each state and total number of borders of each type (nation land, nation sea, colonly land, colony sea).
[d] For factor analytic and other results, see Wilkenfeld et al. (1978, 1980).

References

ABELSON, R. P. (1971) "The Ideology Machine." Presented at the Annual Meeting of the American Political Science Association. Chicago, September.
──── and J. D. CARROLL (1965) "Computer Simulation of Individual Belief Systems." American Behavioral Scientist 8: 24-30.
ABRAHAMSEN, D. (1977) Nixon vs. Nixon: Am Emotional Tragedy. New York: Farrar, Straus, and Giroux.
ADORNO, T. W., E. FRENKEL-BRUNSWIK, D. J. LEVINSON, and R. N. SANFORD (1950) The Authoritarian Personality. New York: Harper and Row.
ANDERSON, J. E., Jr. (1973) "The 'Operational Code' Approach: The George Construct and Senator Arthur H. Vandenberg's Operational Code Belief System." Presented at the Annual Meeting of the American Political Science Association. New Orleans, September.
ANDRIOLE, S. J., J. WILKENFELD, and G. W. HOPPLE (1975) "A Framework for the Comparative Analysis of Foreign Policy Behavior." International Studies Quarterly 2 (June): 160-198.
ASHBY, N. (1969) "Schumacher and Brandt: The Divergent 'Operational Codes' of Two German Socialist Leaders." Stanford, Ca.: Stanford University, mimeo.
ASPATURIAN, V. V. (1967) "Soviet Foreign Policy," in R. C. Macridis (ed.) Foreign Policy in World Politics. Englewood Cliffs, N.J.: Prentice-Hall.
AXELROD, R. (1977) "Argumentation in Foreign Policy Settings: Britain in 1918, Munich in 1938, and Japan in 1970." Journal of Conflict Resolution 21 (December): 727-744.
──── (ed.) (1976) Structure of Decision: The Cognitive Maps of Political Elites. Princeton, N.J.: Princeton University Press.
──── (1972a) Framework for a General Theory of Cognition and Choice. Research Series No. 18. Berkeley, Ca.: University of California, Institute of International Studies.

_____(1972b) "Psycho-Algebra: A Mathematical Theory of Cognition and Choice with an Application to the British East India Committee in 1918." Papers, Peace Research Society (International) 18: 113-131.

BALL-ROKEACH, S. J. (1976) "Receptivity to Sexual Equality." Pacific Sociological Review 19: 519-540.

BANKS, A. S. (1971) Cross-Polity Time-Series Data. Cambridge, Ma.: Massachusetts Institute of Technology Press.

BARBER, J. D. (1977-78) "The Nixon Brush with Tyranny." Political Science Quarterly 92 (Winter): 581-605.

_____(1972) The Presidential Character: Predicting Performance in the White House. Englewood Cliffs, N.J.: Prentice-Hall.

BEN-ZVI, A. (1978) "The Outbreak and Termination of the Pacific War: A Juxtaposition of American Preconceptions." Journal of Peace Research 15: 33-49.

_____(1976) "Hindsight and Foresight: A Conceptual Framework for the Analysis of Surprise Attacks." World Politics 28 (April): 381-395.

_____(1975) "American Preconceptions and Policies Toward Japan, 1940-1941: A Case Study in Misperception." International Studies Quarterly 19 (June): 228-248.

BERELSON, B. (1952) Content Analysis in Communication Research. New York: Free Press of Glencoe.

BOBROW, D. B., S. CHAN, and J. A. KRINGEN (1979) Understanding Foreign Policy Decisions: The Chinese Case. New York: Free Press.

_____(1977) "Understanding How Others Treat Crises: A Multimethod Approach." International Studies Quarterly 21 (March): 199-223.

BONHAM, G. M. (1975) "Cognitive Process Models and the Study of Foreign Policy Decision-Making." Presented at the Annual Meeting of the International Studies Association. Washington, D.C., February.

_____and M. J. SHAPIRO (1979) "The Cognitive Process Approach to Planning and Policy Analysis," in L. S. Falkowski (ed.) Proceedings of the Symposium on Biopolitics and Political Psychology. McLean, Va.: International Public Policy Research Corporation.

_____(eds.) (1977) Thought and Action in Foreign Policy. Basel and Stuttgart: Birkhauser Verlag.

_____(1976) "Explanation of the Unexpected: The Syrian Intervention in Jordan in 1970," in R. Axelrod (ed.) Structure of Decision. Princeton, N.J.: Princeton University Press.

_____(1973) "Simulation in the Development of A Theory of Foreign Policy Decision-Making," in P. J. McGowan (ed.) Sage International Yearbook of Foreign Policy Studies, Vol. I. Beverly Hills, Ca.: Sage.

_____ and T. L. TRUMBLE (1979) "The October War: Changes in Cognitive Orientation Toward the Middle East Conflict." International Studies Quarterly 23 (March): 3-44.

BONHAM, G. M., D. HERADSTVEIT, O. NARVESEN, and M. J. SHAPIRO (1978) "A Cognitive Model of Decision-Making: Application to Norwegian Oil Policy." Cooperation and Conflict 8: 93-108.

BONHAM, G. M., M. J. SHAPIRO, and G. J. NOZICKA (1976) "A Cognitive Process Model of Foreign Policy Decision-Making." Simulation and Games 7 (June): 123-152.

BORGEN, C. A. and L. I. GOODMAN (1976) "Voice Print Analysis of Anxiolytic Drug Effects: Preliminary Results." Clinical Pharmacology and Therapeutics 19: 104 (Abstract).

BRAMSON, L. and G. W. GOETHALS (1964) War: Studies from Psychology, Sociology, and Anthropology. New York: Basic Books.

BRECHER, M. (1979a) Decisions in Crisis: Israel, 1967 and 1973. Berkeley and Los Angeles, Ca.: University of California Press.

_____ (1979b) "State Behavior in International Crisis: A Model." Journal of Conflict Resolution 23 (September): 446-480.

_____ (ed.) (1978) Studies in Crisis Behavior. The Jerusalem Journal of International Relations 3: 1-374.

_____ (1977) "Toward a Theory of International Crisis Behavior: A Preliminary Report." International Studies Quarterly 21 (March): 39-74.

_____ (1975) Decisions in Israel's Foreign Policy. London: Oxford University Press and New Haven: Yale University Press.

_____ (1972) The Foreign Policy System of Israel. New Haven, Ct.: Yale University Press.

_____ (1968) India and World Politics: Krishna Menon's View of the World. New York: Praeger.

_____ and M. RAZ (1977) "Images and Behavior: Israel's Yom Kippur Crisis 1973." International Journal 32 (Summer): 475-500.

BRECHER, M., B. STEINBERG, and J. STEIN (1969) "A Framework for Research on Foreign Policy Behavior." Journal of Conflict Resolution 13: 75-101.

BRENNER, M., H. H. BRANSCOMB, and G. E. SCHWARTZ (1979) "Psychological Stress Evaluator - Two Tests of a Vocal Measure." Psychophysiology 16 (July): 351-357.

BRIM, O., D. C. GLASS, D. E. LAVIN, and N. GOODMAN (1962) Personality and Decision Processes. Stanford, Ca.: Stanford University Press.

BRODIE, B. (1963) "A Psychoanalytic Interpretation of Woodrow Wilson," in B. Mazlish (ed.) Psychoanalysis and History. Englewood Cliffs, N.J.: Prentice-Hall.

BROWNELL, J. R., Jr., T. SPISAK, and A. SPISAK (1975) "The Application of New Methodologies to Analyze the Soviet

Perceptions of U.S. Policies, Volume I." Arlington, Va.:
CACI, Incorporated, Final Technical Report, October.
BURGESS, P. M. (1968) <u>Elite Images and Foreign Policy Outcomes:
A Study of Norway</u>. Columbus, Oh.: Ohio State University Press.
⎯⎯⎯⎯⎯ and R. W. LAWTON (1972) "Indicators of International Behavior: An Assessment of Events Data Research." Beverly Hills, Ca.: Sage.
CALDWELL, D. (1977) "Bureaucratic Foreign Policy-Making." <u>American Behavioral Scientist</u> 21 (September/October): 87-110.
CAMPBELL, D. T. and D. W. FISKE (1959) "Convergent and Discriminant Validation by the Multitrait-Multimethod Matrix." <u>Psychological Bulletin</u> 56: 81-105.
CANTRIL, H. (ed.) (1950) <u>Tensions That Cause Wars</u>. Urbana, Il.: University of Illinois Press.
CENTER FOR BIOPOLITICAL RESEARCH (1978a) "The Psychological Stress Evaluator as a Research Instrument." DeKalb, Il.: Northern Illinois University, prepared for the Cybernetics Technology Office of the U.S. Defense Advanced Research Projects Agency.
⎯⎯⎯⎯⎯ (1978a) "Research Strategies for the Application of Psychophysiological Measurement Techniques to the Management of International Crises." DeKalb, Il.: Northern Illinois University, September.
CHAN, S. (1979) "The Intelligence of Stupidity: Understanding Failures in Strategic Warning." <u>American Political Science Review</u> 73 (March): 171-180.
⎯⎯⎯⎯⎯, J. A. KRINGEN, and D. B. BOBROW (1979) "A Chinese View of the International System," pp. 271-289 in J. D. Singer and M. D. Wallace (eds.) <u>To Augur Well: Early Warning Indicators in World Politics</u>. Beverly Hills, Ca.: Sage.
CHRISTIE, R. and F. L. GEIS (1970) <u>Studies in Machiavellianism</u>. New York: Academic Press.
COLEMAN, J. S. (1975) "Methods and Results in the IEA Studies of Effects of School on Learning." <u>Review of Educational Research</u> 45: 335-386.
⎯⎯⎯⎯⎯ et. al. (1966) <u>Equality of Educational Opportunity</u>. Washington, D.C.: Department of Health, Education, and Welfare.
CONVERSE, P. E. (1964) "The Nature of Belief Systems in Mass Publics," pp. 206-261 in D. Apter (ed.) <u>Ideology and Discontent</u>. New York: Free Press.
CORNING, P. A. (1978) "Biopolitics: Toward a New Political Science." Presented at the Annual Meeting of the American Political Science Association. New York, September.
⎯⎯⎯⎯⎯ (1971) "The Biological Bases of Behavior and Some Implications for Political Science." <u>World Politics</u> 23: 321-370.
CUMMINS, H. W. (1973) "Value Structure and Political Leadership." Sage Professional Papers in International Studies.

Beverly Hills, Ca.: Sage.
D'AMATO, A. A. (1967) "Psychological Constructs in Foreign Policy Prediction." Journal of Conflict Resolution 11 (September): 294-311.
DEVINE, D. J. (1972) The Political Culture of the United States: The Influence of Member Values on Regime Maintainance. Boston: Little, Brown.
DONCHIN, E. (1979) "Event-Related Potentials: A Tool in the Study of Human Information Processing," in H. Begleiter (ed.) Evoked Potentials in Psychiatry. New York: Plenum Press.
_____ and J. B. ISRAEL (n.d.) "Event-Related Potentials--Approaches to Cognitive Psychology." Champaign, Il.: Cognitive Psychophysiology Laboratory, Department of Psychology.
DRUCKMAN, D. (1979) "Social-psychological Factors in Regional Politics," in W. Feld and G. Boyd (eds.) Comparative Regional Systems. New York: Pergamon Press.
_____ (ed.) (1977a) Negotiations: Social-Psychological Perspectives. Beverly Hills, Ca.: Sage.
_____ (1977b) "The Person, Role, and Situation in International Negotiations," pp. 406-456 in M. G. Hermann (ed.) A Psychological Examination of Political Leaders. New York: Free Press.
_____ and R. SLATER (1979) "Nonverbal Communication: Information Processing and Impression Management." Bethesda, Md.: Mathtech, Incorporated, September.
DUNCAN-JOHNSON, C. C. and E. DONCHIN (1977) "On Quantifying Surprise: The Variation in Event-Related Potentials with Subjective Probability." Psychophysiology 14: 456-467.
DURBIN, D. F. M. and J. BOWLBY (1939) Personal Aggressiveness and War. London: Kegan Paul.
DYE, D. R. (n.d.) "A Developmental Approach to the Political Style of Getulio Vargas." Stanford, Ca.: Stanford University, mimeo.
EAST, M. A. (1978) "The International System Perspective and Foreign Policy," in M. A. East, S. A. Salmore, and C. F. Hermann (eds.) Why Nations Act: Theoretical Perspectives for Comparative Foreign Policy Studies. Beverly Hills, Ca.: Sage.
_____ S. A. SALMORE and C. F. HERMANN (eds.) (1978) Why Nations Act: Theoretical Perspectives for Comparative Foreign Policy Studies. Beverly Hills, Ca.: Sage.
EASTON, D. (1976) "The Relevance of Biopolitics to Political Theory," pp. 237-248 in A. Somit (ed.) Biology and Politics: Recent Explorations. Paris and the Hague: Mouton.
ECKHARDT, W. (1967) "Can This Be the Conscience of a Conservative? The Value Analysis Approach to Political Choice." Journal of Human Relations 15: 443-456.

_____(1965) "War Propaganda, Welfare Values, and Political Ideologies." Journal of Conflict Resolution 9: 345-358.
EDINGER, L. J. (1965) Kurt Schumacher: A Study in Personality and Political Behavior. Stanford, Ca.: Stanford University Press.
ETHEREDGE, L. S. (1979) "Hardball Politics: A Model." Political Psychology, 1 (Spring): 3-26.
_____(1978a) "Personality Effects on American Foreign Policy, 1898-1968: A Test of Interpersonal Generalization Theory." American Political Science Review 72 (June): 434-451.
_____(1978b) A World of Men: The Private Sources of American Foreign Policy. Cambridge, Ma.: Massachusetts Institute of Technology Press.
EYSENCK, H. J. (1954) The Psychology of Politics. London: Rutledge and Kegan Paul.
_____(1950) "War and Aggressiveness: A Survey of Social Attitude Studies," in T. H. Pear (ed.) Psychological Factors of Peace and War. London: Hutchinson.
FALKOWSKI, L. S. (ed.) (1979a) Proceedings of the Symposium on Biopolitics and Political Psychology. McLean, Va.: International Public Policy Research Corporation.
_____(ed.) (1979b) Psychological Models in International Politics. Boulder, Co.: Westview.
_____(1978) Presidents, Secretaries of State, and Crises in U.S. Foreign Relations: A Model and Predictive Analysis. Boulder, Co.: Westview Press.
FARBER, M. (1955) "Psychoanalytic Hypotheses in the Study of War." Journal of Social Issues 1: 29-35.
FISCHHOFF, B., P. SLOVIC, and S. LICHTENSTEIN (1979) "Subjective Sensitivity Analysis." Organizational Behavior and Human Performance 23: 339-359.
FISHER, R. (1964) International Conflict and Behavioral Science: The Craigville Papers. New York: Basic Books.
FRANK, J. D. (1964) Sanity and Survival: Psychological Aspects of War and Peace. New York: Random House.
FRANK, R. S. (1977) "Nonverbal and Paralinguistic Analysis of Political Behavior: The First McGovern-Humphrey California Primary Debate," pp. 64-79 in M. G. Hermann (ed.) A Psychological Examination of Political Leaders. New York: Free Press.
_____(1973) "Linguistic Analysis of Political Elites: A Theory of Verbal Kinesics." Sage Professional Papers in International Studies, 2, 022. Beverly Hills, Ca.: Sage.
FREUD, S. and W. C. BULLITT (1967) Thomas Woodrow Wilson. Boston: Houghton Mifflin.
FRIEDLANDER, S. and R. COHEN (1975) "The Personality Correlates of Belligerence in International Conflict: A Comparative Analysis of Historical Case Studies." Comparative Politics 7 (January): 156-186.

GALLHOFER, I. N. and W. E. SARIS (1979) "Strategy Choices of Foreign Policy Decision Makers." Journal of Conflict Resolution 23 (September): 425-445.
GEBELEIN, C. A., C. E. PEARSON, and M. SILBERGH (1978) "Assessing Political Risk of Oil Investment Ventures." Journal of Petroleum Technology (May-June): 725-730.
GEORGE, A. L. (1979) "The Causal Nexus Between Cognitive Beliefs and Decision-Making Behavior: The 'Operational Code' Belief System," pp. 95-124 in L. S. Falkowski (ed.) Psychological Models in International Politics. Boulder, Co.: Westview.
_____ (1969) "The 'Operational Code': A Neglected Approach to the Study of Political Leaders and Decision-Making." International Studies Quarterly 13: 190-222.
_____ (1959) Propaganda Analysis: A Study of Inferences Made from Nazi Propaganda in World War II. Evanston, Il.: Row, Peterson.
_____ and J. L. GEORGE (1964) Woodrow Wilson and Colonel House: A Personality Study. New York: Dover.
GERBNER, G. et al. (1969) The Analysis of Communication Content. New York: John Wiley and Sons.
GIBBINS, R. (n.d.) "The Political Leadership of William Lyon MacKenzie." Stanford, Ca.: Stanford University, mimeo.
GILBERT, J. D. (1975) "John Foster Dulles' Perceptions of the People's Republic of China: An Assessment of Accuracy." Presented at the Annual Meeting of the Southwestern Political Science Association. San Antonio, Texas, March.
GLAD, B. (1973) "Contributions of Psychobiography," pp. 296-321 in J. N. Knutson (ed.) Handbook of Political Psychology. San Francisco, Ca.: Jossey-Bass.
_____ (1969) "The Significance of Personality for Role Performance as Chairman of the Senate Foreign Relations Committee: A Comparison of Borah and Fulbright." Presented at the Annual Meeting of the American Political Science Association. New York, September.
_____ (1966) Charles Evans Hughes and the Illusions of Innocence. Urbana, Il.: University of Illinois Press.
GOLD, H. (1978) "Foreign Policy Decision-Making and the Environment: The Claims of Snyder, Brecher, and the Sprouts." International Studies Quarterly 22 (December): 569-586.
GOMER, F. E., L. R. BEIDEMAN, and S. H. LEVINE (1979) "The Application of Biocybernetic Techniques to Enhance Pilot Performance During Tactical Missions." St. Louis, Mo.: McDonnell Douglas Astronautics Company, Final Report MDC E2046, October.
GOTTFRIED, A. (1962) Boss Cermak of Chicago. Seattle: University of Washington Press.
GREENFIELD, N. S. and R. A. STERNBACH (eds.) (1972) Handbook of Psychophysiology. New York: Holt, Rinehart and

Winston.
GREENSTEIN, F. I. (1975) Personality and Politics: Problems of Evidence, Inference, and Conceptualization, rev. ed. Chicago: Markham.
GUTIERREZ, G. G. (1973) "Dean Rusk and Southeast Asia: An Operational Code Analysis." Presented at the Annual Meeting of the American Political Science Association. New Orleans, September.
HANDEL, M. I. (1977) "The Yom Kippur War and the Inevitability of Surprise." International Studies Quarterly 21 (September): 461-502.
HARARY, F., R. Z. NORMAN, and D. CARTWRIGHT (1965) Structural Models: An Introduction to the Theory of Directed Graphs. New York: John Wiley.
HARPER, R. G., A. N. WIENS, and J. D. MATARAZZO (1978) Nonverbal Communication: The State of the Art. New York: John Wiley and Sons.
HART, J. A. (1977) "Cognitive Maps of Three Latin American Policy Makers." World Politics 30 (October): 115-140.
HASSETT, J. (1978) A Primer of Psychophysiology. San Francisco: W. H. Freeman.
HERMANN, C. F. (1969) "International Crisis as a Situational Variable," pp. 409-421 in J. N. Rosenau (ed.) International Politics and Foreign Policy. New York: Free Press.
_____ and M. G. HERMANN (1967) "An Attempt to Simulate the Outbreak of World War I." American Political Science Review 61: 400-416.
HERMANN, M. G. (1979a) "Indicators of Stress in Policymakers During Foreign Policy Crises." Political Psychology 1 (Spring): 27-46.
_____ (1979b) "Who Becomes a Political Leader? Some Societal and Regime Influences on Selection of a Head of State," pp. 15-48 in L. S. Falkowski (ed.) Psychological Models in International Politics. Boulder, Co.: Westview.
_____ (1978) "Effects of Personal Characteristics of Political Leaders on Foreign Policy," pp. 49-68 in M. A. East et al. (eds.) Why Nations Act: Theoretical Perspectives for Comparative Foreign Policy Studies. Beverly Hills, Ca.: Sage.
_____ (ed.) (1977) A Psychological Examination of Political Leaders. New York: Free Press.
_____ (1976) "When Leader Personality Will Affect Foreign Policy: Some Propositions," pp. 326-333 in J. N. Rosenau (ed.) In Search of Global Patterns. New York: Free Press.
_____ (1975) "Explaining Foreign Policy Behavior Using Personal Characteristics of Political Leaders." Presented at the Annual Meeting of the American Political Science Association. San Francisco, September.

_____ (1974) "Leader Personality and Foreign Policy Behavior," pp. 201-234 in J. N. Rosenau (ed.) Comparing Foreign Policies: Theories, Findings, Methods. New York: Halsted.

_____ (1972a) "Effects of Leader Personality on National Foreign Policy Behavior: A Theoretical Discussion." Columbus, Oh.: Ohio State University Press, mimeo.

_____ (1972b) "How Leaders Process Information and the Effect on Foreign Policy." Presented at the Annual Meeting of the American Political Science Association. Washington, D.C., September.

_____ and C. F. HERMANN (1979) "The Interaction of Situations, Political Regimes, Decision Configurations, and Leader Personality in Interpreting Foreign Policy." Presented at the International Political Science Association Congress. Moscow, USSR, August.

HERNES, H. (1977) "Classical Theories of Foreign Policy Making as Cognitive Archetypes," pp. 242-262 in G. M. Bonham and M. J. Shapiro (eds.) Thought and Action in Foreign Policy. Basel and Stuttgart: Birkhauser Verlag.

HOBERMAN, J. M. (1977) "The Psychopathology of an Abortive Leadership: The Case of Vidkun Quisling," pp. 175-201 in R. S. Robins (ed.) Psychopathology and Political Leadership. Tulane Studies in Political Science, Volume 16. New Orleans, La.: Tulane University.

HOGARTH, R. M. (1975) "Cognitive Processes and the Assessment of Subjective Probability Distributions." Journal of the American Statistical Association 70: 271-291.

HOLSTI, O. R. (1977) "The 'Operational Code' as an Approach to the Analysis of Belief Systems: Final Report to the National Science Foundation," Grant No. SOC 75-15368. Durham, N.C.: Duke University.

_____ (1976) "Foreign Policy Decision Makers Viewed Psychologically: 'Cognitive Process' Approaches," pp. 120-144 in J. N. Rosenau (ed.) In Search of Global Patterns. New York: Free Press.

_____ (1972) Crisis, Escalation, War. Montreal: McGill-Queen's University Press.

_____ (1970) "The 'Operational Code' Approach to the Study of Political Leaders: John Foster Dulles' Philosophical and Instrumental Beliefs." Canadian Journal of Political Science 3 (March): 123-157.

_____ (1969) Content Analysis for the Social Sciences and Humanities. Reading, Ma.: Addison-Wesley.

_____ (1967) "Cognitive Dynamics and Images of the Enemy: Dulles and Russia," in D. Finlay, O. R. Holsti, and R. R. Fagen (eds.) Enemies in Politics. Chicago: Rand McNally.

_____ (1962) "The Belief System and National Images: A Case Study." Journal of Conflict Resolution 6 (September): 244-252.

HOOLE, F. W. and D. A. ZINNES (eds.) (1976) Quantitative

International Politics: An Appraisal. New York: Praeger.

HOPPLE, G. W. (1979a) "Elite Values & Foreign Affairs: Illuminating the Nexus," in L. S. Falkowski (ed.) Proceedings of the Symposium on Biopolitics and Political Psychology. McLean, Va.: International Public Policy Research Corporation.

―――― (1979b) "Elite Values and Foreign Policy Analysis: Preliminary Findings," pp. 211-249 in L. S. Falkowski (ed.) Psychological Models in International Politics. Boulder, Co.: Westview.

―――― (1979c) "Soft Modeling in the Social Sciences: Applications of Partial Least Squares in Political Science." Presented at the Conference on Soft Modeling in the Social Sciences, University of Geneva. Geneva, Switzerland, October.

―――― (1978) "Final Report of the Cross-National Crisis Indicators Project." College Park, Md.: University of Maryland.

―――― and A. J. FAVIN (1978) "The Domain of Command Psychophysiology: A Scientific/Technical Literature Review." McLean, Va.: International Public Policy Research Corporation, Cybernetics Sciences Evaluation Project, December.

HOPPLE, G. W. and J. A. KUHLMAN (eds.) (1980) Expert-Generated Data: Applications in International Affairs. Boulder, Co.: Westview Press.

HOPPLE, G. W. and P. J. ROSSA (1980) "International Crisis Analysis: A Review and Assessment," in D. Zinnes, P. T. Hopmann, and J. D. Singer (eds.) Cumulation in International Relations. Denver, Co.: University of Denver Monograph Series in World Affairs.

HOPPLE, G. W., P. J. ROSSA, and J. WILKENFELD (1980) "Threat and Foreign Policy Analysis: Assessing the Overt Behavior of States in Conflict," in P. J. McGowan and C. W. Kegley, Jr. (eds.) Threats, Weapons, and Foreign Policy Behavior, Vol. 5. Sage International Yearbook of Foreign Policy Studies. Beverly Hills, Ca.: Sage.

HOPPLE, G. W., J. WILKENFELD, P. J. ROSSA, and R. N. McCAULEY (1977) "Societal and Interstate Determinants of Foreign Conflict." Jerusalem Journal of International Relations 2 (Summer): 30-66.

HORVATH, F. (1978) "An Experimental Comparison of the Psychological Stress Evaluator and the Galvanic Skin Response in Detection of Deception." Journal of Applied Psychology 63: 338-344.

International Public Policy Research Corporation (IPPRC) (1979) "Early Warning and Monitoring System: Sample Output." McLean, Va.: Early Warning and Monitoring Project, International Public Policy Research Corporation, June.

JACKMAN, M. R. (1973) "Education and Prejudice or Education

and Response-Set? *American Sociological Review* 38 (June): 327-339.
JANIS, I. L. (1972) *Victims of Groupthink*. Boston, Ma.: Houghton Mifflin.
_____ and L. MANN (1977) *Decision-Making: A Psychological Analysis of Conflict, Choice, and Commitment*. New York: Free Press.
JAROS, D. (1972) "Biochemical Desocialization: Depressants and Political Behavior." *Midwest Journal of Political Science* 16: 1-28.
JERVIS, R. (1976) *Perception and Misperception in International Politics*. Princeton, N.J.: Princeton University Press.
_____ (1970) *The Logic of Images in International Relations*. Princeton, N.J.: Princeton University Press.
_____ (1968) "Hypotheses on Misperception." *World Politics* 20 (April): 454-79.
JOHNSON, L. (1977) "Operational Codes and the Prediction of Leadership Behavior: Senator Frank Church at Midcareer," pp. 80-119 in M. Hermann (ed.) *A Psychological Examination of Political Leaders*. New York: Free Press.
KATZ, D. (1973) "Patterns of Leadership," in J. Knutson (ed.) *Handbook of Political Psychology*. San Francisco: Jossey-Bass.
KAVANAGH, D. (1970) "The Operational Code of Ramsey MacDonald." Stanford, Ca.: Stanford University, mimeo.
KELMAN, H. C. and A. H. BLOOM (1973) "Assumptive Frameworks in International Politics," pp. 261-295 in J. N. Knutson (ed.) *Handbook of Political Psychology*. San Francisco: Jossey-Bass.
KENT, R. S., M. BLATNIKOFF, and D. COVINGTON (1980) "Divisions Within the Cuban Leadership: A Simulated Opinion Poll," in G. W. Hopple and J. A. Kuhlman (eds.) *Expert-Generated Data: Applications in International Affairs*. Boulder, Co.: Westview.
KINDER, D. R. and J. A. WEISS (1978) "In Lieu of Rationality: Psychological Perspectives on Foreign Policy Decision Making." *Journal of Conflict Resolution* 22 (December): 707-735.
KIRK, E. J. (1976) "International Perception and Foreign Policy: Literature Survey and Assessment." Bethesda, Md.: Mathematica, Analytic Support Center.
KRIPPENDORFF, K. (1969) "Introduction to Part l," in G. Gerbner et al. (eds.) *The Analysis of Communication Content*. New York: John Wiley and Sons.
LAMPTON, D. M. (1973) "The U.S. Image of Peking in Three International Crises." *Western Political Quarterly* 26: 28-50.
LANE, R. (1962) *Political Ideology*. New York: Free Press.
LANGER, W. L. (1972) *The Mind of Adolph Hitler*. New York:

Basic Books.
LASSWELL, H. D. (1948) Power and Personality. New York: Viking.
───── (1930) Psychopathology and Politics. Chicago: University of Chicago Press.
───── and D. LERNER (1965) World Revolutionary Elites. Cambridge, Ma.: Massachusetts Institute of Technology Press.
LAWRENCE, D. (1975) "The Operational Code of Lester Pearson." University of British Columbia, Ph.D. dissertation.
LAZARUS, R. (1966) Psychological Stress and the Coping Process. New York: McGraw-Hill.
LEITES, N. (1953) A Study of Bolshevism. Glencoe, Il.: Free Press.
───── (1951) The Operational Code of the Politburo. New York: McGraw-Hill.
LOCKHART, C. (1977) "Problems in the Management and Resolution of International Conflicts." World Politics 29 (April): 370-403.
LODGE, M. and B. TURSKY (1979) "Comparisons between Category and Magnitude Scaling of Political Opinion Employing SRC/CPS Items." American Political Science Review 73 (March): 50-66.
LODGE, M., D. CROSS, B. TURSKY, J. TANENHAUS, and R. REEDER (1976) "The Psychophysical Scaling of Political Support in the 'Real World.'" Political Methodology 2: 159-182.
LODGE, M., D. CROSS, B. TURSKY, and J. TANENHAUS (1975) "The Psychophysical Scaling and Validation of a Political Support Scale." American Journal of Political Science 19: 611-649.
LONDON, H. and J. E. EXNER, Jr. (eds.) (1978) Dimensions of Personality. New York: John Wiley and Sons.
McCARTHY, G. and E. DONCHIN (1978) "Event-Related Brain Potentials - Manifestations of Cognitive Activity." Presented at the Bayer Symposium on the Evaluation of Old Age Related Changes and Disorders of Brain Function. Grosse Ledder, West Germany, October.
McCLELLAND, C. A. (1975) "Crisis and Threat in the International Setting: Some Relational Concepts." Los Angeles, Ca.: International Relations Research Institute, Threat Recognition and Analysis Project Technical Report 28, University of Southern California, June.
───── (1972) "The Beginning, Duration, and Abatement of International Crises: Comparisons in Two Conflict Arenas," pp. 83-108 in C. F. Hermann (ed.) International Crises: Insights from Behavioral Research. New York: Free Press.
───── (1968) "Access to Berlin: The Quantity and Variety of Events, 1948-1963," pp. 159-186 in J. D. Singer (ed.) Quantitative International Politics: Insights and Evidence. New York: Free Press.

McCORMICK, D. M. (1975) "Decisions, Events and Perceptions in International Crisis - Volume I." Ann Arbor, Mi.: First Ann Arbor Corporation, Final Report, July.

McGowan, P. J. (1976) "The Future of Comparative Studies: An Evangelical Plea," pp. 217-235 in J. N. Rosenau (ed.) In Search of Global Patterns. New York: Free Press.

―――― and H. B. SHAPIRO (1973) The Comparative Study of Foreign Policy: A Survey of Scientific Findings. Beverly Hills, Ca.: Sage.

McGRATH, J. E. (1978) "Small Group Research." American Behavioral Scientist 21 (May/June): 651-674.

McLELLAN, D. S. (1969) "Comparative 'Operational Codes' of Recent U.S. Secretaries of State: Dean Acheson." Presented at the Annual Meeting of the American Political Science Association.

McNEIL, E. B. (1959) "Psychology and Aggression." Journal of Conflict Resolution 3 (September): 195-293.

MALONE, C. S. (1971) "The Operational Code of Lyndon Baines Johnson." Stanford, Ca.: Stanford University, mimeo.

MANIS, M. (1978) "Cognitive Social Psychology and Attitude Change." American Behavioral Scientist 21 (May/June): 675-690.

MARVICK, D. (1977) "Elite Politics: Values and Institutions." American Behavioral Scientist 21 (September/October): 111-134.

MASTERS, R. D. (1978a) "Attention Structures and Political Campaigns." Presented at the Annual Meeting of the American Political Science Association. New York, September.

―――― (1978b) "Classical Political Philosophy and Contemporary Biology." Presented at the Conference for the Study of Political Thought, Loyola University of Chicago. Chicago, April.

―――― (1978c) "The Importance -- and Limitations -- of Sociobiology." Manuscript prepared for E. White (ed.) Sociobiology and Politics (mimeo).

―――― (1978d) "Jean Jacques is Alive and Well: Rousseau and Contemporary Sociobiology." Daedalus (Summer): 93-105.

―――― (1978e) "Of Marmots and Men: Animal Behavior and Human Altruism," in L. Wispe (ed.) Altruism, Sympathy, and Helping. New York: Academic Press.

―――― (1976) "The Impact of Ethology on Political Science," pp. 197-233 in A. Somit (ed.) Biology and Politics: Recent Explorations. Paris and the Hague: Mouton.

―――― (1975) "Politics as a Biological Phenomenon." Social Science Information 14: 7-63.

MAY, E. R. (1973) "Lessons" of the Past: The Use and Misuse of History in American Foreign Policy. New York: Oxford University Press.

MAZLISH, B. (1972) In Search of Nixon: A Psychohistorical

Inquiry. New York: Basic Books.
MEDDIN, J. (1975) "Attitudes, Values and Related Concepts: A System of Classification." Social Science Quarterly 55 (March): 889-918.
MEHRABIAN, A. (1972) Nonverbal Communication. Chicago: Aldine-Atherton.
———and S. R. FERRIS (1967) "Inference of Attitudes From Nonverbal Communication in Two Channels." Journal of Consulting Psychology 31: 248-252.
MEHRABIAN, A. and M. WIENER (1967) "Decoding of Inconsistent Communications." Journal of Personality and Social Psychology 6: 109-114.
MENNIS, B. (1972) American Foreign Policy Officials: Who They Are and What They Believe Regarding International Politics. Columbus, Oh.: Ohio State University Press.
MUELLER, D. J. (1970) "Physiological Techniques of Attitude Measurement," pp. 534-552 in G. F. Summers (ed.) Attitude Measurement. Chicago: Rand McNally.
NELSON, S. D. (1975) "Nature/Nurture Revisited II: Social, Political, and Technological Implications of Biological Approaches to Human Conflict." Journal of Conflict Resolution 19 (December): 734-761.
OSGOOD, C. E. (1959) "The Representational Model and Relevant Research Methods," in I. de Sola Pool (ed.) Trends in Content Analysis. Urbana, Il.: University of Illinois Press.
PAIGE, G. D. (1968) The Korean Decision. New York: Free Press.
PARKER, R. W. (1977) "An Examination of Basic and Applied International Crisis Research." International Studies Quarterly 21 (March): 225-246.
PEAR, T. H. (ed.) (1950) Psychological Factors of Peace and War. London: Hutchinson.
PENNER, L. A. (1971) "Interpersonal Attraction Toward a Black Person as a Function of Value Importance." Personality 2: 175-187.
———and T. ANH (1977) "A Comparison of American and Vietnamese Value Systems." Journal of Social Psychology 101: 187-204.
PETERSON, S. (1979) "Foreign News Gatekeepers and Criteria of Newsworthiness." Journalism Quarterly 55: 116-125.
PETERSON, S. A. and A. SOMIT (1978) "Methodological Problems Associated with a Biologically-Oriented Social Science." Journal of Social and Biological Structures 1: 11-25.
POOL, I. de S. (1970) The Prestige Papers: A Comparative Study of Political Symbols. Cambridge, Ma.: Massachusetts Institute of Technology Press.
——— (1959) Trends in Content Analysis. Urbana, Il.: University of Illinois Press.
———and A. KESSLER (1965) "The Kaiser, the Tsar, and the Computer." American Behavioral Scientist 8: 31-38.

POPPER, K. R. (1963) Conjectures and Refutations: The Growth of Scientific Knowledge. New York: Harper and Row.
POWELL, C. A. et al. (1974) "Determinants of Foreign Policy Behavior: A Causal Modeling Approach," pp. 151-170 in J. N. Rosenau (ed.) Comparing Foreign Policies: Theories, Findings, Methods. New York: Halsted.
PRZEWORSKI, A. and H. TEUNE (1972) The Logic of Comparative Social Inquiry. New York: Wiley.
PUTNAM, R. D., R. LEONARDI, and R. Y. NANETTI (1979) "Attitude Stability Among Italian Elites." American Journal of Political Science 23 (August): 463-494.
QUANDT, W. B. (1970) "The Comparative Study of Political Elites." Sage Professional Papers in Comparative Politics. Beverly Hills, Ca.: Sage.
ROBINS, R. S. (ed.) (1977) Psychopathology and Political Leadership. Tulane Studies in Political Science, Volume 16. New Orleans, La.: Tulane University.
ROGOW, A. A. (1969) "Psychiatry and Political Science: Some Reflections and Prospects," in S. M. Lipset (ed.) Politics and the Social Sciences. New York: Oxford University Press.
―――― (1963) James Forrestal: A Study of Personality, Politics, and Policy. New York: Macmillan.
ROKEACH, M. (1979a) "From Individual to Institutional Values," in M. Rokeach (ed.) Understanding Human Values: Individual and Social. New York: Free Press.
―――― (ed.) (1979b) Understanding Human Values: Individual and Social. New York: Free Press.
―――― (1979c) "Value Theory and Communication Research: Review and Commentary," in D. Nimmo (ed.) Communication Yearbook III. New Brunswick, N.J.: Transaction Books.
―――― (1974) "Change and Stability in American Value Systems, 1968-1971." Public Opinion Quarterly 38: 222-228.
―――― (1973) The Nature of Human Values. New York: Free Press.
―――― (1968) Beliefs, Attitudes, and Values: A Theory of Organization and Change. San Francisco, Ca.: Jossey-Bass.
―――― (1967) Value Survey. Sunnyvale, Ca.: Halgren Tests.
―――― (1960) The Open and Closed Mind: Investigations into the Nature of Belief Systems and Personality Systems. New York: Basic Books.
―――― R. HOMANT, and L. PENNER (1970) "A Value Analysis of the Disputed Federalist Papers." Journal of Personality and Social Psychology 16 (October): 245-250.
ROSENAU, J. N. (ed.) (1969) Linkage Politics: Essays on the Convergence of National and International Systems. New York: Free Press.
―――― (1968) "Private Preferences and Political Responsibilities: The Relative Potency of Individual and Role Variables in the Behavior of United States Senators," in

J. D. Singer (ed.) <u>Quantitative International Politics: Insights and Evidence</u>. New York: Free Press.

_____ (1966) "Pre-Theories and Theories of Foreign Policy," in R. B. Farrell (ed.) <u>Approaches to Comparative and International Politics</u>. Evanston, Il.: Northwestern University Press.

_____ and G. HOGGARD (1974) "Foreign Policy Behavior in Dyadic Relationships: Testing a Pretheoretical Extension," in J. N. Rosenau (ed.) <u>Comparing Foreign Policies: Theories, Findings, Methods</u>. Beverly Hills, Ca.: Sage.

ROSENAU, J. N. and G. RAMSEY (1975) "External vs. Internal Sources of Foreign Policy Behavior," in P. J. McGowan (ed.) <u>Sage International Yearbook of Foreign Policy Studies</u>, Vol. III. Beverly Hills, Ca.: Sage.

ROSSA, P. J. (1979) "Explaining International Political Behavior and Conflict Through Partial Least Squares Modeling." Presented at the Conference on Systems under Indirect Observation (Causality/Structure/Prediction). Geneva, Switzerland, October.

_____, G. W. HOPPLE, and J. WILKENFELD (1979) "Crisis Indicators and Models." <u>International Interactions</u>.

ROUS, G. L. and D. E. LEE (1978) "Freedom and Equality: Two Values of Political Orientation." <u>Journal of Communication</u> (Winter): 45-51.

SARTORI, G. (1969) "Politics, Ideology, and Belief Systems." <u>American Political Science Review</u> 63 (June): 398-411.

SCHNEIDMAN, E. S. (1969) "Logic Content Analysis: An Explication of Styles of Concludifying," pp. 261-279 in G. Gerbner et al. (eds.) <u>The Analysis of Communication Content</u>. New York: Wiley.

_____ (1963) "Plan II: The Logic of Politics," pp. 178-199 in L. Arons and M. A. May (eds.) <u>Television and Human Behavior</u>. New York: Appleton-Century-Crofts.

_____ (1961) "A Psychological Analysis of Political Thinking: The Kennedy-Nixon 'Great Debates' and the Kennedy-Khrushchev 'Grim Debates.'" Cambridge, Ma.: Harvard, mimeo.

SCHUBERT, G. (1973) "Biopolitical Behavior: The Nature of the Political Animal." <u>Polity</u> (Winter) 6: 240-275.

SCHWARTZ, D. C. (1976) "Somatic States and Political Behavior: An Interpretation and Empirical Extension of Biopolitics," pp. 15-44 in A. Somit (ed.) <u>Biology and Politics: Recent Explorations</u>. Paris and the Hague: Mouton.

SCOTT, J. P. (1978) "What Are the Expectations Regarding the Scope and Limits of Exploring the Biological Aspects of Political Behavior? Considerations of Methodology." Presented at the Annual Meeting of the American Political Science Association. New York, September.

SEARING, D. D. (1978) "Measuring Politicians' Values: Administration and Assessment of a Ranking Technique in the

British House of Commons." *American Political Science Review* 72 (March): 65-79.

SEMMEL, A. K. (1976) "Some Correlates of Attitudes to Multilateral Diplomacy in the U.S. Department of State." *International Studies Quarterly* 20 (June): 301-324.

―――― (1975) "Deriving Perceptual Data From Foreign Policy Elites: A Methodological Narrative." *Political Methodology* 2: 29-49.

SHAPIRO, H. B. and P. L. CUMMINGS (1976) "Problems in the Use of Ad Hoc Structures in DOD Crisis Management and Implications for Change." McLean, Va.: Human Sciences Research, Incorporated, Final Report, March.

SHAPIRO, H. B. and M. A. GILBERT (1975) "Crisis Management: Psychological and Sociological Factors in Decision Making." McLean, Va.: Human Sciences Research, Incorporated, Final Technical Report, March.

SHAPIRO, M. J. and C. M. BONHAM (1973) "Cognitive Processes and Foreign Policy Decision-Making." *International Studies Quarterly* 17 (June): 147-174.

SHINN, A., Jr. (1969) "An Application of Psychophysical Scaling Techniques to the Measurement of National Power." *Journal of Politics* 31: 932-951.

SINGER, J. D. (ed.) (1968) *Quantitative International Politics: Insights and Evidence*. New York: Free Press.

―――― (1964) "Soviet and American Foreign Policy Attitudes: Content Analysis of Elite Articulations." *Journal of Conflict Resolution* 8 (December): 424-485.

―――― and M. D. WALLACE (eds.) (1979) *To Augur Well: Early Warning Indicators in World Politics*. Beverly Hills, Ca.: Sage.

SLOVIC, P., B. FISCHHOFF, and S. LICHTENSTEIN (1977) "Behavioral Decision Theory." *Annual Review of Psychology* 28: 1-39.

SMART, C. and I. VERTINSKY (1977) "Designs for Crisis Decision Units." *Administrative Science Quarterly* 22 (December): 640-657.

SNIDERMAN, P. M. (1975) *Personality and Democratic Politics*. Berkeley and Los Angeles: University of California Press.

SNYDER, G. H. and P. DIESING (1977) *Conflict Among Nations: Bargaining, Decision Making, and System Structure in International Crises*. Princeton, N.J.: Princeton University Press.

SNYDER, J. L. (1978) "Rationality at the Brink: The Role of Cognitive Processes in Failures of Deterrence." *World Politics* 30 (April): 344-365.

SNYDER, R. C., H. W. BRUCK, and B. SAPIN (1962) "Decision-Making as an Approach to the Study of International Politics," pp. 14-185 in R. C. Snyder, H. W. Bruck, and B. Sapin (eds.) *Foreign Policy Decision-Making*. New York: Free Press.

SOMIT, A. (ed.) (1976a) Biology and Politics: Recent Explorations. Paris and the Hague: Mouton.
_____(1976b) "Introduction," pp. 3-14 in A. Somit (ed.) Biology and Politics: Recent Explorations. Paris and the Hague: Mouton.
_____(1976c) "Review Article - Biopolitics," pp. 293-323 in A. Somit (ed.) Biology and Politics: Recent Explorations. Paris and the Hague: Mouton.
_____(1968) "Toward a More Biologically Oriented Political Science: Ethology and Psychopharmacology." Midwest Journal of Political Science 12 (November): 550-567.
_____and S. A. PETERSON (1978) "Biopolitics: 1978." Notes (DeKalb, Il.: Center for Biopolitical Research, Northern Illinois University, October): 3-4.
_____and W. D. RICHARDSON (1978) "The Literature of Biopolitics, 1963-1977." DeKalb, Il.: Center for Biopolitical Research, Northern Illinois University.
STAGNER, R. (1965) "The Psychology of Human Conflict," in E. B. McNeil (ed.) The Nature of Human Conflict. Englewood Cliffs, N.J.: Prentice-Hall.
STANTON, A. H. and S. E. PERRY (eds.) (1951) Personality and Political Crisis: New Perspectives from Social Sciences and Psychiatry for the Study of War and Politics. Glencoe, Il.: Free Press.
STARR, H. and B. A. MOST (1976) "The Substance and Study of Borders in International Relations Research." International Studies Quarterly 20 (December): 581-620.
STASSEN, G. H. (1972) "Individual Preference Versus Role-Constraint in Policy-Making." World Politics 24 (October): 96-119.
STEIN, J. G. (1978) "Can Decision-Makers Be Rational and Should They Be? Evaluating the Quality of Decisions." Jerusalem Journal of International Relations 3 (Winter-Spring): 316-339.
_____and M. BRECHER (1976) "Image Advocacy and the Analysis of Conflict: An Israeli Case Study." Jerusalem Journal of International Relations 1 (Spring): 33-58.
STEINBRUNER, J. D. (1974) The Cybernetic Theory of Decision: New Dimensions of Political Authority. Princeton, N.J.: Princeton University Press.
STEPHENS, J. (1970) "Some Questions About a More Biologically Oriented Political Science." Midwest Journal of Political Science 14: 687-707.
STONE, P. J. et al. (1966) The General Inquirer: A Computer Approach to Content Analysis. Cambridge, Ma.: Massachusetts Institute of Technology Press.
STRACHEY, A. (1957) The Unconscious Motives of War. London: Allen and Unwin.
STRAUSS, H. J. (1973) "Revolutionary Types: Russia in 1905." Journal of Conflict Resolution 17 (June): 297-316.
STUPAK, R. J. (1971) "Dean Rusk on International Relations:

An Analysis of His Philosophical Perceptions." Australian Outlook 25 (3): 13-28.
SUEDFELD, P., and P. TETLOCK (1977) "Integrative Complexity of Communications in International Crises." Journal of Conflict Resolution 21 (March): 169-184.
―――― and C. RAMIREZ (1977) "War, Peace, and Integrative Complexity: UN Speeches on the Middle East Problem, 1947-1976." Journal of Conflict Resolution 21 (September): 427-442.
TANTER, R. (1978) "International Crisis Behavior: An Appraisal of the Literature." Jerusalem Journal of International Relations 3 (Winter-Spring): 340-374.
THORDARSON, B. (1972) Trudeau and Foreign Policy: A Study in Decision-Making. Toronto: Oxford University Press.
TOLMAN, E. C. (1942) Drives Toward War. New York: Appleton-Century.
TUCKER, R. C. (1977) "The Georges' Wilson Reexamined: An Essay on Psychobiography." American Political Science Review 71 (June): 606-618.
―――― (1973) Stalin as Revolutionary 1878-1929: A Study in History and Personality. New York: Norton.
TURSKY, B. (1977) "A Psychophysical and Psychophysiological Approach to the Assessment of the Direction, Intensity and Meaning of a Political Attitude." Presented at the Annual Meeting of the Society for Psychophysiological Research, Philadelphia.
―――― , M. LODGE, and R. REEDER (1979) "Psychophysical and Psychophysiological Evaluation of the Direction, Intensity, and Meaning of Race-Related Stimuli." Psychophysiology 16 (September): 452-462.
TURSKY, B., M. LODGE, and D. CROSS (1976a) "A Bio-Behavioral Framework for the Analysis of Political Behavior," pp. 59-96 in A. Somit (ed.) Biology and Politics: Recent Explorations. Paris and the Hague: Mouton.
TURSKY, B., M. LODGE, M. A. FOLEY, R. REEDER, and H. FOLEY (1976b) "Evaluation of the Cognitive Component of Political Issues by Use of Classical Conditioning." Journal of Personality and Social Psychology 34: 865-873.
TWERASER, K. (1974) "Changing Patterns of Political Beliefs: The Foreign Policy Operational Code of J. William Fulbright." Sage Professional Papers in American Politics, 04-016. Beverly Hills, Ca.: Sage.
WALKER, S. G. (1979) "Psychological Explanations of International Politics: Problems of Aggregation, Measurement, and Theory Construction," in L. S. Falkowski (ed.) Proceedings of the Symposium on Biopolitics and Political Psychology. McLean, Va.: International Public Policy Research Corporation.
―――― (1977) "The Interface Between Beliefs and Behavior: Henry Kissinger's Operational Code and the Vietnam War." Journal of Conflict Resolution 21 (March): 129-168.

WATTS, M. W. (1978) "Physiological Studies of Violence - Related Attitudes." Presented at the Annual Meeting of the American Political Science Association. New York, September.
_____ and D. SUMI (1979) "Studies in the Physiological Component of Aggression-Related Social Attitudes." American Journal of Political Science 23 (August): 528-558.
WEINSTEIN, E. A., J. W. ANDERSON, and A. S. LINK (1978) "Woodrow Wilson's Political Personality: A Reappraisal." Political Science Quarterly 93 (Winter): 585-598.
WIEGELE, T. C. (1979a) Biopolitics: Search for a More Human Political Science. Boulder, Co.: Westview.
_____ (1979b) "The Case for a Biological Perspective in the Study of International Relations," in L. S. Falkowski (ed.) Proceedings of the Symposium on Biopolitics and Political Psychology. McLean, Va.: International Public Policy Research Corporation.
_____ (1979c) "The Dominican Crisis: A Voice Stress Analysis." DeKalb, Il.: Center for Biopolitical Research, Northern Illinois University, Working Paper.
_____ (1979d) "Methodological Aspects of Voice Stress Analysis." DeKalb, Il.: Center for Biopolitical Research, Northern Illinois University, Working Paper.
_____ (1979e) "Signal Leakage and the Remote Psychological Assessment of Foreign Policy Elites," pp. 71-93 in L. S. Falkowski (ed.) Psychological Models in International Politics. Boulder, Co.: Westview.
_____ (1978a) "Physiologically-Based Content Analysis: An Application in Political Communication," in B. Ruben (ed.) Communications Yearbook II. New Brunswick, N.J.: Transaction Books.
_____ (1978b) "The Psychophysiology of Elite Stress in Five International Crises: A Preliminary Test of a Voice Measurement Technique." International Studies Quarterly 22 (December): 467-511.
_____ (1978c) "Toward a Human Science of Politics: The Real Post-Behavioral Revolution." Presented at the Conference for the Study of Political Thought, Loyola University of Chicago. Chicago, April.
_____ (1977) "Models of Stress and Disturbances in Elite Political Behavior: Psychological Variables and Political Decision-Making," pp. 79-111 in R. S. Robins (ed.) Psychopathology and Political Leadership. Tulane Studies in Political Science, Volume 16. New Orleans, La.: Tulane University.
_____ (1973) "Decision Making in an International Crisis: Some Biological Factors." International Studies Quarterly 17 (September): 295-336.
WHITE, G. (1969) "A Comparison of the 'Operational Codes' of Mao Tse-tung and Liu Shao-ch'i." Stanford, Ca.: Stanford University, mimeo.

WHITE, R. K. (1970) Nobody Wanted War: Misperception in Vietnam and Other Wars. Garden City, N.Y.: Doubleday.
_____ (1951) Value-Analysis: The Nature and Use of the Method. Glen Gardner, N.J.: Libertarian Press.
_____ (1949) "Hitler, Roosevelt, and the Nature of War Propaganda." Journal of Abnormal and Social Psychology 44: 157-174.
WHITEY, S. and D. KATZ (1965) "The Social Psychology of Human Conflict," in E. B. McNeil (ed.) The Nature of Human Conflict. Englewood Cliffs, N.J.: Prentice-Hall.
WILKENFELD, J., G. W. HOPPLE, P. J. ROSSA, and S. J. ANDRIOLE (1980) Interstate Behavior Analysis. Beverly Hills, Ca.: Sage.
WILKENFELD, J., G. W. HOPPLE, and P. J. ROSSA (1979) "Indicators of Conflict and Cooperation in the Interstate System, 1966-1970," pp. 109-151 in J. D. Singer and M. D. Wallace (eds.) To Augur Well: Early Warning Indicators in Interstate Conflict. Beverly Hills, Ca.: Sage.
WILKENFELD, J., G. W. HOPPLE, S. J. ANDRIOLE, and R. N. McCAULEY (1978) "Profiling States for Foreign Policy Analysis." Comparative Political Studies 11 (April): 4-35.
WILLHOITE, F. H. (1978) "Rank and Reciprocity: Notes Toward a Sociobiological Political Theory." Presented at the Conference for the Study of Political Thought, Loyola University of Chicago. Chicago, April.
WILLHOITE, F. H. (1977) "Evolution and Collective Intolerance." Journal of Politics 39: 667-684.
WILLHOITE, F. H. (1971) "Ethology and the Tradition of Political Thought." Journal of Politics 33 (August): 615-641.
WILLIAMS, P. (1976) Crisis Management: Confrontation and Diplomacy in the Nuclear Age. New York: John Wiley and Sons.
WINHAM, G. R. (1970) "Developing Theories of Foreign Policy Making: A Case Study of Foreign Aid." Journal of Politics 32 (February): 41-70.
WINTER, D. G., and A. J. STEWART (1977) "Content Analysis as a Technique for Assessing Political Leaders," pp. 28-61 in M. G. Hermann (ed.) A Psychological Examination of Political Leaders. New York: Free Press.
WOLD, H. (1979) "Model Construction and Evaluation When Theoretical Knowledge is Scarce: An Example of the Use of Partial Least Squares," in J. Kmenta and J. Ramsey (eds.) Evaluation of Econometric Models.
_____ (1978) "Ways and Means of Multidisciplinary Studies," pp. 1071-1095 in the Transactions of the Sixth International Conference on the Unity of the Sciences, San Francisco. New York: The International Cultural Foundation.

WOLFENSTEIN, E. V. (1974) "The Two Wars of Lyndon Johnson." Politics and Society 4: 357-396.
⎯⎯⎯ (1967) The Revolutionary Personality: Lenin, Trotsky and Ghandi. Princeton, N.J.: Princeton University Press.
ZIMMERMAN, W. (1970) "Elite Perspectives and the Explanation of Soviet Foreign Policy." Journal of International Affairs 24: 84-98.
ZINNES, D. A. (1976) "The Problem of Cumulation," pp. 161-166 in J. N. Rosenau (ed.) In Search of Global Patterns. New York: Free Press.
⎯⎯⎯ (1966) "A Comparison of Hostile Behavior of Decision-Makers in Simulate and Historical Data." World Politics 18 (April): 474-502.
⎯⎯⎯, J. L. ZINNES, and R. D. McCLURE (1972) "Hostility in Diplomatic Communication: A Study of the 1914 Crisis," pp. 139-62 in C. F. Hermann (ed.) International Crises: Insights From Behavioral Research. New York: Free Press.